Daniel Köhler
The Mereological City

Architecture | Volume 36

Daniel Köhler (Dr.) teaches urban design at the University of Innsbruck and digital design strategies at the Vilnius Academy of Arts. His research incorporates digital methods into the study of the city, its history and architecture.

Daniel Köhler
The Mereological City
A reading of the works of Ludwig Hilberseimer

[transcript]

This publication was printed with financial support from the funds of the Vice-Rector for Research, the Faculty of Architecture and the Institute of Urban Design at the Leopold-Franzens-Universität Innsbruck.

Bibliographic information published by the Deutsche Nationalbibliothek
The Deutsche Nationalbibliothek lists this publication in the Deutsche Nationalbibliografie; detailed bibliographic data are available in the Internet at http://dnb.d-nb.de

© 2016 transcript Verlag, Bielefeld

All rights reserved. No part of this book may be reprinted or reproduced or utilized in any form or by any electronic, mechanical, or other means, now known or hereafter invented, including photocopying and recording, or in any information storage or retrieval system, without permission in writing from the publisher.

Cover layout: Kordula Röckenhaus, Bielefeld
Cover illustration: Daniel Köhler, Plan of Chicago, according to Ludwig Hilberseimer's schema of removing street segments, 2015
Proofread by Emanuel Binder, Lucie Sedlaková

Print-ISBN 978-3-8376-3466-2
PDF-ISBN 978-3-8394-3466-6

Contents

1 Prologue: Architecture as a Discipline of Composition | 7
1.1 Acknowledgements | 16

2 Introduction: Topic, State of Knowledge, Method | 19
2.1 Ludwig Hilberseimer: Life and Work | 19
2.2 Scientific Recension of the Work Hilberseimer's | 23
2.2.1 Society follows Form: Society is predetermined by form | 25
2.2.2 Form follows Society: The form as product of social factors | 28
2.2.3 The Schemata of Design | 34
2.3 The method: A mereological reading | 34
2.3.1 The term form in philosophy and architecture | 35
2.3.2 The house and the city: a classic formal thesis | 38
2.3.3 An introduction to Mereology | 42
2.3.4 A mereological composition of a line | 47

3 The Large City: The will to elemental architecture | 61
3.1 Creation and development | 61
3.1.1 The Kunstwollen as frictional contrast | 62
3.1.2 The Dionysian and the Apollonian | 73
3.2 Groszstadt Architecture | 79
3.2.1 The abstraction as a discursive experiment | 81
3.2.2 The large city as an elemental task | 84
3.2.3 The Vertical-City as vertical composition | 87
3.3 Towards an Autonomous Architecture | 116
3.3.1 The definition of the smallest architectural element | 118
3.3.2 The city as a new compositional task | 119

4   The unfolding of a planning idea | 123
4.1   From Vertical-City to Flat-Building | 123
4.1.1   The Welfare City | 123
4.1.2   The Proposal to City-Building | 125
4.1.3   Flat buildings | 128
4.2   Flat-building and city space | 131
4.2.1   In the shadow of Mies | 141
4.3   Studies on room insolation | 143
4.4   Elements of City Planning | 148

5   The punctualisation as architectural method | 165
5.1   The concept of form in the work of Hilberseimer | 165
5.2   Punctualisation as method | 168
5.2.1   The punctualisation at Hilberseimer | 172
5.3   Room, House, Town, Region: a mereological analysis | 182

6   Conclusion: The Art of City-Planning | 209

Notes | 215
Prologue: Architecture as a Discipline of Composition | 215
Introduction: Topic, State of Knowledge, Method | 217
The Large City: The will to elemental architecture | 223
The unfolding of a planning idea | 229
The punctualisation as architectural method | 233
Conclusion: The Art of City-Planning | 237

List of Figures | 239

Bibliography | 247

1 Prologue:
Architecture as a Discipline of Composition

> Forms are no longer superimposed but the result of order which in itself has already to some extent form quality.
> LUDWIG HILBERSEIMER. ARCHITECTURE: STRUCTURE AND FORM

Architecture is about the many, the composition of a collective[1]. Architecture starts when a plurality, more than two, enter into relations with each other, on a longer term basis without an ascertainable horizon. Architecture is the physical constitution, the attempt of a translation, and at best, a projection of a collective. Regimes of content articulate architectural features according to their specific will and Zeitgeist. However, architecture always deals with the arrangement and joining of figures. The basic scheme of the disciplinary being remains the same. But what is the nature of joining and arranging? Which specific methods are used in the discipline of architecture? In order to present my work clearly, I will narrow down the discussed topic to the work of the art critic, architect, urbanist, teacher and curator Karl Ludwig Hilberseimer. I will clarify and discuss my question in the following way: What is Ludwig Hilberseimer's understanding of architectural order? What is the relationship of his architectural elements to each other? And more precisely: What is the relationship between the individual house and its arrangement in a settlement in the work of Ludwig Hilberseimer?

I will mereologically consider the work of Ludwig Hilberseimer's, that is, in the resonance of the determining parts of his project. I will come to the conclusion that Ludwig Hilberseimer developed a design method, which describes the parthood relations of house and settlement circularly rather than hierarchical. The description of a settlement as a *whole as part of the part as a whole* provides a new urban definition of ground as figurative composition. A settlement as a compositional intervention is designed with specific architectural elements. The design of the house depends on its projection as Many, the settlement. This is the punctualisation as architectural method.

The actuality of my search is based on an already ordinary question of our time, which in my opinion has only just started to be considered seriously : It is the question of the possibility of an ecological architecture. The common sense – in the following the first hits of a simple search of the internet – today gives us a response of exclusively technical artifacts, such as solar panels, heat registers, K-values, U-values, thatched roofs, hemp fiberboards, wood casement windows, mud bricks, rainwater cisterns, geotherms, waste paper insulations. Whether on the house, in the house, or under the house: In any case, the ecological integrity of an architectural object is judged by means of a technical, extra-disciplinary artifact. But not by the articulation of the architecture itself. And so the question arises: Can we show an architectural strategy that is congruent with the essence of ecological thought? Is there a disciplinary knowledge in architecture that can be described as ecological?

The work of Ludwig Hilberseimer and its previous review seems to me to be a good start to look for an answer. In architecture Hilberseimer's drawings take a kind of key position when it comes to show the method of modernity and their failure. It is precisely because the work Hilberseimer is an example of an epoch, which need to be overcome, I want to search for approaches here. If we declare global urbanization, the project of modernity, as complete, external criticism is no longer possible. Everything is interiority[2], based on modernity. Therefore, here I would like to propose a different approach: instead of a negative departure as the project of postmodernism, I recommend the *revaluation of modernist method*[3].

Several times was the work Hilberseimer a fruitful source of friction, the basis of various architectural positions. The list of recipients is long and impressive: Oswald Matthias Unger's *city-archipelago*[4], Christopher Alexander's *anti-tree-city*[5], Andrea Branzi's *weak urbanism*[6], Archizoom's *non-stop-city*[7], Aldo Rossi's *city in the city*[8], Albert Pope's eliptical urban space[9], Rem Koolhaas's *imagine nothingness*[10], Manfredo Tafuri's *critique of the assembly line*[11], Michael Hays's analysis of *mass ornament*[12], Pier Vittorio Aureli's *project of autonomy*[13], Patrik Schumacher's *fluid urbansim*[14], to name just the most influential. All the above mentioned critiques are dealing in a way with the work Hilberseimer, which seems typical to me for the postmodernist discourse: The critique of the content of the formal figure. In the words of Marx these analyzes builds on a direct link between praxis and practicing, ie infrastructure and social fabric[15]. Each approach accepts the direct, but dichotomous combination of content and figure. Each consequential argument remains a further alteration of the two opposites. Similar to a mathematical equation, an argument on one side leads to a conclusion on the other. In architecture we are familiar with this equation in the framework of typology: On the one hand we comprehend content with its figure, e.g. the patio-house, or on the other hand we comprehend the figure with its program, e.g. the Single-family-house. As postmodernists we learned from Robert Venturi to adress these both sides ironically as the duck or the shed. An illustration: Through the linear coupling of social interaction and the pattern the roads, Christopher Alexander concludes an argument against modernist building assemblies, due to lack of interaction (=intersections) of roads. The monotone facades in Hilberseimer highrise city Hays defines as a mass ornament of a mass society, which as a further conclusion Schumacher draws on for the demand for a variable architecture for a flexible society. None of the analyzes deals satisfactorily with the architectural design of the figure in itself: the study of the composition of parts, as an alternative to a purely opposing coupling between content and form. With the semantical steps of critique and improvement is connected the idea that each crisis keeps inherent an account of criticism as the necessary fruit of progress, growth and wealth. But such rhetorical eloquence as a negative departure from modernism seems to be more and more irrelevant. In this sense, I propose the reorientation of the architectural type that is an historical product of modernism[16]. I propose the reading of the architectural design of the figure in itself: its *mereological composition.*

The search for an alternative is not new and is at the core of our epoch of crises, or more precisely the ecological crisis. We find approaches in other disciplines under the definition of ecological politics[17], within the texts of the theoretican of science, philosopher and sociologist Bruno Latour[18], and the anthropologist Philipe Descola[19]. Ecological politics does not attempt a response to a crisis of nature, but ontologically, to a crisis of objectivity, naturalism and its dichotomy between nature and society. An initial enrichment of society with concerns of nature led to new compositions. The development demanded new ontological schemes, caused by their mixing and equal treatment of human and non-human beings. These schemes are engaged in the common definition of human and non-human beings, their groups, types of relationships and institutions[20]. In a flat ontology, an equal coexistence of people, institutions, creatures, ecosystems, machines, so *objects*, it is on the one hand not the representation, the hierarchization of content: the One, or on the other hand the formal characteristic[21] which is the material expression of the Many, but the negotiation of the One and the Many: the *resonance of parts*[22].

Here, I will mereologically consider the work of Ludwig Hilberseimer's, that is, in the resonance of the determining parts of his project. I will come to the conclusion that Ludwig Hilberseimer, coming from a scale based dialectic, developed a design method that weaves together the needs and scales of a house and a settlement, so that the figure of a settlement is always in a state of transition between part and whole. One can also say: The ground is in itself a figurative composition. Even more: the operations that are necessary to link the scale of the single house and a settlement accept no scale. In Hilberseimer's settlement-studies, the whole of a city is only negotiable as part of the part, so the house as a whole. The class of a settlement can only be understood by the consistency of its houses. There is no settlement without its elements: its houses and their consolidating negotiation. Sense of scale undergoes a revaluation and becomes the *disposition* of One and the *colocation* of Many. In such a reading the form of the architectural type is the way of composing parts.

Of course, Hilberseimer is rooted in his era. His layout of the world is clearly based on the dichotomous opposition between nature and culture. But by shifting his focus to a dialectic of part and whole, Hilberseimer developed a synthesis of form, which does without the question of content. Content alters form quantitatively. However, form is not determined by content, neither morphologically, typologically or topologically. Alone architectural operations on architectural figures create (more complex) architectural figurative compositions. The architectural object is defined by its simultaneity of that in which it is and that which is in[23]. It is therefore also a difference between the One and the Many. Another aspect is crucial here: The architectural object, as poietic object is not created theoretically by its assumption, but poietically: in its design. The operational step which summarizes a figural composition to an object epistemologically, in the philosophy of science is defined by the concept of punctualisation[24]. This work builds transdisciplinary on this definition and translates it into architecture.

If architecture as poietic discipline[25] communicates knowledge through the development and reference of architectural design-objects, a disciplinary scientific work should also use their specific media to communicate. Thus, in addition to a textual description, the work consists of complementary drawings and associative constructions. These representations serve as architectural explanations for poietic examination of the theoretical description. Designed objects are not limited to physical objects, figurations may exists textual as well. The format of the Poietics in this way can articulate the theoretical side of an investigation. This is another point that speaks for Hilberseimer's work as an object of investigation. Hilberseimer's planning was always criticized as unrealistic by its degree of abstraction and hermeneutic coherence. But it is precisely the accusation of the hermeneutic approach that can be used as an advantage here. The planning method in itself is treated by Hilberseimer as poietic object. This process can be divided into three design steps: The theoretical texts of Hilberseimer first of all, are descriptions of the zeitgeist, the phenomena of the city or region. The analysis is used for abstraction of an era or a territory in their recognizable, historical, cultural, social, economic or technical factors. In the following, the abstracted factors are related to each other. They become a presentation of a territory as figuration. Thus, it is possible for Hilberseimer to provide criticique compositional. The critique becomes a requirement for the fabric of the territory. It is translated in a parthood-relationship to be established within the represented figuration of the region. In his planning Hilberseimer transforms theoretically-abstracted figuration into urban schemata; as compositions of architectural elements and their parthood towards each other. The application of a schema leads to speculation about compositional interventions in the city. Indirectly, through the parthood-relationship the specifity of the city can be sensed. The speculation of the city is expressed in the design of a specific architectural element.

Both sides, theory and design, build the instrument of composition: The theoretical abstraction leads to the idea of figuration. Critique is translated into a parthood relationsship to be designed. The urban scheme generates speculation to the city by proposing specific elements described by the raised parthoods of the schema.

I will divide this study into five chapters. The study begins with an introduction to the work of Ludwig Hilberseimer, his person and the recent scientific review of his work. Because this study is a formal reading, I will also introduce the concept of form and mereology. In the second chapter, I shall cite aspects on why the project of Ludwig Hilberseimer can be read mereologically. This is apparent from an arthistorical and philosophical classification Hilberseimer's. The third chapter describes Hilberseimer's low rise building studies. In the fourth chapter, I compare the method of punctualisation with the design method of the low rise building studies and thereby translate the sociological method of punctualisation into the architecture. The method of punctualisation is a key element to analyze the urban structure Hilberseimer's of room, house, settlement and region mereologically. The fifth chapter concludes this study with a categorization of the work and outlook on the value within the field of architecture.

As already mentioned, in the first chapter I will carry out that previous reviews either make conclusions on architectural form with regards to content such as cultural analyzes, or criticize social aspects by means of an analysis of form. An examination of the form of Hilberseimer's work, as the schema of an architectural design in itself, is still pending. In order to assess the schema of Hilberseimer properly, in the following I will give a transdisciplinary overview of the concept of form. I will present approaches to form in the aesthetics to specific definitions of form in architecture.

In this regard, I will point out parallels between the work of Hilberseimer and Leon Battista Alberti. In the comparative study of both works can be seen, that Hilberseimer worked on a classical problem of form in architecture: the relationship of parts to a whole. The relationship between the house and a settlement, Hilberseimer designs as a parthood-relationship. For this reason, this work is a mereological examination. I will extensively introduce philosophical and mathematical definitions of mereology. Based on the geometric example of a line, I want to discuss how mereology can also be applied transdisciplinary on to architecture. In doing so, I am going to transform the line and its possible figuration into a mereological model, analoge to Bodo Rasch's and Frei Otto's wool-threads-model, and discursively position it as an alternative to spline curve. The wool-threads-model serves as a design analogy to the model of the settlement Hilberseimer's. As a model of form-finding, it is closest to the model of the settlement.

Before Hilberseimer became acquainted with urban designs, he was mainly an art-critic. Therefore, I will place, in the second chapter, the project of Hilberseimer art-historical and philosophical based on his early theoretical texts. That is not been done in this detail. Hilberseimer integrated formal methods of art history in his work. To be specific: methods of the art historian Alois Riegl. Analoge into Alois Riegl, Hilberseimer puts the materiality of a time in a tense relationship to artistic expression, the so called *Kunstwollen*. The tension between the material and the artist opposes the real with representation by the method of abstraction. Works of art are not imitations of nature, but compositions of figurations from simple elements. In a similar way Hilberseimer describes the history of architecture as compositions, as increasingly complex arrangements building on each other. The column as a design evolution of a pillar, building typologies as the result of various transformation of architectural elements or even as a composition of different building types. In order to assess works of art as compositions, Riegl used the relation of form to plane. The ratio sets the figure in contrast to their figuration. Riegl's formal relationship between figure and figuration will play a central role in Hilberseimer's design of the mixed development (Mischbebauung) and the subsequent settlement unit. In Riegl's writings, we also find the origin of Hilberseimer's distinction of geometric and organic order. The geometric order is the view of the nomad, a magical and centripetal: a planning from the outside. The organic order is the view of the farmer, a mystical and centrifugal: a planning from the inside. Geometric and Organic are no descriptions of an expression, whether perpendicular or amorphous, but formal descriptions of part-to-whole relationships. Hilberseimer himself uses the organic order. This is evident in the design of the Vertical City. The design is a critique of Le Corbusier's Ville Radieuse as geometric, horizontal harmonization of the city. In contrast, Hilberseimer describes the Vertical City as a collection of relations between the various parts of the city.

The second major theoretical influence on Hilberseimer's work is the philosophy of Friedrich Nietzsche. This can be verified by direct transfer of text passages Nietzsche's in Hilberseimer's early texts. The tension between Kunstwollen and material also corresponds to Nietzsche's writings struggle between Apollonian and Dionysian. The contrast between the corporeal and sensual, body and idea in its union leads Nietzsche to the *Rausch*: the eternal return of perpetual sameness. Through Nietzsche's Rausch, for the first time the concept of form can be defined in the work of Hilberseimer: As the zone of content. On the example of the design of the Chicago Tribune Tower is noticeable that the facade of the skyscraper is the expression of the addition of ceilings and columns. As a close of an interior the facade is the closure of an autonomous element. The facade is not a hull, no interface to an outside and therefore no information carrier of a society. There is no direct connection between the bare representation of the facades in Hilberseimer's visualizations and a conscious social expression and criticism, as mentioned in earlier reviews of his work[26]. In terms of Alois Riegl's method of abstraction as representation of the real Hilberseimer developed his geometrically rigid high-rise concept from the perception of existing, American skyscrapers. The design of the skyscraper becomes the schema of the American metropolis.

As defined region of form, the sensual-corporeal is distinguished from others by the end of the self. With this form creates duration and continuity. The random properties of a thing become the contrast to form. A recognition is only possible from the corporeal view. The recognition of a corporeal is therefore an interpretation, a perspective on others, participating in the other. For the design this means, that architectural elements as compositions are described by a specific part-hood-in-the-other, thereby mereologically. In subsequent designs Hilberseimer reduces buildings to representations of consciously designed parthood relationships. Buildings become placeholders, the city becomes a schema. The schema character of Hilberseimer's designs is presented on several examples. As schemata, they are no architectural representations and despite their rigid representation they contain an idea of variation. The comparison of plan-schema and perspectives of the Vertical City will show that the punctuated facade shown in the perspectives is not the perforation of a wall with window openings, but an opening signifies a loggia, and thus it is the significant of an apartment. The perspectives show no architectural parts of a structure, but the disposition of residential units into a major figure. As schema, the design of Vertical City includes enough free space to design each unit of the city individually. Especially the reduction of representation embodied the idea of variation. In the Vertical City, a house is described by limits. So the city block stretches between two metro stations, the house is described as the distance of two staircases. The whole is described as a partial relationship for the part of the whole.

In the third chapter I will show, that the decentralized planning of Flat Housing and Settlement-Units not represent a break with the Vertical City. By the skyscraper as stacking of workshops, offices and housing in one unit, a solution for the dense city is found for Hilberseimer. The model of the Welfare City as concentric representation of urban morphology at different density, shows that high- and low-rise buildings for Hilberseimer coexist. If Hilberseimer begins to develop single storey settlements, the flat is the urban theme of his time. In a textual discussion, I will describe the mereological links in the Flat Housing. I shall suggest that the so-called L-Houses are to be regarded as a schema. As schemata they are representations of parthood-relationships of house and settlement. This is evident in comparison to the atrium houses of Mies van der Rohe. Atrium- and L-house studies both emerged at the same time as student projects in the so-called Bauseminar at the Bauhaus, under the direction of Mies and Hilberseimer. While L-houses represent simple and mostly minimum solutions for family homes, the atrium buildings are architecturally highly differentiated. However, both are mereologically congruent. The questions of Hilberseimer's semester tasks show: The house is designed as an axiom in itself, but always in its simultaneous arrangement of a settlement. The projected settlement is part of the planning of a house. The evaluation of the One through the Many is Hilberseimer's implementation of Riegl's ratio of form to plane. The difference between axiomatic and quantitative evaluation of a design is architecturally the difference between Poché and linear expression. In studies of Flat Housing Hilberseimer changes from the representation of Poché, as a distinction from One and the Other, to representations of the linear, as a distinction from One and the Many. Vertical City and studies of flat housing are described by Hilberseimer as associative models.This makes Hilberseimer a precursor of associative design strategies in the field of urban design.

With reference to the study of Room-Insolation, I will give an example, how external parameters are transformed into specific parts of an architectural element. By transferring human characteristics to the space, the assessment of the figur moves from the external view of a subject in the form of the designed house. The shift is a transfer of Kant's synthetic model. The relationship between subject-object transformes into a relationship between object-object. The architectural scale of modernity always designed with humanistic roles: The form of existence of an object is reflected in its form of effect as part of a subject. The urban operation of the shift of the form of effect in the architectural figure finally allows a revaluation of modernity, as a contrast between nature and culture. By multiplying the form of effect in the neighborhood fabric of the settlement, the humanistic contrast becomes a compositional parthood-relationship.

In the fourth chapter I link Hilberseimer's urban shift with contemporary approaches to ecology policy. The definition of punctualisation is transmitted transdisciplinary from the theory of science into a method for architecture. Literally shifts in Hilberseimer planning of a settlement from the evaluation, the $\nu o \mu o \varsigma$ of a house / $o \iota \kappa o \varsigma$, to the relationship of houses, so $\lambda o \gamma o \varsigma$. The economic requirement to consider a house as a utility, leads through the projection of the economy as a settlement structure to the transformaion of an economic to an ecological analysis: the Synoikism. Hilberseimer defines ground figurative comparable to Alois Riegl's formal descriptions as an essential urban element.

A mereologically-graphical analysis of room, house, settlement and region presents Hilberseimer's settlement unit as a material model. The compositional way of describing the model, builds on later models of the Form-Findung. With the specific translation of a mathematically-founded mereology, the schemes of the Vertical-City and Settlement-Unit can be compared compositionally. In the comparison of the two schemes will apparent, that punctualisations only gain expression when they are mereologically described as Bottom *and* Bound. The simultaneous description as part and as whole can indirectly be sensed in the proportion of the settlement: the gap. The analysis of regional studies shows, that the description of the region is bound to fail. In the region, the largest whole, a mutually considered mereological description as a bottom and bound is not possible.

This leads to the conclusion, the fifth chapter of the study. If one positions Hilberseimer's schemata in the discourse of architecture, architecture is conceived here fully in line with Aristotle poiesis: The intersection of disposition and colocation designes a poietic object. First, the disposition of the object gives knowledge about the quality of the colocation of the composition. This is reflected in the interaction of house and settlement: The disposition of the house in the settlement decides on the design of the house. In this step, the disposition is crossed and inseparable from the colocation: The settlement is part of the house, more precisely: The whole is part of the part as a whole: this is the punctualisation as architectural method.

1.1 Acknowledgements

This work is the result of several years of research, which concluded in writing a dissertation at the institute of urban design at the University of Innsbruck. I would like to thank Peter Trummer, for the support and the opportunity to realize my work at his institute. I thank the Independent Architecture Research Colloquia Innsbruck for friendship and innumerable discussions with Peter Griebel, Thomas Mathoy, John Ladinnig, Christoph Zimmel, Raphael Petrovic. I thank the many guests and critiques of the IoUD and the IARC for their advice in specific: Jeffrey Kippnis, Toni Kotnik, Michael Hensel, Robert Stuart Smith, Mario Carpo, Francois Roche, David Ruy, Michael Young, Graham Harman, Johan Bettum and Stefano de Martino. I thank Joost Meuwissen for his insights on the works of Karl Friedrich Schinkel. I thank Ulrich Metschl for assistance in the field of formal logic and mereology. Each work begins with inspiration. For this I thank Casey Reas. In particular, I would like to thank Lars Spuybroek to whom I owe the basic framework of this work.

This work is based on extensive research of the work of Ludwig Hilberseimer and would be unthinkable without the generous help of: Stephanie T Coleman und Seth Vanek of the Ryerson & Burnham Archive, Chicago Art Insitute; Kimberly Soss, Head of Architecture Library of IIT, Chicago, und Ralph Pugh, from the IIT Archiv. I thank George Schipporeit, for the insight into the work of the IIT at times Hilberseimer. I thank the Bauhaus Archive in Berlin for the overview in the teaching at the Bauhaus.

Finally, I thank my parents, Barbara and Jürgen Köhler, for their encouragement and faith. And I thank Rasa Navasaityte for the Priceless.

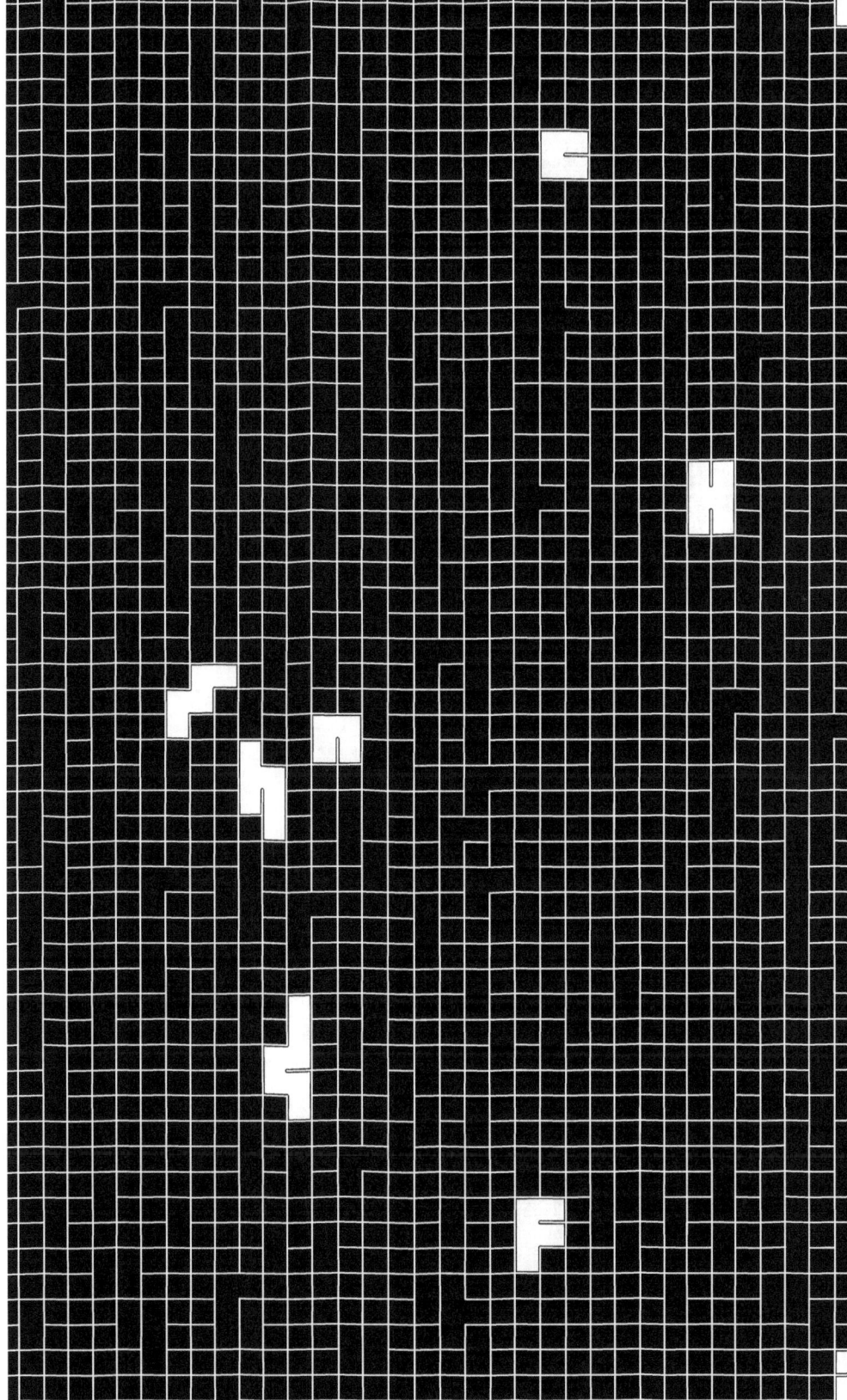

2 Introduction:
Topic, State of Knowledge, Method

> Like the poet, the architect too can, by mastering conditions and means, free himself from their determinations
> LUDWIG HILBERSEIMER. THE ART OF ARCHITECTURE

2.1 LUDWIG HILBERSEIMER: LIFE AND WORK

Brief biographies of Ludwig Hilberseimer have already been published often. This biography is therefore an independent one, however a summary of previous researches and was supplemented by information from the Chicago Architects Oral History Project of the Art Institute of Chicago.

Ludwig Hilberseimer was considered to be introverted, withdrawn into himself, a person who shunned public appearances and only rarely confided in friends in his trust[1]. By most of his built projects little is known. His influence is located in an immense number of articles, books and academic projects. He was known as an outstanding teacher, always focused on content. According to his students is known that Hilberseimer was also extremely well-read and well-versed. There is evidence that in his own biography Hilberseimer tried to present his work in a better light. There is also evidence that Hilberseimer realized much more buildings than is commonly known. There is no knowledge, plans, photographs of his buildings before the First World War, and it is clear from various correspondence that Hilberseimer realized several projects at this time. It is known that during this period Hilberseimer traveled to construction sites (e.g. in Croatia) several times. Precise information on locations unfortunately does not exist. Ludwig Hilberseimer did not found a family and devoted his life to his work and studies. From the descriptions of his apartments, one can assume that he used a modest, almost ascetic lifestyle[2].

Ludwig Hilberseimer was born September 14, 1885 in Karlsruhe in moderate conditions. Between autumn 1906 and summer of 1910 Hilberseimer studied architecture at the Polytechnic University of Karlsruhe. However, Hilberseimer studied only as a trainee an academic degree was denied him due to the fact that he did not finish high school with baccalaureate[3]. His teachers at the university known to us were Joseph Durm, Marcus Rosenberg (applied art), Friedrich Ostendorf[4] and Reinhard Baumeister[5]. On his own account Hilberseimer also attended lectures in art history and philosophy. It seems that Friedrich Ostendorf had the most impact on the development Hilberseimer's. In contrary to the emerging theories at that time, such as the Werkbund that modern culture produces a product from the transformation of functions, use and techniques[6], Ostendorf represented the need to reflect on the essential principles of architecture. He insisted on the structural unit of the functional plan of a house and its architectural manifestation. The central point of Ostendorf's criticism was directed to the irrelevance of a culture that results from the progressive advancement of techniques and reforms. Architecture here is understood in a parent, timeless setting[7]. In his study books the student Hilberseimer cites Ostendorf:

"It (Architecture) must have a simple appearance within the meaning of the organism: [...] When the talk should be of an architectural expression it means designing: Due to processing of the room layout, the situation and spatial requirement it includes one be taken out of several or many ideas for the building in your mind. Design therefore has nothing to do with drawing."[8]

In the consolidation of Ostendorf's teaching, Hilberseimer will develop an architecture theoretical approach of seeing the artistic zeitgeist of an era always in friction with material and technology. In his early writings references to Alois Riegl's Kunstwollen, Nietzsche's Great Style, Worringer Abstraction and Empathy and Schopenhauer's Will to Power are clearly visible[9].

After leaving the university and a half-year internship in Bremen, Hilberseimer moved to Berlin, where he lived until his departure for America. During the First World War, Hilberseimer was Executive Board in an architectural firm that built several air plane buildings. We know about a plane workshop, a hangar (by Staaken, Berlin) and the "Institute of Aeronautical Training and Research" (at Lake Müritz). From last drawings only a bird's eye view published in his latest book *Entfaltung einer Planungsidee*[10] is available. In Berlin, Hilberseimer seeks contact to the art scene, befriends with contemporary artists and in 1919 becomes a member of the *November Gruppe* and a little later of the *Arbeitsrat für Kunst* and *Die Kommune*. Furthermore, Hilberseimer was active in the Berlin Dadaists scene. All groups have the combination of art with a left-wing, political motivation in common. To his own socialist beliefs, Hilberseimer will always remain faithful. In 1919, an intensive phase as an art critic begins for Hilberseimer. Hilberseimer published in a multitude of Berlin's magazines, such as: *Der Einzige, G, Freie Zeitung, Feuer, Die Form, Vesc, Zeitschrift für sozialistische Politik, Das Kunstblatt*. From 1920-1926 Hilberseimer is a columnist for the *Sozialistischen Monatshefte*. In these writings, Hilberseimer developed his core theses, which he will always follow. Correspondence from this period shows, that Hilberseimer at that time planned a collection of articles under the title *Schöpfung und Entwicklung* (Creation and Development). Until 1922 Hilberseimer writes about art in general, from 1923 he turned his attention back to architecture.

Unfortunately, Hilberseimer cannot use his success as a theorist in practice. Until 1938, Hilberseimer runs a small architecture firm in Berlin and builds several small houses, which are briefly summarized. Again and again, Hilberseimer takes part in competitions, but without coming to a commission. However, he understands to combine his prototypical designs with his work as a critique and thus with the projects of the avantgarde. He succeeds to be included in exhibitions. His books *Groszstadtbauten*[11] and *Groszstadtarchitektur*[12] are a mixture of architectural history, collection of contemporary projects entered with his own designs. Through his work as architecture critique, he is able to make important contacts to the architects of the European avantgarde. In 1925, he traveled to Holland and met the protagonists of De Style, in Paris it seems he has had contact to Le Corbusier. Back in Berlin, he became a member of the *Zehnerring*, other members are: Bartning, Behrrendt, Gropius, Haring, Mendelsohn, Mies van der Rohe, Poelzig, Bruno and Max Taut.

He is one of the architects invited to build at the Weissenhofsiedlung. But even more important, Mies van der Rohe invoked Hilberseimer to organize the exhibition: *Internationale Plan- und Möbelausstellung Neuer Baukunst*. It served as a pendant and complement Weissenhofsiedlung. The exhibition brought together international examples of modernist movement. The projects were presented only with the help of large format photos. The exhibition was a great success and was sent on a journey through 17 different European cities. This resulted in the demand for an exhibition catalog, which appeared as a special print of the magazine *Moderne Bauformen* in September 1927. This publication is one of the first, featuring the modernist architecture as an international movement, as style. Hilberseimer has reached the center of the avantgarde. The photo exhibition of the material also forms the basis for Hilberseimer following publications, where he used materials originally part of the International Building repeatedly[13].

In 1928, Hilberseimer was appointed by Hannes Meyer to the Bauhaus, first as a guest lecturer, two years later Hilberseimer becomes "Meister" and teaches classes *Urban Planning* (1930-1933) and *Settlement Planning* (1931-1933)[14]. The academic research is becoming increasingly important for Hilberseimer. His following publications are made entirely of results of his research and teaching. With the closing of the Bauhaus Hilberseimer plays a key role. To allow a continuation of the Bauhaus, the Nazis demanded Mies, who was director at that time, to dismiss Kadinsky as Russian painter and Hilberseimer as socialist planner. In order to avoid this, Mies closed the Bauhaus with the approval of the Collegium. His latest designs in Germany, e.g. for the *Freie Universität Berlin*, due to the political conditions were only studies for a private circle of people and published by Hilberseimer only later on. This circle Hilberseimer found in the "Friday Group", a group of former Bauhaus students who met with the objective for intellectual resistance weekly in Hilberseimer's office. In this context, the development studies to Dessau emerged, which together with his 1933 manuscript *Grundlagen des Städtebaus*, formed the basis for *New City*[15]. Under the Nazi regime, he almost does not face any more architectural commissions. On July 27, 1938 Hilberseimer left Germany to go to London, under the pretext to have found a publisher for his publications and finally followed the invitation from Mies van der Rohe's to Chicago.

In the fall of 1938, Hilberseimer begins to teach with Mies van der Rohe and Walter Peterhans at the Armour Institute Chicago, later IIT. Until 1965, that is until he was 80 years old, he remains an active member of the faculty[16]. On the side of Mies van der Rohe, Hilberseimer was a complementary partner, who worked on analogous problems on the urban level[17]. As Mies recognized architecture as tectonic problem, Hilberseimer dealt with the tectonics of the city, that shapes a compositional order from the juxtaposition of architectures. Starting out in more chaotic conditions, accommodated without own premises in an attic, with a low number of students and in German language with a student interpreter, the IIT has developed steadily to one of the most important schools of architecture in America after the Second World War. Despite the high number of students who Hilberseimer supervised during this period, opinions regarding his influence vary strongly. Neither Hilberseimer himself nor none of his students were ever able to realize a Settlement-Unit[18]. Multiple times Hilberseimer tried to realize his Settlement-Unit, but except for the master plan for Lafayette Park in Detroit, he never succeeded. Lafayette is congruent with Hilberseimer theses, pedestrian throughway, an interweaving of landscape and architecture, but not even recognizable as a settlement unit. Here, the diagram turned into architecture. As Mies, who was commissioned to design the IIT campus, and his own office were very busy with the planning of the campus buildings, Mies handed the design of student and teacher Apartments to Hilberseimer. Based on the L-shape studies, a settlement east of the campus should emerge. Unfortunately, Hilberseimer could not prevail with the clients and SOM got the job, what SOM opened the doors for the

Figure 2.1: Ludwig Hilberseimer Portraits; A: Portrait 1912; B: Photo in front of the stacked highrise models of the welfare city model 1928, C: Portrait n.d.

final adoption of the whole campus project[19]. Hilberseimer's great plan of Chicago is indeed originated as a research project in its entirety at IIT. However, archived correspondence confirms that Hilberseimer repeatedly suggested excerpts for implementation to city committees. Many of his former students occupied key positions in the city planning committees of the American cities. Therefore, at least Hilberseimer as teacher gave an influence.

In 1963, for the first time since his departure from Germany Hilberseimer takes an extended trip to Europe. In Berlin, he was honored by the Technical University with an honorary Doctor of Technical Sciences. It is Hilberseimer's only academic title. To a Berlin reporter and the question on his merits Hilberseimer replies: He had achieved nothing.

On May 6, 1967 Ludwig Hilberseimer died in Chicago, at the age of 82 years.

2.2 SCIENTIFIC RECENSION OF THE WORK HILBERSEIMER'S

The Estate: The work of Hilberseimer is easy to follow because of his own numerous publications. Overall, Hilberseimer published twelve books and over one-hundred articles. We owe it to his acribic work style that he left behind a well-ordered collection of manuscripts, sketches, secondary literature, which is now owned by the

Ryerson and Burnham Archives, Art Institute of Chicago[20]. Due to his teaching at the Bauhaus there is a further estate at the Bauhaus-Archiv in Berlin. And yet, there are some voids. Hilberseimer left Germany in 1938 under the pretext of wanting to find a publisher. Although there were early sketches from the Berlin time under the holdings of the Chicago apartment, Hilberseimer was forced to leave the majority of his estate in Berlin. The work of his office and his built projects can only be traced from photographs, at that time published material or indirectly via official documents, correspondence, etc. The resulting works in conjunction through the Bauhaus are sparse. They are fragmented due to fire damage or were lost totally during the Second World War[21]. At the Illinois Institute of Technology in Chicago, due to the lack of space, no architectural projects could be archived. Thus, nearly no original plans or models of student work from the era of Mies and Hilberseimer have been preserved[22]. Since Hilberseimer had no office in Chicago and worked either at home or at IIT, one can assume that the original data of its research projects were also discarded. For legal reasons, the Master's thesis work has been archived in the letter format only. Most plans are preserved only as photographs.

The Review: Due to the scope and coherence of his thoughts, the number of authors who were related to Hilberseimer to support their own theories is large. However, comments on Hilberseimer during lifetime are sparse. A serious critical consideration of the theses Hilberseimer's started only in the sixties.

A contemporary commentary was delivered by Hugo Häring 1926 in the essay "Zwei Städte" (two cities)[23]. In this article, Häring already developed two contrary critical points, which are exemplary for the further review of Hilberseimer's work. In the article, Häring is impressed by Hilberseimer spotless "thought and will capacity." On the other hand, he rejects the proposal of the Vertical City vehemently, with the following two arguments: Firstly, from an aesthetic point of view, Häring denotes Hilberseimer's Vertical City as inhuman and technocratic in its Gestalt. The mechanically-uniform architecture of Vertical City lacks any contextualization, any interaction between city and landscape. The city remains an idea, it lacks the confrontation with Nature. On the other hand, Häring criticizes the negotiating of human needs through mechanical forms. "The planned setting of man leaves no space for the living, de-dignifies man to a thing." Further he carries out his own ideas of an organic city. His ideas of society here are directly transformed into the image of a landscape.

Both critical points are based on a direct dependency of content and figure. On the one hand of the critique *society is predetermined by form*: That is, this type of reading is based on the assumption that an architectural figure determines social processes, actions. An analysis of the form leads to conclusions about an inscribed social model.

The deterministic model can be used on one hand to reject the architectural figure, due to the lack of formal properties which are necessary to carry out desired social actions. On the other hand, the extracted social model can also reveal unsuspected political and social impacts, assigning an inherent potential to the architectural figure. Its formal abstraction and paranoid amplification results in new figurations. Social interventions pass through architectural form. On the other side of the critique is *form is the product of social factors*: social, technical, material properties provide the architectural figure. The figure is evaluated by an epistemological description of social conditions, analogous to the time of the creation of the design, in Hilberseimer's case the architectural figure, the result of the states of the Weimar Republic. Here likewise, a content weighting lead to a rejection or approval of the figure. Architecture is situated in a passive role and is the result of a materialistic worldview.

2.2.1 Society follows Form: Society is predetermined by form

Those who have not yet heard from the name Hilberseimer, probably already stumbled over the perspective views of the Vertical City as a negative example of the effects of the modernism. To put his work of the Settlement-Unit in the foreground, Hilberseimer himself in 1963 brands the Vertical City himself as "Necropoli"[24], and therefore opens the gates for a phenomenological-architectural interpretation of his studies, which has survived to this day. Since then, especially the two perspectives of the Vertical City were used again and again as polemic example to demonstrate the weaknesses of a modernist society and its failure[25]. This side of the critique on the works of Hilberseimer uses a phenomenological interpretation of his architectural Gestalt: the figure.

Absence: In his seminal article *The city is not a tree*[26] of 1966, Christopher Alexander compares the image of a (data-) tree with a semi-lattice. Based on the set theory of mathematics, Alexander in this paper developed a formal analysis method that allows him to translate the road layout of canonical modern urban plans into path diagrams. Alexander points out, that the urban models of modernism structurally are based on the organizational form of a tree. Tree structures as likewise abstracted human relation schemes lead to the insights of sociology, to the separation and isolation of social neighborhoods. In short circuit of both path diagrams, physically manifested tree structures lead to isolation in urban structures. In the case of Hilberseimer's Settlement Unit, the translation of the fishbone structure of the settlement into a tree diagram similar to Figure 2.2, is an almost trivial step. The elimination of intersections, one of Hilberseimer's main demands for urban planning, Alexander

26 The Mereological City: a reading of the works of Ludwig Hilberseimer

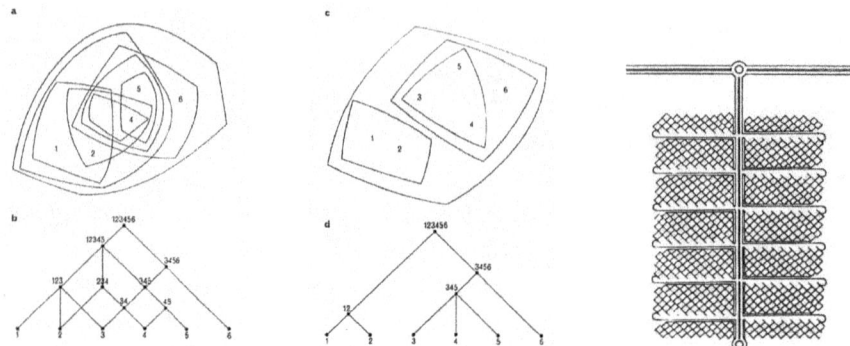

Figure 2.2: left, middle: Christopher Alexander: diagram: lattice – semi-lattice; left: overlapping spatial structure is transferred in a heterogeneous network; middle: nested spaces are transferred to a hierarchical tree structures; right: Ludwig Hilberseimer: Schema of a street layout of a Settlement-Unit

uses equal to the elimination of social contact in the city. In short, Hilberseimer's Settlement Unit is anti-social. Alexander opposes the tree structure with the image of the semi-lattice: The organizational superposition of spatial structures leads to densification and diversity of social structures. As drawed conclusion: Social neighborhoods emerge at the junctions of the city, where people meet, communicate and maintain social networks. In the subsequent conclusion: the number and figure of intersections determines the social health of a city.

I would like to confront this with Hilberseimer's concept of "Open Space". Most clearly Hilberseimer defined the term in a manuscript for a not published, book with the title *City Architecture, The Trend towards openess*:

"We no longer need Agoras, forums or public squares, because we have parliaments, assembly halls and auditoriums. We also do not need anymore market squares, because we have shopping centers, super markets and department stores. We also have little use for architectural squares. But what we really need and do not have in our cities is open space! [...] Should not this open space gained be in direct connection with nature, should not the city itself be penetrated by nature?"[27]

What now Hilberseimer means by open space? First, he notes that in contrary to all predecessors, for the contemporary city the object of the city architecture is no longer planning assembly facilities as physical manifestations of a collective. The task of urban architecture is reduced to the creation of "Open Space". His comment that a

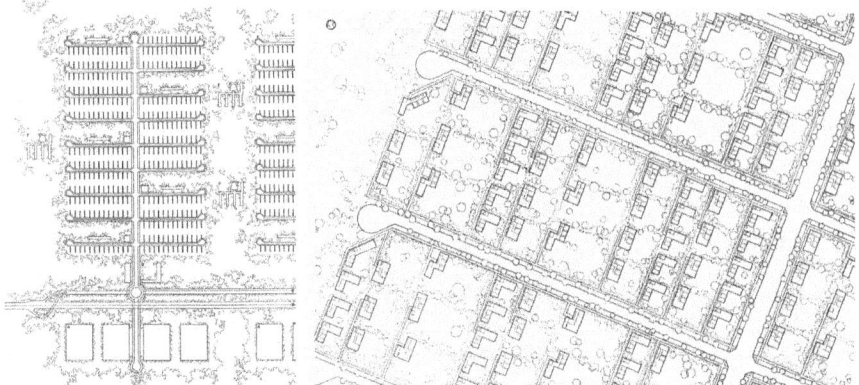

Figure 2.3: left: schema of a Settlement-Unit; right: detail of a Settlement-Unit

link between nature and city can create this open space, finally will let us will find it in the peripheral areas of the Settlement-Unit. Here, single-family houses are only accessible from the street from one side of the ground. Three sides of the plot are adjacent to neighboring properties. Whereby there are no properly fixed boundary lines, a property determination is not shown. However, on the center lines between the houses we find footpaths, which bundle themselves and lead out of the Settlement-Unit into the open landscape. As part of the Settlement-Unit there are no plans at all from Hilberseimer for public buildings. In the aerial photographs volumetric forms of places of assembly assigned to the Commercial Areas can be seen. The only public building we know is planning a school. Furthermore, there are plan drawings for playgrounds and parks, remarkably organic in nature. Schools such as parks are located outside and mostly between the settlement units.

With Open Space, Hilberseimer refers to the possibility of free development of each individual. Collective space is not caused by a quantitative size, but by the absence of any territorialisation. The elimination of road junctions not only minimizes the length of road, but also a universal territorialized (state) interaction. On the other hand, the free space, or rather the interaction between landscape and settlement is maximized, as well as the space of personal evolvement. Hilberseimer finds this in the settlement unit, a translation of the urban (Hobbesian) role model of American society: The free, individual development and opportunities far from an integration into a (state) global structure. By shifting the collective space from the architectural street space into the urban void, Hilberseimer developed a city that actually already precedes the demands of Alexander for neighborhoods. However, for Alexander's method of analysis, this city is invisible as the shift from form to content is not transformed from the traditional city and thus cannot be morphologically reconstructed.

Eliptical Space: Albert Pope points out in his book *Ladders*[28], that Hilberseimer in advance accesses the urban space of postmodernism of Late-Capital[29]. Pope speaks of the urban inscription of the subject[30] that changes the basic infrastructure. The "Ladder" leads to the implosion of urban space. Architecture itself becomes the city. The street becomes a tunnel and corridor. The street is only a pure extension and connection between indoor spaces[31]. The city becomes a network of cul de sacs. Pope sees the facing of cul de sacs similar to opposing of settlement units, a way to a new kind of urbanity. The absence of planning creates a space free of any territorialization and economic links[32].

Rem Koolhaas developed a similar idea in his essay: *Imagining Nothingness*[33]. Here, referring to Oswald Matthias Ungers Green Archipelago project of 1976[34], the city is divided into "Urban Solids" and "Metropolitan Voids". Both are independent of each other, two levels of planning and perception of the city, but intertwined. Koolhaas sees the void in Hilberseimer's "Zero Degree Architecture". As urban intervention Koolhaas suggests to fill the void, the absence, with program in order to bring the two parallel models of the city and content in conjunction. With this Koolhaas intensifies Albert Pope's approach and relocates the area of absence from the space of the city to the generic building mass of the city.

2.2.2 Form follows Society: The form as product of social factors

On the other hand, there is one side in the review of Hilberseimer that indicates Hilberseimer's Large-City-Buildings as a product of social factors during the Weimar Republic. With this, the project of Hilberseimer becomes as a consequently conducted intellectual performance Hilberseimer's, an exemplary comprehension of an era.

Hilberseimer's planning as urban materialism: This is a historical interpretation, which, in Manfredo Tafuri's *Architecture and Utopia*[35], has its beginning in 1976. For Manfredo Tafuri, modernist projects for the city reproduce the reality of industrial production. Based exemplary on the review of Hilberseimer's *Groszstadt Architektur*, Tafuri describes how modern urbanism reflects the industrial assembly line. The methods of industrial production methods are part of the organization of the object. From the standardized element to the cell, to each block, to the settlement and finally to the city, a hierarchical chain is described, in which each parent object must be seen as an assemblage of small objects. The architecture does no describe anymore a form, but organizes the economic, social, technological forces, relations and conditions of the city. In Tafuri's analysis for Hilberseimer the "object" is not considered. For Tafuri, Hilberseimer focused exclusively on laws of the organization. Through their total elaboration Tafuri goes as far as to call his approach to the city as a "social machine". This bears the role of architecture as an assemblage of single cells reciprocally influenced by the planimetric conditions of the Large City.

Certainly Tafuri's analysis is conclusive and correct. But I would like to put into question, to what extent Tafuri's historical linkage may allow conclusions about, or even a rating of Hilberseimers architecture[36].

Firstly, Tafuri's description is a materialist interpretation but Hilberseimer projects, taking into account Hilberseimers own architecture-theoretical writings which especially builds on Alois Riegl's terms of the Kunstwollen, cannot be interpreted as a purely materialistic approach to design.

Second, in his metaphor of the social machine, Tafuri places cell and organism on the same level with the individual and the collective. But cell and machine is a common connotation of the former discourse on urbanism. Karl Scheffler, for example, already in 1913 compares the city to an organism and the family economy as the smallest cell in the urban organism[37]. Later, the work of Patrick Geddes will affect Hilberseimer. Geddes, in the *The Coming Polity*[38] calls the family a cell and the city an organism. I would rather like to represent the assumption that Hilberseimer took over from the former discourse, that is the definition of the cell as the home of a single family and the city as the accumulation of those. Its focus was on the relationship of the parts and its assemblies on different scales. Unlike Scheffler and Geddes equivalent of the cell to the biological family, Hilberseimer sees the cell as a composition of needs and circumstances. The cell is a purely architectural element, which is based on their internal laws of form. Consequently, for Hilberseimer, room and residents are farmost separated. The room is a logical arrangement of furniture, walls, floor, ceiling and room openings. The resident moves into a fix furnished room only with a suitcase, his personal clothing. The house as a hotel is completely contrary to semperianian theory of architecture as clothing[39]. The resident finds room (german: Raum) and space (german: Raum[40]) which is not produced specifically for him. For Hilberseimer, architecture is not the extension of biological and materialistic conditions of the people, as in Tafuri's reading. As architecture, it is opposed to them.

Several authors have built on Tafuri's materialistic interpretation. So Sabine Hake in the book *Topographies of Class*[41] describes the *Groszstadt Architektur*[42] by Hilberseimer in a similar manner as the architectural equivalent of, quoting Siegfried

Krakauer, the "space images" of the Weimar Republic. In addition, there are a two arguments from Pier Vittorio Aureli, which I would like to discuss in more detail:

The City-Archipelago: In *The Possibility of an Absolute Architecture*[43], Aureli argues for the possibility of a finite architecture, as a counterpart to the city as a process of endless urbanization. An architecture as Archipelago – a city within a city[44] – takes a clear position to its limitations. Its similiarity to an island produces a complete mode of relations as a political form. The relationship intended as a confrontation of parts is a fundamental metaproject with which architecture can obtain its critical position to the city[45]. By confronting ordinary, existing, everyday pieces the specific evolves, the basic definition of architecture here as a "State of Exception"[46].

The roots of Aurelis argumentation go back to Aristotle's distinction between politics and economics, precisely between *techne politike* and *techne oikonomike*[47]. For Aristotle, techne politike (the art of politics) is the area where decisions are made for the good of the public interest, possibilities like different groups living together. In this sense, politics arise from the existence of the polis. The polis is the space of the crowd (the many), the space exists between individuals or groups of individuals when they co-exist with each other. The basis of politics here is decision making, which can resolve conflicts in Co-Existence. Techne Oikonomike, the economy, is concerned with the administration of the private space of the house: the oikos. For Aristotle, the oikos is a complex organism of relationships. But unlike the political sphere, in the space of the Oikos, human relations are given, unchangeable and despotic. Economy therefore is concerned with the administration of the house and the control of its members. The Greek city was divided into two parts as well: the oikoi, the agglomeration of houses, and the political space of the agora, where opinions were exchanged and public decisions were made. Going further, Aureli distinguishes the Greek concept of the polis, which finds the mode of their relationships as their essential political form of the condition of the island and the Roman term urbs, that describes more the material constitution, the pure agglomeration of houses with no political intention. Urbs reduced the protected living-together to the principle of the house and its material conditions. The urbanization is based on the Roman concept of urbs and replaced politics with economics as a mode of city control.

Aureli describes it in reference to three canonical projects: Ildefons Cerdas Plan for Barcelona, Ludwig Hilberseimer's Vertical-City and Archizoom's Non-Stop-City. He describes the fundamental space shifts like human relations from the political space of the city to the economic space of the house. Aureli outlines Hilberseimer's Large-City-Architecture, inspired by Tafuri's interpretation, as a project that consists of the coordination of two extremes: the individual cell and productive and economic forces of the city[48]. As key element Aureli argues Hilberseimer's project of the Vertical City solely as a polemical stance against Le Corbusier's City for Three Million Inhabitants. For Aureli, Hilberseimer's Vertical City consists of the uniform repetition of a single type of building. A hybrid between city block and slab, where all the city activities such as housing, production, commercial are merged. A functional separation does not exist. The repetition takes place in a uniform circulational grid that can apparently be extended indefinitely in all directions. Aureli says, that architectural form is understood here not as a representation, but as a process, as assemblage of all elements of the city. He emphasizes the uniform character of the Vertical City, which he interpreted as a lack of any figurative or individual element. The city is reduced to its reproductive condition. So any distinction between public and private space disappears in favor of a totalitarian, organic understanding of city without any limit. The methods of economics institutionalize the private space of the city as the administration of the private house.

The trend towards architectural autonomy: Cynically, precisely Hilberseimers Vertical City and its research on the Settlement-Unit can be seen as a precursor to Oswald Matthias Ungers City Archipelago and thus to Aureli's autonomous architecture. From the first moment on, Hilberseimers sets a limit to his urban schemes. Inspired by Raymond Unwin's scheme of Suburbs, Hilberseimer developed his Residential City in 1923, building on a satellite town model. The city as a framework of multiple, self-contained, districts and not as an endless expansion of a grid as posttulated by Aureli[49]. In a comparison of the current development of Berlin overlaid with an island-like distribution of settlement units in 1932, Hilberseimer even contributes as a forerunner to the idea of the city in the city.

Furthermore, Hilberseimer defined the minimum and maximum size of his city units very well and thus follows analogously the demands of Aristotle to the size of the city. Size is bound by Aristotle and Hilberseimer to the plurality of a community. On the one hand, diversity should establish individual choice and development, on the other hand, for both the size of the city is limited so that the effect of individual participation does not vanish into the mass[50]. Instead of searching instruments for a materialistic, endless urbanization, Hilberseimer aims exactly at the opposite. He is concerned with the conscious design of the Large City. From the city in its current state, he draws a picture of an ocean of houses, an endless urbanization which is to overcome[51]. In a late book: *Contemporary Architecture – It's Roots And Trends*[52], Hilberseimer describes the various developments of architecture as a continuous tension between individual artistic expression and the technical, material circumstances. Looking back to the 1920s, Hilberseimer describes architecture as a trend towards architectural autonomy, a phase during which architecture liberated itself from external influences and discovered its elements in their purest form. Hilberseimer in his own words:

"The architecture of the Twenties was characterized by its objectivity, its directness, and its simplicity. Its trend was toward architectural autonomy. It aimed to free itself from all external influences, from all traditional bonds, to be self-determined, and to realize its goals by the true means of architecture. It tried to discover the elements of architecture and to use them in their purest form."[53]

Architecture is free from any economic speculation as the materialization of global urbanization. Architecture rather is an independent science of architectural elements and their distribution.

The design of the Vertical City was created in response to the traffic problem in Corbusier's City of 3 million inhabitants. For this purpose, Hilberseimer dispensed the required functional separation of Corbusier and stacked labor, offices and residential into one city block. Modeled on the medieval town, the city blocks of the Vertical City are nothing more than the enlargement of a medieval town house. This means, that Hilberseimer's city blocks are autonomous units: a house as a city. By linking the workplace with the apartment, transport between the blocks is reduced to a minimum. Community life is displaced into the interior of the city blocks, making the street and any other external infrastructure stripped of its benefits to society. So the streets of the Vertical City also appear empty and oversized, questioning their redundancy. As a result, precisely the infinity of the street network indicates the limit of urbanization. In the Settlement-Unit, Hilberseimer finally minimizes the street network, deprived of its architectural task and develops an alternative in the "Absence".

Barbarians: In a further paper *Architecture for Barbarians*[54] Aureli develops Hilberseimer's Large-City-Architecture to a critical project of a capitalist city, which especially through its gray, generic design, the political void, sets a chance for a new societal beginning. Aureli bases his assumption on the work of Walter Benjamin and his definition of "Barbarians": man without memory, history or tradition, who is given the chance to start new[55]. For Benjamin, the mode of a Tabula Rasa is the only salvation for the residents of the city, who in the face of increasing impoverishment of their human experience (the workers), plunge into an enhanced substitute of entertainment. Instead of this pathetic resistance against the inhuman condition of city, Benjamin proposes rather more accepting the real production conditions of the city as a new beginning of the city. With a city that can be extended to infinity without

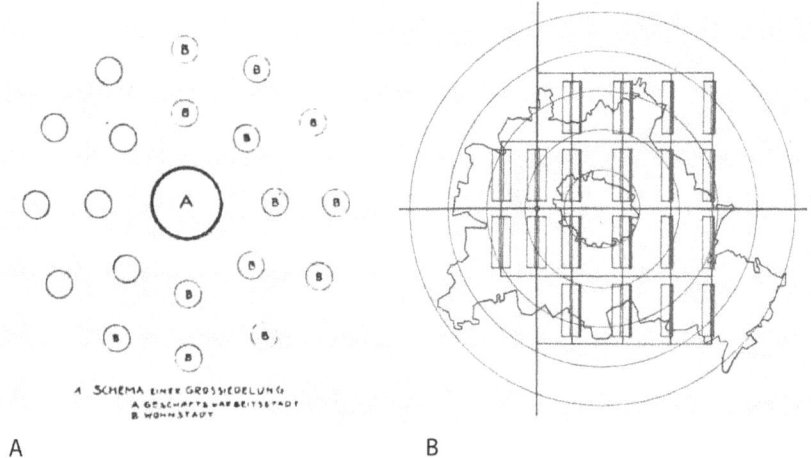

Figure 2.4: A: Hilberseimer, Trabantenstadt, 1925; B: Hilberseimer, Combination of Elements of a City for 4,000.000 People, 1940

specific characteristics, Hilberseimer developed a city of and for the mass of workers. The city develops from the power of the labor and production. Due to its extreme reduction, Hilberseimer unmasks the true purpose of the industrial city to bring its residents to work. If we understand Hilberseimer's project as a critical project for the capitalist city, as a representation of the urban condition of mankind, there are parallels to Benjamin's essay, which sees the generic condition of our city as a new beginning for a differentiated society.

It should be stated critically, that the deliberately designed Barbarics, so architecture as Void, the opposite is of the later shigt Hilberseimer's of the architecture into the urban Void. A "naked", commonly same design is also a kind design, and hence a kind of territorialization. As Michael Hays been able to show[56], it was precisely the conception of the naked but predefined territory, that totalitarian regimes of the 20th century knew to exploit. The nakedness of the mass ornament, the Barbarian was already an unintended but shocking reality. Also Kilian argues that the concept of "Primitive" and "Barbarian" for Hilberseimer is the possibility for an art-critical analysis of the emergence of a piece of art and Hilberseimer did not aim at the "barbaric" as a template for a new style[57].

2.2.3 The Schemata of Design

In his paper *An End to Speculation*[58] as introduction of the English translation of: Hilberseimer 1927b. Richard Anderson moves one step further. Based in the materialist tradition Tafuri's, Anderson calls Hilberseimer's naked aesthetics an alternative to speculative design models. For Anderson, Hilberseimer project is therefore a current possible solution to crises triggered by a speculative real estate market, driven by speculative models for architecture[59]. According to Anderson, the solution of Hilberseimer lies in the shift of his attention from form towards the law of form, from the interest on the aesthetics of form to the organizational possibilities of architecture[60] Care should be taken with Anderson's concept of form. As we shall see in the following, based Hilberseimer's approach on a concept of form not as an appearance, but as an organization. Anderson's understanding of form can therefore be not equated with Hilberseimer's form-term. With this, Anderson takes on a side note of Manfredo Tafuri:

"Hilberseimer did not offer "models" for designing, but rather established, at the most abstract and therefore most general level possible, the Coordinates and dimensions of the design itself."[61]

It is the scheme of the design itself, which Hilberseimer worked out. Although Tafuri almost 40 years ago noted this aspect, a deeper insight is still pending. It is this point, that I will investigate in this work.

2.3 THE METHOD: A MEREOLOGICAL READING

What exactly is a scheme? For the first time the term scheme was described by Kant. Scheme for Kant denotes the "Representation of a general procedure of the imagination; to find a concept its image"[62]. Martin Heidegger considered Kant's definition more closely and it turned out that a scheme is not the sensualisation of an empirical vision, but the directory of the norm of image acquisition. "The rule is shown in the how of their regulating, ie in which, the representation regulating, as it is dictated into the descriptive aspect of it."[63]. With this is "although the scheme distinguishable from the image, but nevertheless relative on something like image, i.e. the image character belongs necessarily to the schema."[64]. The scheme therefore as the determination of the image character; of the expression of the image, is not the definition of the picture itself.

In the architectural context the schema is different from the concept of the diagram. A diagram refers to the production of the image. Let's remain with Heidegger: In Heidegger's sense, the formulation of a diagram arises from the sensualisation of the empirical vision of similar images. But the empirical vision by the formed signifier always incorporates more as the term itself contains. Thus, the vision and ultimately a diagram is one of an infinite number. An empirical abstraction will always be incomplete. A scheme however, stands for "one that applies to man"[65].

This definition of the schema is important for the understanding of the work of Hilberseimer. His schemes are concerned with the ways of organizing elements (architecture) to a larger whole (the city). Thus Hilberseimer deals with the architectural problem of the part to the whole. However, not only as a full-scale problem between the house and settlement, but as a planning problem, the search for a valid understanding of any whole. For this purpose, Hilberseimer developed architectural schemes as sensualisation of the term settlement for the planning of a house as part of the settlement. These schemata have the potential, which is expressed best by Heidegger:

"The individual has disbanded the arbitrariness, however, is thereby a possible example for the one that governs the much valid arbitrariness as such. In this regulation but has the general its specific structured determination and is by no means compared to the isolated an indefinite blurring anything and everything"[66]

In its broadest sense, a scheme therefore is a particular type of form. The form of a figure is obtained by *abstraction* of the content from the figure. When taking away the content of a figure the form of the figure remains. The form of a sentence, for example, is its grammar[67]. So you can say, formal methods deal with the schemes of real objects. The correct method for the study of Hilberseimer's work is so at first a *formal* method.

2.3.1 The term form in philosophy and architecture

At first glance, it seems to be very easy to talk about form. On closer examination however, it is found that the concept of form was used throughout the history of philosophy, mathematics, logic, art and architecture in extremely diverse manners. For this reason, it is important to define the concept of form more closely before commencing an investigation. The term can be refined from two sides. On the one hand, based on the nature of the scheme at Hilberseimer, as a relationship between the house and settlement and on the other hand through the historical context of Hilberseimer taking into account his art historical– and philosophical sources.

Let us first frame the concept of form by the kind of its schemes[68]. The word form goes back to the Latin word forma and replaced the Greek words μορφη und ειδος. While the first stands for the Gestalt of a form, so the physical form, the second stands for the idea of a form, so the conceptual form. The Latin summary of two very different meanings is the root of the variety and complexity of today's definitions. The easiest way is to classify the different meanings by their opposites.

If we take as opposite content, form means the *appearance* of a thing. The term form here is applied to what acts directly on the viewer's senses. Form is the direct appearance, a sound, a color – content its meaning. The concept originated in poetry and stood for the difference between the sound of the words and their meaning. The probably oldest example is the difference between Homer's hexameter and the deeds of a much-traveled man. Impressionism in the visual arts is a good example. Extreme formalists, following this tradition, deny content, try to detach from each reference and work only with the appearance: form as a shape. *The life of forms*[69] from Henri Focillon is a good example for this: Forms for Focillon are no symbols or images, but an expression of themselves. Even in one of the first reviews on Focillon's proposal, Wassily Kandinsky countered, by himself an abstract painter: "An artist loves the forms passionately as he loves his tools and the smell of turpentine, because they are all powerful means in the service of content."[70] Especially nothingness emphasizes the absence of what it removed[71].

Another antithesis of form is materiality (German: Stofflichkeit). Form becomes a *contour* and the limit of a material. When content is understood as a materiality, form describes a hull, an envelope. This idea of form is found in the historic French Poché and the Italian concept of drawing. When drawing the outline of a person, a figure emerges. Therefore, in this concept the figure is of a synonym of form. This definition clearly distinguishes itself from the definition of the form and appearance. In the visual arts, this is perhaps most clearly illustrated by Wölfflin's contrast between the linear and the painterly[72]. The contour distinguishes two things from each other, a contour-shape can be determined only by an Other. If form in architecture is understood as a boundary, two tasks for architecture arise: At first: to distinguish figures, as in Collin Rowe's Figure-Ground Analysis[73], or Pier Vittorio Aureli's absolute space as a containment[74]. Secondly, overlaying with the first concept of form as appearance: the envelope is the narrative carrier of the enclosed, as with the historic facades of Semperianians, Robert Venturi's Decorated Shed[75] or Patrick Schumacher's parametric semiology[76].

The third contrast to form is the part. Thus form is equivalent to the arrangement of parts. Form is the *order of parts* to a whole. For example, the form of a portico is the arrangement of its columns. With this term ςυμμετρια, αρμονια and ταχις becomes to synonyms of form. The consonance of parts is also probably the primordial concept of form in architecture, first described by Leon Battista Alberti[77]. According to Alberti, the order of elements enables the measurement of the beauty of a building by "lawful agreement of all parts, whatever a thing could be, which consists in that you could not take away something to add or change, without making them less pleasing" [78]. The concept of form as the organization of the parts of an objects the definition, to which the current use of the adjective *formal* is probably the closest.

Form generates duration and continuity. With this view, the coincidence or the random properties of an object are the contrast of form. This approach was first developed by Aristotle as $ευτελης$. Form becomes the opposite of the fluctuating properties, the *essence of the object*. That is why it is also referred to substantial form. It should be noted that there is a difference between Plato's $ιδεα$ and Aristotle $ευτελης$. Plato's $ιδεα$ is designated to an abstract archetype of a thing, $ευτελης$ stands for the thing as actualization of an inherent will. Expressed in design terms: Something complex, which occurs when a large number of simple elements are composed together. The Entelechy was a forerunner of today's concept of self-organization. As Helmut Müller-Sievers could show[79], Aristotle's form concept was re-established in the literature of the 18th century. In contrast to the concept of pre-formation, the concept of Entelechy helped the biologists of the 18th century to argue organisms as autonomous beings.

It is these literature sources on which Kant builds later on. From the autonomous object and its subjective view, Kant draws the conclusion, that form is an *addition of the subjective thought* to the perceived object. Kant shows that in aesthetics there is no a-priori-form. Therefore, beauty for Kant is not based on a constant state of mind, but on the creative talent of an artist[80]. This approach was further developed by Konrad Fiedler and Adolf von Hildebrand and differentiated form of existence (German: Daseinsform) from form of effect (German: Wirkungsform)[81]. This term was transferred almost parallel by Alois Riegl to the concept of the Kunstwollen[82] and led to one of the first art-historical analyzes based on the effect of form of an epoche. When Hilberseimer began to publish his first articles at the beginning of the 1920s, the influence of Riegl's writings is clearly visible.

For the architecture of Hilberseimer we can now determine a formal method more accurately. We evaluate the previous definitions: If form is the direct appearance, as opposite of content, the example of the hexameter shows, that appearance is describable only by a kind of composition, the distances between its elements, ie through form as the arrangement of its parts. The contrast of content therefore is obsolete as a matter of closer evaluation. If form is seen as a boundary, it is possible to separate one thing from one another, but only from an external point of view, in a kind of

Cartesian view. An idea for the actual design is not included in this definition of form. It is a method of observation and thus falls into the category of theoretical sciences. Although form as contour can distinguish things, mark them, but does not describe the relationship between two or more things, such as a house and settlement. The notion of form as an arrangement of parts here comes closest to the used definition of architecture as a composition. We find this concept of form in a similar manner by Hilberseimer, in the moment, when he compares architecture with poetry and its basis on structural elements[83].

2.3.2 The house and the city: a classic formal thesis

Hilberseimer's understanding of form has very classical roots in architecture theory. Often, Hilberseimer refers to Leon Battista Alberti's theories on the city. As described for the first time in 1452, in *De Re Aedificatoria*[84] it is Alberti's image of the city as a large house and the sum of its elements to which Hilberseimer refers[85]:

"The city is like some large house, and the house is in turn like some small city."[86]

In a similar way Hilberseimer formulates architecture as an interplay between House and City:

"A satisfactory solution of the problems of city planning can be achieved only when plans for the whole city and plans for the houses in it are both taken into consideration. [...] The plan of a house must relate each room to the other rooms and to the house as a whole."[87]

This quote is part of *The New City* from 1944. However since its first publication to the city: *Groszstadtbauten*, Hilberseimer describes the interaction, that the single cell of the room affects the urban organism and vice versa the city plan the formation of the room[88]. To understand Hilberseimer's relationship between house and settlement architecturally, it is instructive to read Alberti's quote in the original Latin:

"Quod si civitas, Philosphorum sententia, maxima queda est domus, et contra domus ipsa minima quaedam est civitas."[89]

For Alberti a city is civitas. Civitas means a city as city-state. The Roman notion of Civitas embodies the city in its political form, the whole as the co-existence of its citizens (lat. cives). Civitas is opposed to the Roman Urbs, the city as a purely administrative-economic unit. In an Urbs the elements follow a pattern of organization, a grid, the conditions of the market. The pattern of organization is located outside of the elements and does not correspond to the internal order of the parts. For this reason, Urbs has no limit, in contrast to Civitas, which is clearly defined by the region of its elements. The political form of co-existence then for architecture is the negotiation and consistency of the architectural elements. Architecture is thus a theory of formation, composition. It is the embodiment of a political form. Architecture becomes a spatial concept as manifested negotiating strategy. So how to relate the parts and the whole to each other in Alberti's work? In the ninth book, fifth chapter, Alberti describes architecture as a proportional relationship between the parts and the whole. Beauty arises in the clear expression of order[90]. In Latin expressed by the word: Concinitas. With the term Concinnitas, Alberti describes the desire for a well assembled whole by the harmony and symmetry of parts towards each other. Concinnitas for Alberti is the request to determine "the figure, the dignity and beauty" of buildings from the parts of the body[91]. When Hilberseimer begins to enumerate the design elements of City Architecture [92], they are the same means as for Alberti's beautiful figure. First, in Alberti's original Latin text:

"Tria esse que precipue ad pulchritudinem acuenustatem edificioru faciant, *numerum* scilicer, *figuram* et *collocarionem*."[93]

In a similar way Hilberseimer writes:

"Architecture is arising from three things, namely the *number*, the *figure* and *collocation* of the different parts. The architectural problem is then to join and unite certain numbers of parts into a whole, by an orderly and sure coherence and agreement of all those parts."[94]

Instead of figure, dignity and beauty, in a more sophisticated determination, Hilberseimer summarizes the terms together with Architecture. City-Architecture for Hilberseimer always is figure (German: Gestalt) because the instruments are purely physical in nature, the design elements are the buildings themself, the location and relation to each other.[95]. Alberti's Concinnitas, so the dignity and beauty, in Hilberseimer we find as a specific requirement for a whole as the agreement and coherence of its parts. When Alberti talks of a whole and its parts, Hilberseimer talks of the city. The proportions, the proportional ratio of the masses and their appearance, are the corresponding requirements of city architecture. Its main task is first to define laws, as negotiation, which is what Hilberseimer means when he speaks of a theoretical abstract solution. City architecture is the order and design of the space with the buildings and the free spaces that constitute a city[96].

The number, the figure and the colocation: What do Hilberseimer and Alberti now mean by a figure describing a proportional relationship? For Alberti a Gestalt is determined by three factors: the number, the figure and the colocation. These three terms go back to medieval scholasticism, or more precisely to the definition of order in the work of St. Augustine. Eventually, this root has been known by Hilberseimer; an indication can be found in the introduction to *The New City*, written by Mies van der Rohe. As a bridge between the settlements of Hilberseimer and medieval scholasticism, Mies quoted from the doctrine of beauty by St. Augustine:

"The disposition of equal and unequal things, attributing to each its place"[97].

In the Original from St. Augustine, De Ordine we read about the ideal of beauty:

"Et (ratio) terram coelumque collustrans, sensit nihil aliud quam pulchritudinem sibi placere, et in pulchritudine figuras, in figuris dimensiones, in dimensionibus numeros"[98].

For Augustine, Beauty is treated equally to the order in which the figure is composed of rhythms. Rhythm is a number and a number can be seen as the interval between two figures. The individual, the entity designated by Alois Riegl as a form of seclusion[99] is generated with rhythm. According to Augustine, rhythm is the universal means of visual art to generate an individual form of seclusion in an art work. By means of rhythm, two objects are not simply added, but objects and rhythm together produce a third, a new unit. Saint Augustine states a tree as an example. The tree is a self-contained unit with its individual shape and at the same time has no less individual, branches, twigs and leaves. The tree owes its parts to its development, its movement, its expression[100]. According to Riegl, this collective character of natural things is what the artist endeavors in the art work, the Abstraction and Empathy of nature, to bring it "to unilaterally increased expression"[101].

This results in two directions of the composition. Downwards when a number as a cohesive unit can only be retrieved through its relation, within the interval to one-another, immediately the question arises: Where in the depth you will you stop if order is only described by the type of addition? Without the Many, the One can only be read as Many through the opening of the One; an infinite chain emerges. In Hilberseimer's work we find the same in-depth relations, from the city to the houses, to the rooms, to the furniture and utensils[102]. Augustine finds a solution in abstraction. In the reason and the perception of objects. In the English Version:

"And she considered in herself, if there were lines and curves, shapes and forms that correspond to what hid her mind within. Under all that was available to the eyes, she found only inferior, which could stand no comparison with what the mind recognized. Also, this was distincted and divided and handed over to a science called Geometry"[103].

The representation of order is not the order of nature, but of the mind. A representation of nature is an abstraction. It is thus clear, that a logical order from numbers, that is their intervals, that is their proportional relationships build on top of each other[104]. For Augustine, the classification and figuration begins with the invention of geometry. The beginning of abstraction – the designation of the terms of perception – determines the smallest elements. It should be noted that Augustine means the One mind, and holds only an intuition for the only One. But we want to state that order arises from the contemplation of nature, therefore abstracted and the things contrary to and not a part of the things themselves. The smallest part is thus one which is still recognizable, viewable. The smallest part is not an object in itself, but it is an abstraction as part of another object. In *Groszstadt Architektur*, Hilberseimer will determine the smallest parts of architecture with the parts of the room. The room is the first element in architecture being composed. From the perception of architecture, and thus for Hilberseimer, the smallest parts are the abstracted parts of the smallest composition: walls, ceilings, floors, windows, doors, furniture.

The Autonomy of form   The concept of Entelechy as a definition of form would allow to consider the object as autonomous, as a (self-)organization of elements. The subsequent symbiosis Kant's of subjective view and object as synthetic form is, at first sight, wedged in the first dichotomous separation of subject and object: Nature and culture. Each investigation building on the dusty contrast between ground and figure would commit to the same categorical error. Also, the attempt to remove one of the two notions would only point to the absence of the other.

However, despite the dichotomous rift, the path of form followed by Kant, has a decisive advantage: Form as the synthesis, diplomacy between two things. Because a synthetic form as a form of effect accepts the autonomy of objects as form of existence. Unlike the form of Concinnitas, the parts have not been subordinated to a whole, they remain autonomous. This approach of form integrates the substantial form as a multiple of the autonomy of the parts. The form of effect thus acts indirectly. Alois Riegl showed, how the Kunstwollen as response to the form of effect of an era, facing the autonomy of objects, thereby multiplying the objects and facing their representation as plurality, as figuration. In this tradition Hilberseimer begins to develop his scheme of the city. As an architect Hilberseimer understands form in the classical architectural sense, as an organization of parts into a whole, however in the Kantian superior to form. As a result, a shift happened: the negotiation of the

Many to One and the concept of form of effects leads to the problem of multiplicity of views. Form becomes diplomacy of effect-forms.

It is already predictable, that a concept of singular perception has to be transformed by the given variety of houses of a settlement. The schemes of Hilberseimer are thus a search for possibilities for negotiation of a multitude. Therefore, to understand the schemes, the relationship between parts and wholes needs to be considered.

2.3.3 An introduction to Mereology

The discipline that deals with the possibilities and definitions of part and whole is called mereology[105]. The mereology is the formal science of parts. It deals with the relationship of a part to a whole and the relationship of parts to parts in a whole. The term derives from the Greek word μερος: part.

Since its beginnings, philosophy analyzes the relationship between parts and whole[106]. Starting with the pre-socratic Atomists, over Plato's dialogue Parmenides, Aristotle's Metaphysics to the writings of other ancient and medieval ontologists, the question of the relation of part and whole immerses again and again. In Aristotle's Metaphysics we find part and whole clearly defined: As a whole, Aristotle refers to something that is complete. Similar as later in Alberti's writings you cannot subtract or add to a whole. That means implicitly that a whole is determined from a sum of parts. If a unit consists of a sum of parts, this further means, that the whole thing must have its own attributes, which is more than the sum of its parts. The whole thing is clearly quantificly determined; it can be distinguished from an other in the same category, such as the difference between water and the whole of a dress[107]. For Aristotle, there are different types of parts: a whole can be either quantitatively or qualitatively divided. So parts are the volume of a whole and the various properties of the whole. The type of dividing or the perception of the parts is itself a kind of part of the whole. In contrast to the phenomenology here, the description, the definition of the object is also a part of the whole[108].

In modern philosophy, the first significant work on mereology is represented by the writings of Franz Brentano and his student Edmund Husserl. Husserl's *Logical Investigations*[109] are considered to be the first detailed study of the part and the whole, without formal means. For Husserl as well as for Aristotle, each whole consists of parts. But instead of through completeness of the whole, Husserl defines the whole through the types of relation of parts to each other. It is the way of compositeness, which describes a whole. Can you tear apart a whole into a plurality of disjoint parts or are the parts indistinguishable from each other? So wholes can be divided into two categories: the simple and the compounded, or the unarticulated and articulated things. For Husserl, every thing is an "actual and possible part" and "there are actual or potential wholes", which include it. It follows, that the number of wholes as compositions is infinite, regardless of the number of things. Husserl thus contradicts Aristotle's description of completeness. If by Aristotle the definition of the whole was a part of it, Husserl introduces the specific case of the *linkage-whole* (German: Verknüpfungsganzes). A link is an entity in which parts are joined together with the help of a concept. A figure/Gestalt is such a linkage. The determination of the whole is here external, a conception of the whole and is not part of the whole itself.

A part is now all that is distinguishable in a whole. But only parts of the real object in itself are counted and not according to parts after the whole is perceived. Since phenomenological perception is an abstraction of the real object, the number of parts of an item would be un-countable. The perceived whole will never correspond to the real whole. The object as a whole eludes observation and will never be fully describable. Any description of the whole remains a linkage-whole. Husserl uses the term grounding as a description of the relationship and linkage of the parts. A unified grounding with which any part or content, directly or indirectly linked, describes a whole. As Lothar Ridder points out a whole can be reduced to the concomitance of its parts. Husserl does not presuppose the concept of the whole. Basically, here the concept of the whole is dispensable[110]. With Husserl's words: "Everything truly unifying, we should say outright, are the ratios of the grounding"[111].

The phenomenology, founded by Husserl, tried to describe objects by perceiving them. In the following, in Husserl's phenomenology almost naturally theories of part and whole were focused. A pioneer work here is provided by Christian von Ehrenfels. Ehrenfels is the first to ask, in *Über Gestaltqualitäten*[112], why a whole is not dependent on its part to exist independently. With the example of a melody, Ehrenfels shows, that a melody is also recognized when it is played only fragmentary or with other sounds or instruments. Ehrenfels wants to point to the fact, that a whole has its own qualities, independent of its parts. This statement today is known as the first Ehrenfels criterion: the whole is more than the sum of its parts. Variation is another aspect: A melody remains recognizable as the same thing, although it is played differently. The conclusion from this is the Second Ehrenfels criterion: A figure, Gestalt remains the same even while changing.

These and subsequent studies[113] lead to the movement of Gestalt theory during the mid-30s of the 20th century. However, the transfer of Gestalt to the human body theory provided cruel arguments for racial selection. For this reason, the Gestalt theory to this day remains almost untouched. During the mid-50s, aspects of Gestalt theory were transferred into logic by Nicolas Rescher and Paul Oppenheim[114]. The transmission also forms a good summary of Gestalt theory. In the tradition of Husserl's writings, Rescher and Oppenheim assume that a real whole can never be fully described. As "Gestalt-logicians", they refer to a whole as what Husserl introduced with the concept of a linkage-whole. Analogous to Husserl, the whole is defined by Rescher and Oppenheim as: First as an attribute of the link, which determines the independent status of the whole. Second, the parts of the whole must be in a specific relation to each other, which allocates them as parts of a clearly definable whole. Third, the whole has a structure, a form of arrangement of its parts.

Further, the whole can be categorized due to the nature of the link. For Rescher and Oppenheim this results to the following definitions of possible properties of a whole [115]: The *D-unshared attribute*, an attribute and which do not have the parts in itself. Also referred to as *Collective Property*. The *D-shared attribute*, an attribute, which possesses the whole but also each part, for example weight. The *D-G-underivable attribute*, an attribute which is not logically derivable from the properties of the parts alone. For example: the weight of a heap is not just the weight of its parts, but also resulting from a physical law, which allows to sum up the weights. The *D-G-derivable attribute* is an attribute which is logically derivable alone from the properties of the parts. The *D-G-T-underiveable attribute* is an attribute of the whole, which can not be explained by a theory. Congruent with the later notion of *Emergence*. The *D-G-T-deriveable attribute*, is an attribute which can be explained by a theory. The whole, the link, the figure, always consists of parts. It is therefore a configuration and is characterized by the relations in which the parts stand to each other, abbreviated configuration(R). The *quantitative attribute* f of the part p, therefore is a part of a functional configuration described by an f-value for a specific relation R(p).

Husserl's linkage and thus the concept of figure in this way describes a system of dependency. Rescher and Oppenheim speak of a *dependence-system*. The description of a whole by means of a relation is equal to the organic, functional and integrated whole. This leads to the following characteristics of a whole: The whole must have a structure. For a structured whole three things are necessary: its parts, a domain of positions, which occupy the parts and an assignment which assigns to the part to a specific position. If the allocation follows topological attributes, one speaks of a *complex whole*[116]. Let us recall Ehrenfels: a figure may also remain under transformations. A property which remains the same under certain transformations, by Oppenheim and Rescher is considered as *complex feature* of a figure. The consistent figure by a group of displacements is a*isomorphic complex*. An example of an isomorphic complex is the figure of a melody. It should be noted: For Gestalt theory, the Gestalt is an attribute of a complex (whole)[117]. With the logical processing of the figure, Rescher and Oppenheim also provide a new determination of structure: as a character of the common relation between the parts of a whole. Structure here is the way things relate to each other.

In the context of postmodernism, so the 2nd half of the 20th century, mereological statements were only marginal notes in philosophy. When postmodernists vehemently tried to emphasize the incompleteness of a whole, they forgot that the incomplete whole still describes a kind of whole. Analogous to the ancient concept of a whole, the incompleteness itself became part of the description it: Incompleteness was reduced to the appearance of its figure. Instead of drawing conclusions from the finding of incompleteness, the postmodernists only replaced the term complete with incomplete, fatally following the same conception. To paraphrase the philosopher of science Bruno Latour: "postmodernists believed in knowledge with the knowledge that others only believe"[118]. With the notion of an impossible completeness any provision of a whole becomes superfluous. The only thing left is the collectives, their affiliations, dependencies and freedom, practically, the relationship between the elements and the parts and the compositions.

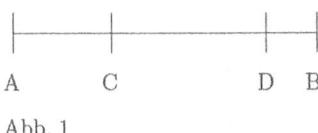

Abb. 1

Figure 2.5: Stanislaw Lesnievki's example of a line as mereological whole through the segments AB and DB or AC and CB

Introduction to Mathematical Mereology The first mathematical formularization of part and whole relationships was provided by Stanislaw Lesniewski in 1916[119]. Since Lesniewski's definition, the mathematical formularization of part and whole relationships is referred to as the discipline mereology. Whereas the mathematical formularization has no direct connection to philosophical concepts of part and whole, or vice versa. As a formal theory, the mathematical mereology describes the generic principles of the relationship between individuals and their constituent parts. Similar to the set theory, which describes the relationship between a class and its members. It is therefore often seen as an alternative to the set theory. But Mereology is based on one crucial difference: In set theory, a class can be defined as an abstract entity, the empty set with no elements. In the mereology, however, all objects are quantified, ie each individual possesses at least one part. As an example of a mereological class Lésniewski indicates a line segment [AB], which is formed by their sections [AD] and [DB] or [AC] and [CB] as constituents[120]. As concrete, spatio-temporal entities, the mereological notion of class is similar to Russell's notion of the *heap* or the *conglomeration*. According to Lothar Ridder[121] a mereological class has the following properties: First, the membership relation is a part to whole relationship. Second, the membership relation is transitive. Third, a null class is not a mereological class since mereological classes consist of its elements. Fourth, if a mereological class consists of only one element, then it is identical with that element.

Through this specific definition of the class, of the set, mereological theories in mathematics offer an alternative to set theory[122]. The mereology is nominal and deals with the negotiation and description of individuals. Relations are reflexive, antisymmetric and transitive. The following four sets are a prerequisite for all that follows[123]: First, everything is part of itself. Second, two different objects can not be part of each other. Third, each part of a part of a whole is also part of that whole. Fourth, an object can be a part of another object, if both exist. The following provides an overview of the most common mathematical formalizations of mereological conditions[124]:

(1) Part: $P(x, y)$; x is part of y.

(2) *Reflexivity*: P(x, x) ; x is part of x.

(3) *Transitivity*: $(P(x, y) \wedge P(y, z) \rightarrow P(x, z))$; is x a part of y and y a part of z, then x is also a part of z.

(4) *Antisymmetry*: $(P(x, y) \wedge P(y, x) \rightarrow x = y)$; is x a part of y and y is a part of x, x and y correspond.

(5) From the Antisymmetry follows *Equality*: $EQ(x, y) = (P(x, y) \wedge P(y, x) \rightarrow x == y)$; is x a part of y and y is a part of x, x and y correspond.

(6.1) *Proper Parthood*: $PPh(x, y) = P(x, y) \wedge x \neq y$; an unambiguous part and whole relationship exists when x is part of y and x is not equal to y.

(6.2) Proper Part: $PP(x, y) = P(x, y) \wedge \neg P(y, x)$; as an unambiguous (enclosed) part holds: if x is part of y and y is not a part of x.

(7) *Overlap*: $O(x, y) = \exists z(P(z, x) \wedge P(z, y))$; as Overlap holds, when z is a part of x and y.

(8): *Overcrossing*: $OX(x, y) = O(x, y) \wedge \neg P(x, y)$; x overcrosses with y, if x overlaps with y and x is not a part of y.

(9) *Proper Overlap*: $PO(x, y) = OX(x, y) \wedge OX(y, x)$; as Proper Overlap holds, when x overcrosses y and y overcrosses x.

(10) *Underlap*: $U(x, y) = \exists z(P(x, z) \wedge P(y, z))$; as Underlap holds, when x is part of z and y is part of z.

(11) *Undercrossing*: $UX(x, y) = U(x, y) \wedge \neg P(y, x)$; x undercrosses with y, if x underlaps y and y is not part of x.

(12) *Proper Underlap*: $PU(x, y) = UX(x, y) \wedge UX(y, x)$; as Proper Underlap holds, when x undercrosses y and y undercrosses x.

(13) *Disjointness*: $D(x,y) = \neg O(x,y)$; x is a disjoint part of y, if x and y do not overlap. Disjointness can be derived from Overlap.

From the definition of a Proper Part, the following conclusions can be drawn:

(15) *Supplementation*: $PP(x,y) \rightarrow \exists z(P(z,y) \wedge \neg O(z,x))$; is x an unambiguous part of y, then do not overlay all parts of y with x. If there is a Proper Part of a whole, there must be an additional supplement. The conclusion is that parts and wholes exist without their relationship towards each other[125].

(16) *Atom*: $A(x) = \neg \exists y PP(y,x)$; read: x is defined as Atom, if x has no proper parts. A unit without Proper Part is the smallest unit.

(17) *Density*: $PP(x,y) \rightarrow \exists z(PP(x,z) \wedge PP(z,y))$; to produce density in the mereological sense, various part to whole relationships must overlap. The more part-whole relations overlap, the greater the density.

(18) *Bottom*: $\exists x \forall y P(x,y)$; x is defined as Bottom, if x is part of all y.

(19) $\zeta - Bound$: $\zeta(x,y) \rightarrow \exists z(P(x,z) \wedge P(y,z))$; compositionally the largest whole is described as Bound: for the sum of all part-relationships of x and y exists the whole z, which has x and y as parts.

(20) *Sum*: $Sz(x,y) = \forall w(O(z,w) \leftrightarrow (O(w,x) \vee O(w,y)))$; compositionally can sums or fusions formed by the description of Overlaps. Sums are new objects. Simply speaking: From part-whole relationship creates a 3rd, a new object[126]. To simplify one can write: $Sz = x + y$

(21) *Product*: $Rz(x,y) = \forall w(P(w,z) \leftrightarrow (P(w,x) \wedge P(w,y)))$; read: z is the Product of x and y, if all parts w of z are parts of x and y. To simplify one can write: $Rz = x \times y$

(22) *Difference*: $Dz(x,y) = \forall w(P(w,z) \leftrightarrow (P(w,x) \wedge \neg O(w,y)))$; z is the Difference of x and y, if all parts w of z are parts of x and do not overlap with y. To simplify one can write: $Dz = x - y$

(23) *Complement*: $Cz(x,y) = \forall y(P(y,z) \leftrightarrow \neg O(y,x))$; z is the Complement of x and y, if all y are part of z and do not overlap with x.

2.3.4 A mereological composition of a line

The description of Husserl's linkage whole corresponds quite well with today's description of a parametric figure in architecture[127]. Compositionally, one can describe it as a figure consisting of a number of components[128], which are oriented to an outward positioned parameter. The figure corresponds to the function of the relation of the parts to the function of subordination. Aside from the aesthetic effect, the concept of linking as a whole is not profoundly implemented in the parametric design process. As crucial difference to Husserl, the parametric figure is not using Husserl's method of foundation – that is the part relationship as a definition of a whole – but describes a new whole through the outward positioned, parametric linkage. This matter I would like to explain on the example of the parametric line – the spline. With the line as an interface between architectural and mereological discussion, I would like to also link with Lésniewski's geometric example of the line for a mereological composition. Using the spline as a further development of the line from a criticism of the modernist line, I would like to show how parametric strategies indeed aesthetically worked with the link as a form, but mereologically still constructed to a complete whole in the ancient sense.

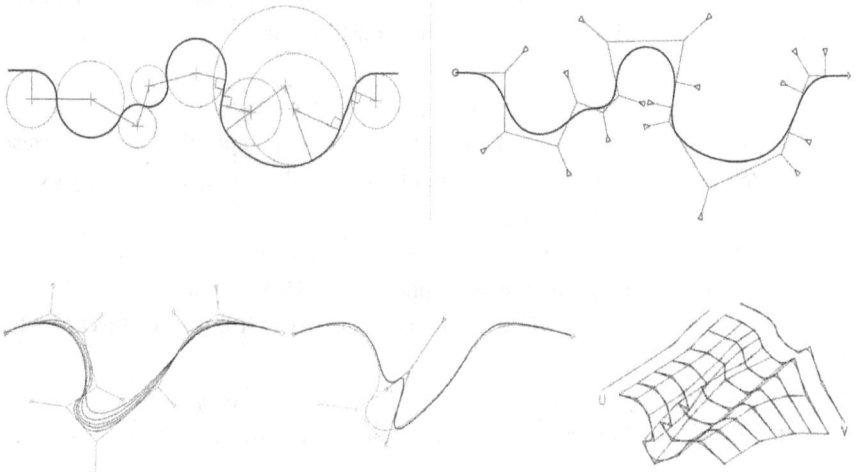

Figure 2.6: Greg Lynn, Spline-Diagram; top left: composite curve described by radial and straight curve segments; top right: curve described using spline geometry; bottom: an array of splines describes a surface

If you follow Greg Lynn's argument in *Animated Form*[129], the continuous curve is the result of a criticism of modernism. Building upon Tafuri's materialist reading of architectural history, the segmented line of the modernists Lynn reads as a reference to the Industrial Age. The line of modernists consists of separate, precisely described individual segments, more precisely circular arc segments that are joined together to form a line. Analogous to the industrial product, each segment is precisely described in itself, but the self-reflexive description of segments lack a possible way of linking to each other. The only way to compose as a modernist is the simplest: the linear sequence. As the car will be produced serially in arrays, the circular arc segments are lined up only tangentially. The circular arc segment line so becomes the connotation of an assembly line. The missing form of composition leads to the reproduction of

Introduction 49

a part as a whole, the repetition of the same and finally the loose juxtaposition of buildings in the city. The notion of a line is equal and may be held accountable for the mistakes of modernism. The loose array of the figurative line segments leads to the architectural criticism: the modernists have forgotten the ground.

Greg Lynn finds his solution, which was the solution for a whole generation of architects, by constructing a spline: The spline, the NURBS curve that unfolded later in the style of parametricism. The continuous drawing of the curve is made possible by a referential description of all elements of a curve in a parametric space. That is, all objects to be linked are referenced in the curve's own space, the parametric space. The space is spanned by a function. The function interpolates the referenced points and represents the interpolation as a curve. So far as within the meaning of Husserl's linkage: The whole is perceived only fragmentary, by reference to a specific singularity with a point. However attention: The curve is seamless, its parts are no longer distinguishable from each other. By the interpolation the points are absorbed by the curve. The curve is created as an image of a negotiation of parts, but without negotiating the actual parts. The point as a value of the function can not reproduce, thus transforming the referenced object. The reference is not real to the referenced figure. An architectural critique could now read as follows: for the Parametricists the ground exists, but they have blurred its figures and figuration.

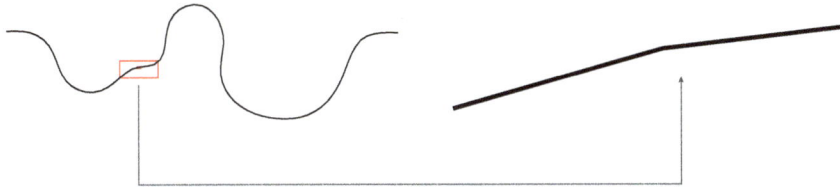

Figure 2.7: Greg Lynn's line as mereological composition; analogous to Lesniewski's example, the line is made up of segments; left: Greg Lynn's contour line rebuilt, right: magnified section

In a parametric line parts can join together and become a whole, but parts cannot become a whole. Greg Lynn's criticism of the modern only shifts the scale of the figure and by this draws the ground as figure. The interpolation of the specific line segments creates a new character, specific, but only shaped by an interpolation function, the link itself. The modernist space is liquified. But due to the displacement, the array of the assembly line in the next compositional scale immersed again: a parametric surface is generated by an array of curves: a loft. Due to the mirror of criticism, the techniques and objections of the moderns reflect in parametric design too. Ultimately, the sequence as a reference in a function causes, that in a parametric figure in the sense of Alberti's Concinnitas, also no point, line or surface cannot be added or subtracted without changing the whole. The uniformity of the moderns thus became the uniformity of one linkage whole.

But alongside Tafuri's metaphor of the Assembly-Line there is another historic reference. It is the metaphor of the railroad rail, the speed and thus the changed perception, so aesthetics, of the industrialization[130]. The railroad rail as line moved in the second half of the nineteenth century more and more into the focus of aesthetic studies and finally became the carrier of various art movements such as the Central European Art Nouveau, the Viennese Secession and the French Art Nouveau. The line became a symbol of the unity of art and industry. The extruded profile of iron production translated the artists of the Art Nouveau almost directly into the cast-iron balustrades and frames of their works[131]. On the one hand, the iron line embodied functional usefulness. On the other hand, the line also was the aesthetic result of the mechanical age. With the speed of the train-railway-stations halls in previously unprecedented dimensions evolved. These results of increased speed and scale could be no more thought and designed with the classic concepts of part relationships. The concept of beauty described by means of subordination and disposition of the part to the whole was no longer possible: In the age of the iron line the whole appeared only fragmentary, due to its shear dimensions or shortened duration of perception.

Husserl's phenomenology and its precursors proposed an alternative way by explaining a whole – or more precise its Gestalt – as result of subjective perception. Amplifying Kant's insight that aesthetic judgements are dependent on compositional synthesis, the synthesis between the observer and the work of art became a thing on its own: described by Husserl as linkage-whole. The raised impression on the perceiver became the subject for art. The notion of beauty turned into the expression of subjective construction. The dynamics in the curves of Art Nouveau was a one to one translation of the dynamics of subjective experience. However, in return lines possessed the power to evoke primary reactions in the observer[132]. The understanding of architectural form as perceptual dynamics: the theatrical tension between observer and geometrical expression led to an overall new concept of space. Latest in August Schmarsow's inauguration lecture *Das Wesen der architektonischen Schöpfung*[133] the new spatial paradigm was fully formated. As Mitchell Schwarzer summarized in an article published in August 1991:

"space became a cognitive process by which spatial images are built up over time. [...] For Schmarsow, the essence of architecture resides in the generation of culturally stimulated rhythmic patterns of movement through enclosed inner rooms, passages, and courtyards."[134]

The next generation of architects transformed Schmarsow's rhythmic patterns of geometry into locomotive patterns of use: function superseded ornament; the organization of the plan replaced the tectonics of the facade. The notion of organic architecture shifted from an expression of geometry to the stimulation of spatial experience.

When Greg Lynn *Curvelinearity* introduced as term into the discourse of architecture, it can be regarded as his achievement to regain the line's connection to Art Nouveau aesthetics and the "unpredicted and contingent influences and external forces"[135]. The Spline questioned the line as locomotional diagram. Also, for Lynn the spline was the first geometric application of his concept of the *multiplicitous body*, originating in Deleuze and Guatarri's *body without organs*. With this reading, the line is decribed as an affiliation of many organs, a sequence of line segments seamless blurred into each other. To achieve a *multiplicitous body* Lynn called for a two-sided deterritorialization: first: "the loss of internal boundaries" and second "the expansion of the interior outward"[136]. But the proposed Spline as a transformation of a multiplicitous whole into an architectural element faces two problems: First, the problem of abstraction between internal and exterior qualities. In the case of the Spline, the influence of external events is always described by a constant and therefore general function. However, the expansion of an interior outwards depends on specific selections of relevant influences. A two-sided deterritorialization induces a circular chain of specific abstractions between that which is in and that in which it is. The specific abstraction of that what is an external event names that which is in and the specific abstraction of that what expands outward names that in what it is. In the case of the functional description of a spline this circular deterritorialization based on specific forms of abstratctions can not take place. The general abstraction of the function leads again to the subordination of parts. This leads to the second problem, a more general problem of parametric design: in parametrics, architectural form is described through its becoming. By this, parts can join together and form a whole, but only through their contribution and subordination. Parts can not become wholes. This is contradictory to the original call for a *multiplicitous body*, which Lynn developed from Elias Canetti's *paradigm of the pack*, as "an assemblage of often disperate morphologies"[137]. Here obviously every part is as well a whole; e.g. a wolf without being a part of the pack in the first place. Comparable to Husserl's method of foundation, in Canetti's paradigm the whole is defined as relation between parts as wholes. The *paradigm of the pack* and therefore the *multiplicitous body* differs from the calculus of spline geometry. The curve's algorithm can not be described as compositional whole between parts. The algorithm is an interpolation of perceived input data. The spline is a transformation of wholes to parts through the general abstraction method of an algorithm. One object is described through the expression of another object. In this point overlaps the model of spline geometry with the theatrical tension of Art Nouveau between subjective experience and the expression of a line. In a manner similar to the algorithms of spline geometry, Art Nouveau constructed a linear relationship between the meaning for a subject and the expression of an object; in short: between content and form. Objects became absorbed into the meaning for a subject. In this equation of form and content the only way to bring several aspects of an object expressed is by a dynamic articulation: the movement of subjective experience over time. For this reason, the form of a *multiplicitous body* was always defined by its unstoppable mode in the becoming.

As shown, Canetti's *paradigm of the pack* or Lynn's *multiplicitous body* are congruent with concepts of early phenomenology and later to Husserl's linkacke whole. As Lars Spuybroek pointed out in *Sympathy of Things*[138], before Art Nouveau and similar art movements transformed the line into a mediator of subjective experience, Kant's insight that aesthetic judgements are dependent on compositional synthesis first led to the theory of *apperzeptive Einfühlung* (lit. apperceptive Empathy = Sympathy). Theodor Lipps, the philosopher who defined the concept of apperceptive empathy, decribed in the article *Concerning the aesthetics of mechanics* the relation between an observer and a line as follows:

"Any form of a spatial figure thus includes my form-creating activity in itself. This is mine and also its, ie the spatial figure activity. The molded figure exists not without this form creative activity for me. [...] As I perceive a spatial figure, I penetrate it with my activity or my life. [...] Aesthetic valuable to us must be forms in which we feel free active [...] Aesthetic valuable ie those forms in which there are movements for us or moving forces be realized."[139]

Here the relationship between subject and object is not linear or based on a form of general abstraction. The relationship between observer and object does not lead to the design of the line for a direct impression on the viewer, but indirectly leads in their synthesis to the line itself, its movement and strength of will. Through specific abstraction the line absorbs an idea of the viewer and becomes autonomous, defined by its specific qualities. The designer's reflection on a speculative observer turns into specific part relationships of the composition. One generation later, at the origins of the modernist formalism, in the writings of the Viennese Alois Riegl, the observer was described as compositional synthesis based on the synthesis of the parts to each other. Riegl's art-critical method consisted in specifying cultural differences through the observation of part-to-whole expressions. Thereby form has been decoupled from the subject and meaning turned into the speculation on the resonance of parts.

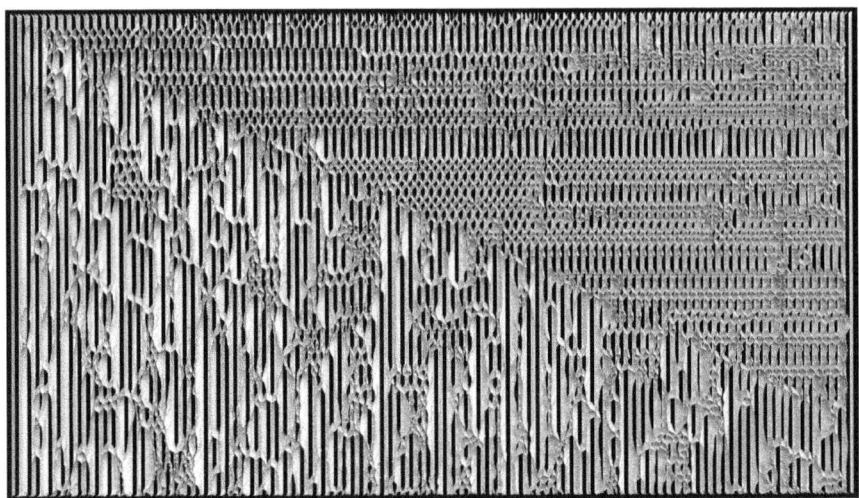

Figure 2.8: compositional line, surface composition, the composition consists of 100x500 lines, each with 1000 line segments, each point is an average of 38 part connecting segments: This composition contains 50000 lines described by 3850000000 parts

In the beginning of the nineties, ie parallel to Lynn's NURBS curve argument, Frei Otto and his team, especially Bodo Rasch, investigated optimized path systems at the Institute for Lightweight Structures in Stuttgart. In the wool thread model, different properties as the thread thickness, thread length, thread number etc. are associated by means of a process – in a quite banal manner that is, by shaking[140]. In the case of Rasch's work the resulting compositions are sorted according to an existing image, the most famous example of the IL is the street network of an unplanned settlement[141]. The aim of the study was to mimic the path systems of unplanned settlements. Using a kind of re-engineering, image and experimental result were compared and then adjusted the decisive parameters in the model. The aim is to imitate the image and thus the development of an analog planning process. The constellation of the design parameters is limited and more specific over several iterations, until they can map the existing object congruent with the elements of their own composition. In the formal language of architecture, one can say, Frei Otto and his team used the method of form finding as the boundary of a Poché to find a contour. But as Lars Spuybroek[142] already pointed out, this form is also designed as composition. The possibility of imitation and optimization is a side effect of the design richness of such a composed figure. The figures of the form correspond to the entanglement of specific

54   The Mereological City: a reading of the works of Ludwig Hilberseimer

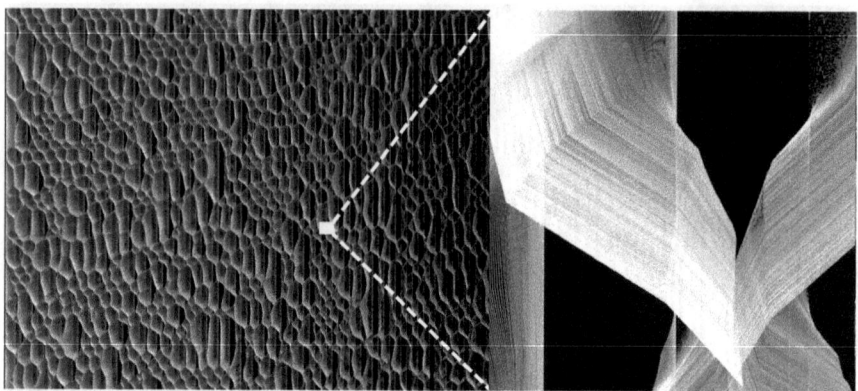

Figure 2.9: compositional line, left: surface composition, right: magnified section

characteristics of real things as parts of the composition. The composition is not explicitly expressed in the shape. Similar to the Hippodamian City plan of Milet, such mereological composition can be completely insignificant in the absence of pressure from the entanglement of the figure. Form and shape are only partially coupled to each other through specific assignments. The partial entanglement reduces the objects not to a reference, but accepts the richness of the object especially through its reduction. The concrete negotiation creates open space, as the unseen gap of the real.

Such mereological compositions are based upon a determination of their material parts, for example wool threads, as specific parts of a composition and principles established on the properties and kinds of the compound, like wool thread length or adhesion of the thread. In the following, I will describe a general mereological surface, as a composition of lines, analogue to the model of a wool thread model. This can be seen as well as the "pseudo-code" description of the digital model in figure 2.8-2.10.

Before one can set up the link conditions, one must identify regions where linkages as part relationships take place. One can specify four regions: point, segment, line and space. Building upon Lésniewski's example of the line, our line consists of parts, the segments. Each line must contain at least one segment in order to not form a null-set. The segments must be specifically locatable, so we need points as regions of localization. The location is an overlap of the region of space held in, which the lines are ultimately shown. A region can be defined in mereological size. The smallest size is the mereological Bottom. A Bottom is a part which is contained in each element. The upper limit is the mereological Bound. As Bound applies another item, of which each element is also part. The composition depends upon the follow-

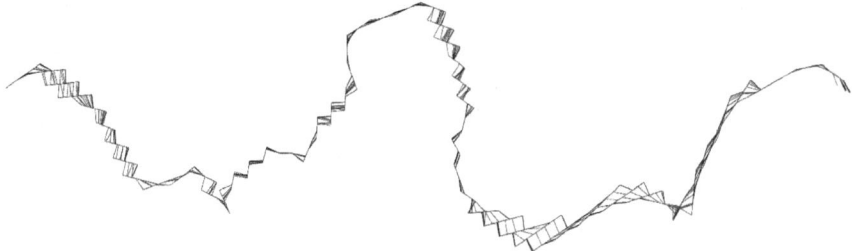

Figure 2.10: mereological line, described by rigid line segments

ing regions: Point as Bottom: A point has a proper underlap with a position and an identity. The identity includes a proper overlap of a position and space. A position includes space as underlap. The Bound of a point: A point is part of at least one segment. The segment is proper bound of the point. Segment as Bottom: A segment has an identity, a length and a diameter as ProperUnderlap. The identity is the sum as proper underlap of the identities of two points. The length is a proper overlap of two point positions. The diameter is an under-crossing of the part length and the segments bound line. The Bound of a segment: A segment is part of a line. Line as Bottom: A line is a composition of segments. A line has proper underlaps with segments. A line has underlaps with the identities of points. Line as Bound: a line is in the space. The space is the Proper Bound line. Space as Bottom Lines are parts of the space. One space has a proper underlap with lines. The Bound of Space: The space is part of positions. Positions are the proper bound of the space.

Here it is immediately obvious, that a mereological description of geometric elements does not follow the hierarchy of a classic geometric description. Mereologically the space is as well part of a point. The point is part of the segment, the segment of the line, the line of the space. Through the concatenation of the mereological relations of point-segment line-space, the space is transitive the mereological bottom of the point and also part of a line. On the other hand, through the mereological Bound relationship, a line is determined as being part of the space. Instead of using a taxonometry, a subordinating structure, like Kadinsiky's point, line, plane: the formal compositions at the Bauhaus[143], a mereological line is described by its overlap with other parts of the composition. Because of the missing ability of a null-set in mereology, the line cannot be pre-determined by the space as an element. The line must first exist as an individual to become a part. A composition is preceded by the autonomy of its elements. The philosopher Levi Bryant describes this as *Flat Ontology*: "no object can be treated as constructed by another object"[144]. No figure is the ground for all the other figures. For this reason, a mereological description has always strange aspects. Parts are always simultaneously wholes and the whole is always a part of the part as a whole. Here, the line is defined by the mereological bound part of the space, but the space through the transitive relationship of the bottom-line is also part of the line for the line as a whole. So far, the mereological regions of a line were defined. For the composition of lines to a surface more mereological axioms to link the regions together are required:

Axioms of incidence: Each line contains at least one segment. Each segment contains exactly two points. The number of point identities of a line corresponds to the number of segments plus one segment. Axioms of order: Each line is limited by their containing segments. Each segment is limited by their containing the points. For each point as part of a line, except for exactly two points of the line, there are exactly two segments that contain this point. Axioms of congruence: The segments as part of a line are different from each other. The points of a segment are different from each other. Points are individually.

To create a surface of lines, one needs axioms for the composition of lines: An overlay of two segments, which are not part of the same line, produce a new segment. One point of one of the overlapping segments will be a part of the new segment. The length is half the distance of the points. Each point has a specific number of possible overlays of segments. Points, segments, lines are brought together in such an areal composition. The elements are part of each other, by partial abstractions, the extraction of parts. Detached from the reference of a single external image, a variety of references are available in the possible figures. A crucial element of the design is the mereological determination of the form.

The line as figurative figuration In this way, you can design a line as a mereological composition and from lines design mereological surfaces. The mereological description here includes any statements on morphological properties of an element. There are no statements that specify the type of the element. More precisely: There are no absolute statements on the character of an element, but relative descriptions of part-relationships between elements. A mereological description is a mutual interlacing of concrete elements. The abstraction of the description is an approximation of an epistemological perception of concrete objects[145]. On closer examination of the mereological definition of a point, it becomes clear that even the smallest element in fact is not described as an axiom. In contrast to a classical axiom such as the Euclidean geometry, a point is not described as an axiom as a whole without parts, but as a specific localization. A point here is the smallest common overlap of the area of the region and the position of the point. It first is an approximation which, depending on

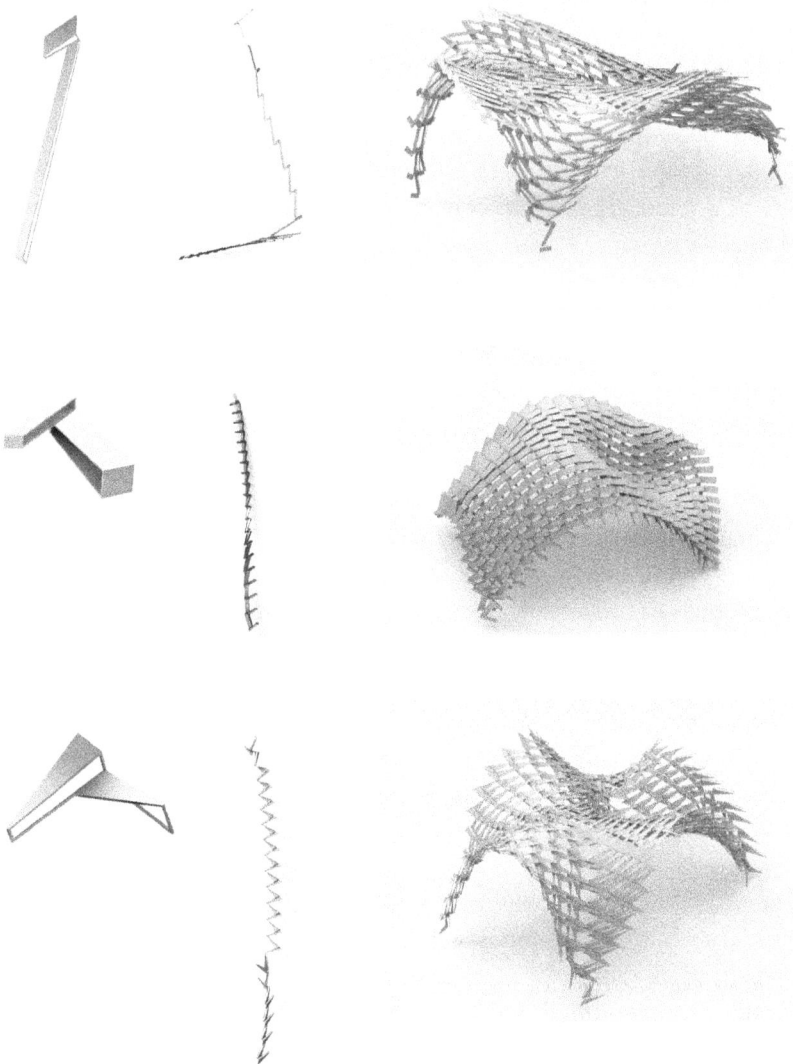

Figure 2.11: from punct to line to surface, student work by Petras Vestartas, seminar: "The Figure and its Figuration", supervisor: Daniel Köhler, Rasa Navasaityte, Vilnius Academy of Arts, 2014

the distance of the observation and the degree of granulation, may be more accurate or coarser. On the other hand, a point is always a compositionally specific element – due to the overlap and the approximation to a limit. Mereological geometries can thus be made of concrete-specific elements.

With the previous composition of the line, a line consists, as a translation of the curvature of a spline geometry, by a plurality of line segments. But through the method of approximation, a boundary region of a smallest common also creates a free space for an indirect design of concrete elements. Point, segment, line need not be smooth Euclidean[146]. Because mereological descriptions are always only parthood relations, elements are mereologically never absolutely determined as a whole. In our example, the mereological description of a segment refers to the overlap of points in a segment and its parthood in a line, but not to its shape. The definition of a segment used above not only allows straight line segments, but also convoluted, branched – just specific – elements as line segments. Due to the absence of the absolute determination, the line-type of the segment is undefined. The segments can be designed from surfaces as well as from volumes. As long as segments may reflect through a parthood the concrete in the composition, they satisfy the mereological requirements. If you replace the line-type of the segments with specific types, it is all the more clear, that the curvature of the line becomes a reflection of its concrete segments, points and parts. The indirect nature of a partial relation is that it possibly makes a line appear strange. As with its own life. It is simply the apparent reduction, the non-description, which creates free space for the unexpected.

My thesis is, that the indirect design of free space is what Ludwig Hilberseimer meant by the goal of city architecture. Similar to the mereological composition of a line Hilberseimer's schemes of house and settlement are reduced models of parthood relations of the architectural elements of the city.

Mereological indications in the work of Ludwig Hilberseimer

We can find hints for Hilberseimer's interest in architecture as the organization of its elements already in his study period. In his transcripts of the lectures Friedrich Ostendorf's you will find page-filling collections of sketches to individual structural elements, such as towers, doors, bay windows, each sorted, regardless of time and style, by their form and purpose texture. Formal condition and its reasonable arrangement in the building fabric here determine the taxonomy of architecture, in contrast to the then usual classification by symbolic and historical significance. One example is the perspective of a cornice, not as a horizontal line of a facade, but as a chain made of bricks, characterized by the profile of the individual stones. Each architec-

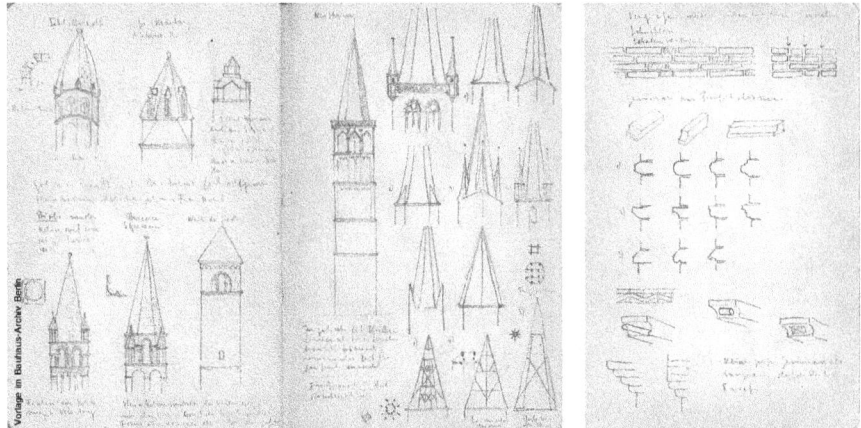

Figure 2.12: Hilberseimer, Sketches from the classroom, work records, 1908-11, Karlsruhe

tural element is characterized by its internal addition. Unfortunately, it can no longer be understood how far the formal grouping in the records already was part of the east village teaching or based on Hilberseimer initiative.

After leaving the university, Hilberseimer begins to design building of building typologies, all of which occurred at first in the large city. He begins to design congruent building types as examples of elements of large city. In the following city his designs are concerned with the determination of a compositional unit and its assembly into an organic whole. From the house to the row house, from the apartment to the city block, from the city block to the large city. Analogue, in Hilberseimer's studies on the Settlement-Unit, he will develop dependencies from the room to the house, the house to the settlement and the settlement to the region. Coherently Hilberseimer's work deals with the relation of the elements to a whole, a mereological method for negotiation of architectural elements.

3 The Large City:
The will to elemental architecture

> The trouble is that architecture cannot be determined by argument. It is its own argument. The logic of the old way of building was in the building. The proof was in the stones.
>
> LUDWIG HILBERSEIMER. ARCHITECTURE: STRUCTURE AND FORM

3.1 CREATION AND DEVELOPMENT

The Architecture of the Large City At the beginning of the 20th century many protagonists are under the spell of the Groszstadt, the Large City[1] and so is Ludwig Hilberseimer. The architectural design of the city is the issue he deals with in his work. From 1908 to the study time of Hilberseimer, August Endell writes in *The beauty of the large city*:

"Because that's the amazing thing that the large city, despite all the ugly buildings, despite the noise, despite what one can blame her, for the one who wants to see a miracle is to beauty and poetry, a fairy tale, colorful, colored, much designed as any that ever told a poet: a home."[2]

This is a literary description of a large city as an affirmation of the material forces of the city as a shaping ideal of their time. In 1911 Otto Wagner: *The large city. A study of these*[3] appears. The large city: The central problem of modernistic urban design. Ludwig Hilberseimer thus names his first manuscript written in 1914: *The architecture of the large city*[4]. The work about the city of Berlin by Karl Scheffler, which appeared only one year earlier, holds the same title[5]. In Hilberseimer's manuscript one can already find the key elements on which he will work his whole life[6]. Not only the title of the text is a reference to the writings of Schefflers: Hilberseimer also starts with the same principles as Scheffler. The large city is declared in both writings to be the central topic of architecture. The new economic conditions of industrialization determine the character of the large city. Thus, the large city differs from the historical city, which evolved from a need for protection and thus a local binding of capital. Up to this point both works are congruent. However, further on Scheffler bypasses the circulation of the economy to changes in family constellations. In this, Scheffler puts the family on the same level as the apartment as the smallest cell of urban morphology The biology of humans is transcribed verbatim on to the urban organism.If the challenge for urban design is to adapt the urban morphology to economic conditions, Scheffler's coupling of family with architecture leads to the urban-political conclusion to group small families to the production sites. By this pairing, it is only logical that the "living cell" of a nuclear family reflects the recurring characteristics of the industrial worker. Drawn together to the large units corresponding to a factory, for Scheffler, the large city consists of uniforms and free-standing blocks.Consequently, the facades of city blocks should express the uniformity of labor life circumstances and are treated in the uniform rhythm. It is Scheffler's point of view of production and the city, which later on reverberates in the words of Tafuri's.

3.1.1 The Kunstwollen as frictional contrast

However, Hilberseimer is not interested in a quantitative adaptation of the city to the social situation. Instead he recognizes, that the industrial large city has generated new architectural typologies. These new types as well as the city in its essence, are reflection of the time events. Instead of wearing the mask of a no longer appropriate architecture, the style should be rooted in the nature of the object, while the inner large city organism remains the same. For this reason, the city will also be combined artistically in a homogeneous, rhythmic articulation. Hilberseimer's argument for Sachlichkeit in architecture is formal by origin. Hilberseimer already in his firs text available to us quotes the Viennese art historian Alois Riegl literally:

"In contrast to this mechanistic view (semperian theory) the nature of the artwork I have represented is teleological, while I saw in the art work the result of a particular purpose and conscious Kunstwollen, which prevails in battle with purpose, material and technology"[7].

This frictional contrast between material needs and the artistic expression of the time becomes Hilberseimer driving force and here shall be my access point for understanding Hilberseimer's project[8]. Alois Riegl's *Kunstwollen* is the starting point for a development in Hilberseimer project that turns on the project along with all of its contents connotation to an interest with the scheme of the architectural design. As Manfredo Tafuri remarked in a footnote[9], Hilberseimer developed the coordinates of the design itself. Hilberseimer found an introduction to the Kunstwollen through his teachers: Friedrich Ostendorf and Richard Baumeister have raised analogous demands to a functional architecture, contrary to the drafts of the "Semperians"[10].

The work of art as a ratio of tension To illustrate: In the beginning of his work, Hilberseimer recognizes the initiating globalization of the world economy and the industrial city caused by this. What constitutes his time are the technical innovations and opportunities. But he complains that the unrestrained development of the economy, the machine above everything, ultimately machinises humans, too. Due to a lack of synthesis of matter and spirit and the material and ethical factors, social progress fails to happen[11]. A synthesis of the material and ethical factors. The formulation of the synthesis will have to be solved architecturally and is read off on a new order to the chaotic large city. The task of architecture will therefore be to hold against the new economic and technological forces of large city.

"Architecture (Baukunst) is monumental expression of metaphysical ideas. This formative metaphysics against the material purposefulness appears minor. For what meant use, purpose and construction, where it is last things. They are only a means to realize the pure idea."[12]

In his theoretical writings Hilberseimer makes it obvious that materiality and construction are secondary and that in first place there is a form of will –

"The Kunstwollen is never subjected as the will to development. [...] The form has become expression of this will is just the artwork"[13].

Yet to one another materiality and will stand in proportion. The art of the era – a style caused from the tension between the idea[14] and the material form. A period of art is now trying to further develop their physical and structural possibilities along with the meaning of the artistic will "A style reached its climax when the material the will to form opposes no resistance. [...] A work of art is a brought up to the harmony ratio of tension."[15] Hilberseimer wrote these texts as an art critic for the magazine *The Only*[16]. His definition of style is not new at the time. This is a common definition of art history at the beginning of the 20th century, similarly formulated e.g. by Worringer:

"The history of architecture is not a story of technological developments, but a history of alternating expression purposes and the type and manner, how technology adapts to these changed purposes by getting new and sophisticated combinations of its basic elements and makes them servant"[17].

Worringer's work *Abstraction and Empathy*[18] was regarded as widely read example of artists of this period. The concept of Kunstwollen and its consequences however, were authentic and decisively developed by Alois Riegl, a Viennese art historian (1858-1905).

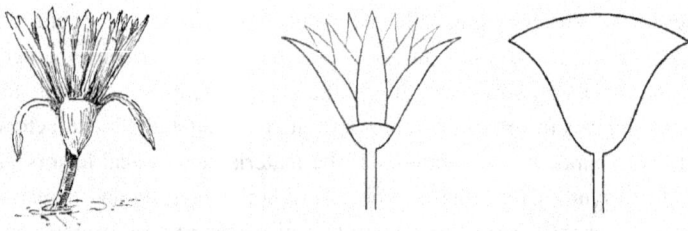

Figure 3.1: Alois Riegl: Abstraction of a lotus flower, left: Lotus flower with mugging sepals by Goodyear; center, right: abstracted lotus flower in profile

The Kunstwollen: The refinement of Semper's formula: A further understanding of the term Kunstwollen starts with Alois Riegl's relationship to Semper. Riegl introduces the concept to liberate art from "dependency theories", as Semper's concept, to emphasize the autonomy of a work of art[19]. According to Harry Mallgrave's analysis[20] however, it is certainly far too simplified to say that the friction of the Kunstwollen can be seen as an opposite to Semper's style theory. On the contrary, one can say Riegl begins with Semper and further developed Semper's theory. Riegl begins his own academic career in an intimate understanding of Semper's theses and like Semper, Riegl takes great interest in clothing, textiles and ornamental techniques. Riegl's first two books published, *Ancient Oriental Carpets*[21] and *questions of style*[22], deal with these topics. As head of textile division of the Austrian Museum for Art and Industry, Riegl built a collection of historic textiles on the model of the 1st volume of Semper's style as follows: to document the history, art and aesthetics of clothing. Once famous for the notion of Kunstwollen, Riegl developed the Kunstwollen in *questions of style* as a defense of Semper's theory against the generalizations and materialistic interpretation of the Semperianians. Riegl indicates, that in the becoming of the art-form, for Semper material and technology came into account, but not exclusively as for the Semperians. Thus, the Kunstwollen in *questions of style* is Riegl's departure to interpret against the Semperianians along with Semper.

It is not until the *Late Roman art industry*[23], that Riegl begins to distantiate himself from Semper. He accused Semper's theory of uncertainty and of having contributed to the misconception that a work of art should be a mechanical product of intended use, resource and technology. In order to dispel this misunderstanding, Riegl lets Semper's theory go and ascribes the three mechanical-physical factors to have an inhibitory, negative role[24]. As a "coefficient of friction"[25] the Kunstwollen is opposed to the material factors. The new confrontation finds its basis in the development of the concept of Kunstwollen. While in *questions of style* Riegl associated the concept with the individual, creative will, in *Late Roman art industry* the Kunstwollen stands for a world view for the zeitgeist, that determines the artistic development of an entire epoch.

Probably, as a theorist and art critic Hilberseimer was aware of the nuances of the relationship between Semper's and Riegl's theses aware. More than thirty years after his first statements on Kunstwollen wrote Hilberseimer:

"Architecture depends on the materials, techniques and structures of a given time – material and rational elements – but it is the spiritual alone that determine its particular expression. The essence of architecture, then, is always apart from, but never in conflict with the conditions and means that produce it."[26]

These words Hilberseimer wrote as an introduction to the architecture of Mies van der Rohe.

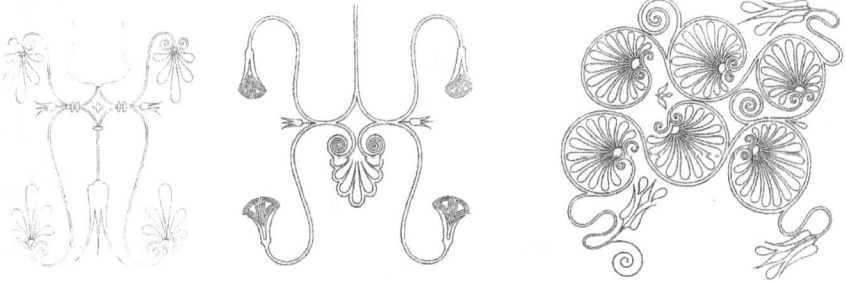

Figure 3.2: Alois Riegl: handle ornaments from Greek amphorae

The world view: the creation of art as a bet with nature The concept of art as an understanding of the nature of a particular epoch, in *questions of style* Riegl developed as a criticism to Semper's work *The style*. Riegl raises the question whether the early works of art really as a next evolutionary stage have really turned to natural conditions. In his study he recognizes, that early "primitive" works were first formed geometrically. They follow the elementary laws of symmetry, proportion and rhythm. The early works of art therefore are confident combinations according to the rules of geometry. Due to a lack of experience in craftmanship, a work of art as an evolutionary step, an imitation of nature, however must be a faulty imitation[27]. More complex figurations in this way do not arise through a more detailed presentation of what is perceived but through combination and multiplication of abstracted schemes.

This concept appears quite familiar to us today and can also explain digital simulation techniques. Take for example the digital visualization of a flock of birds. The representation is not created by the precise mapping of real bird movements but from the reproduction of three simple movement decisions, namely: maintain distance, move towards the center, follow direction, ie the organic in relation to the physical proximity of discrete points in space, so the Cartesian-Geometric, as the inorganic. Complex formations are caused by the composition of three schemes and their multiplication, in short: from simple to complex, or as Hilberseimer claims:

"We must learn to see the intricate simply, even naively. We must disentangle the chaos to find again the basic principles from which general ideas can develop, theoretical principles be established."[28]

The geometric stylization is therefore no replication of nature, but an implementation of its own imagination. The correspondence with one occurring phenomenon represents a quantitative adaptation, reproduction of the abstract concept. Style is no longer the equivalent of the physical characteristics of the world, but the style is the embodiment of an inner world view. Hans Sedlmayr already pointed this out[29]. Accordingly, the concept of Kunstwollen first of all helps to clarify the term "style". The concept of Kunstwollen alone, at first only states that styles change because the view of a group changes, nothing more. But Riegl does not stop there and goes far beyond that. Further, Riegl now begins to inquire for the inner structural principles of a work of art. The Kunstwollen is superordinated, spiritual will, supported by a group of people. This group is not necessarily geographically or temporally localized to achieve the variability that is necessary to explain the co-existence of different styles in the same geographic area[30]. So the Kunstwollen combines the social circumstances of a group and embodies their world view. By bundling otherwise epistemological enumerations of his art historical predecessors, Riegl creates a counterpart to all material, purpose and technology. In summary, Riegl intensified this contrast through its definition: "Art work is betting work with nature to express a harmonious world view"[31]. The art does not attempt to imitate nature, but to express its idea of nature. Each

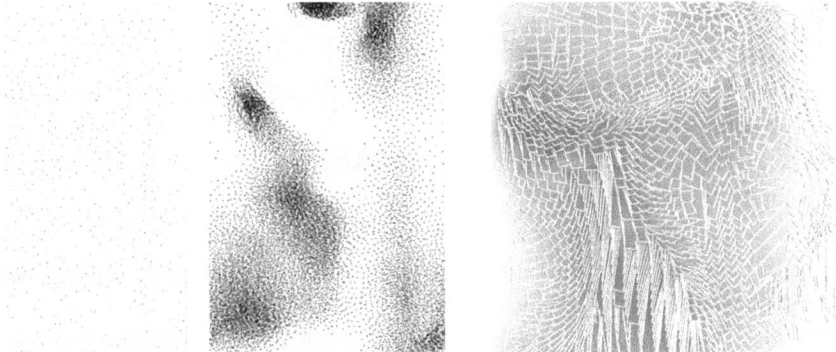

Figure 3.3: left, middle: point distributions as geometric stylization of swarm behavior; right: amplification and differentiation in a context model

artwork is corresponding to a work of nature, which its motive is. This is Riegl's question of "What?" of a work of art[32].

Abstraction as an instrument of perception If the creation of art is not an imitation of nature but a competition to her work, artistic creation will be a representation of nature. Riegl divides nature into inorganic and organic matters. Inorganic things, "dead matter" follow the law the crystallization. Symmetry and sharp demarcation to other things: these are the characteristics of a crystal. Crystals are passive, their figure is broken by movements coming from outside. Organic things however, have an inner cohesion through their very movement. As a result, their symmetry is veiled, refractions of the crystal lead to curves, a feature of the organic form. Organic things are constructed proportional, for Riegl proportion is symmetry in motion. The symmetry so is the law of form of matter, the motion is the law of form of the mind. The man's perception (mind) of nature (material) is in its formal translation and the ratio the expression from symmetry and movement. But man can never reach nature through mimicking and can only compete on the same level. This is achieved through the representation of nature's principles[33]. The abstraction so is the instrument for possible observations of nature.

Crystalline forms are caused by external influences. Organic Forms express an inner movement. The same opposition of geometric and organic law of form we found in Hilberseimer. The geometric city for Hilberseimer is an expression of an autocratic order. An example is the Roman settlement, as an offshoot of a distant city, which follows a geometric order. The organic city is the expression of a free city, just as the medieval city. Its organic urban structure originated from the social order. The organic city adapts to the territory, which is in contrast to the geometric conditions of the site. The Geometrical is not the opposite of Organic. Detlef Mertins already pointed out that Hilberseimer never speaks of the inorganic. For Hilberseimer both formal laws of nature are manifested in two different views of the world[34]. The Organic as well as the Geometric are the fundamental principles for an auto-genetic design of the form[35].

The cultural representatives are the farmer, organic, and the nomad, geometric. The farmer sees no difference between mind and matter. For him, depending on the soil, all things are animated, based on an inner source. The farmer is the carrier of the mystical culture, a centrifugal force. The nomad on the other hand, depending on what already exists, only trusts to the real physical. He acts only based on reality and is suspicious of any irrationality. The Nomad is the carrier of the magical culture, a centripetal force[36]. The Organic works from the inside outwards. The Geometric acts from outside inwards. With respect to the Many, a geometric order means, that each item must be ordered in preset of a principle: an autocratic order. This can be compared to geometric operations such as the subdivision of a mesh, also imposing of a changing transformation. Similar to an array of elements with specification of a grid or the transformation using an underlying map. With respect to the Many, an organic order means, that the elements are designed from their interiority and have to negotiate the principles with each other: a democratic order. This is an order of naturalness, organic in character.

"There is no longer a dominating form concept to which everything must be subordinated. The organic order is autonomous; its guiding principle is that each part must develop according to its own law, that each part must also have its due place, according to its importance and function, within the whole. It means, as St. Augtistine said, "the disposition of equal and unequal things, attributing to each its proper place." "[37]

Geometric and Organic are no distinctions between straight and curved lines, but mereological forms of perception to develop parts and the whole. As Detlef Mertins already pointed out, Hilberseimer distinguished between the city grids of autocratic cities such as Roman settlements and the grids of free cities, cities like as Priene and Miletus planned by Hippodamus. For Hilberseimer, the crucial point were the principles of organic order and allows adaptation and and the possibility of adaption[38]. Between the form the city and its shape by laws of the organic order there is only an indirect relation.

For Hilberseimer the different characters of the cities express different social orders. Formal orders Hilberseimer can only evaluate by building a sign-reference of figure and societal "will". The geometric order so embodies the primal nomad[39] and manifests a centripetal understanding of space. Everything is based on the disposition[40] of inner representations. Roman cities, colonial towns, autocratic cities, are examples of geometric order. The prefixed figure is dispositioned to the ground. However, the organic city is the city of farmers and embodies a centrifugal understanding of space. Everything is based on the co-location towards a center. Examples of the organic order are prehistoric settlements and medieval towns. The figure is formed by merging and negotiating the territorial conditions. The figure is prefixed ground[41].

Hilberseimer did not propagate any formal system as the preferable order. The once defined sign reference allows Hilberseimer to reveal the method of an order . With the detachment of the method from another era, the sign reference becomes obsolete. The geometric arrangement produces knowledge on the disposition of the figures. The organic order produces knowledge on the colocation of the figure. For Hilberseimer the disposition becomes the methodology of territorial adjustment, the colocation later becomes the method to describe a house and a settlement.

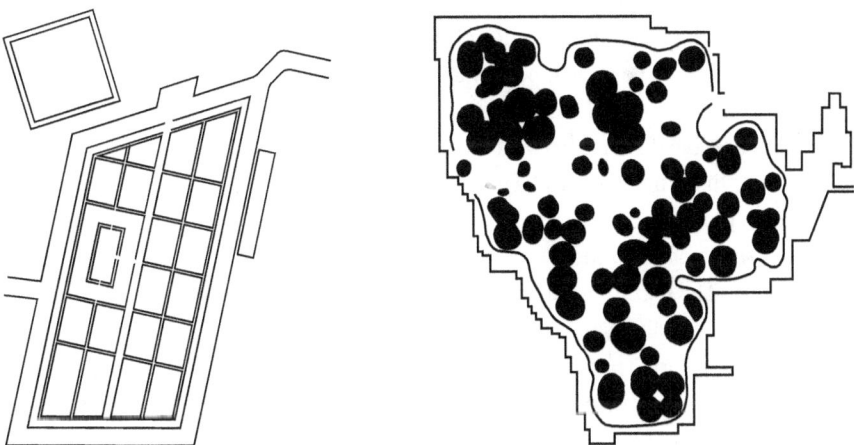

Figure 3.4: left: the geometric City: Castelazzo Di Fontanellato; right: the organic city: Glastonbury

Back to Riegl: Following, that for an aesthetic desire resource, technology, intended use and mental image are excluded, only the Kunstwollen remains to evaluate a work of art[42]. The value of a work of art is given by the degree, of how far it has succeeded in the law of perception of form of the natural motive to be expressed in the piece of art. In this way, Riegl linked the work of art to perception:

"In the perception of the accordance of the work of art with the corresponding work of nature lies the source of all purely aesthetic pleasure"[43].

So Riegl includes findings from the aesthetics of perception and joins the row of art historians, who have coined the conception of aesthetics, formed in the 20th century due to the Phenomenology, albeit in different weightings[44]. According to Hans Sedlmayr, Riegl's point of contact with the Gestalt theory begins here. Riegl recognizes that shapes appear as surfaces and dissolves the Kunstwollen of a group to the relation of form to surface. For Riegl, the proportion of form to surface is the basic means of expression of a work of art.

Riegl recognizes that natural objects are first experienced visually, so with the sense of sight. The outline of a figure and the color determines whether an object displays in isolation or combined to other objects. Due to the possibility of overlay of contours or homogeneous coloration however, a visual observation alone is not sufficient to definitely determine a figure as clearly detached from the context. Only the sense of touch can provide clarity. Only the haptical is able to isolate an object. Optical isolation of an object for Riegl then is a reminiscence of the experience of the sense of touch. The optical perception of touch Riegl therefore calls the Tactical. The Tactical shows the individuality of things. The Optical the coherent whole[45]. In the experienceable distance between art and the viewer, the Kunstwollen can now be categorized. In his main work *The late Roman art industry*, Riegl divides the distance into three regions[46]:

1. Close vision: A tactical consideration based on the sense of touch, Riegl calls close vision. The Close vision is the method of societies who were trying to define and separate the individual. The Tactical avoids the space which individuals would put into relationship. Therefore, the Tactical tries to represent spatial objects, ie volume, as flat as possible. A flat representation can be achieved by the avoidance of shadow, the frontal representation of figures and a cutting of the background. The background is monotone, not figuratively. Each part obtains a clear coloration to distinguish to an Other: The polychromatic arises. In the close vision, the Tactical is also synonymous to the real touch. For Riegl the Egyptian Art is an example for a Close vision. Using the example of the pyramid, Riegl demonstrates that here the figure is most lifted from the background whille the character itself always appears flat.

2. Normal view: Optical and tactical consideration are in balance to one another. Space and time are accepted in it. Several parts form a whole, which is still clearly distinguished from the background. The parts are structured, shadow is used as a

means of art. The surface is articulated. In Normal view, the tactical consideration arises from the experience. The Greek temple is an example of the Normal view. The temple has no interior, but the uniform surface is broken with the rows of columns. Shadows are accepted. The column house is also spatial, a three-dimensional object.

3. Far vision: A visual observation, that is, the relationship between the individual and the whole created here in the understanding of a vision. The figures are detached and differentiated from each other. Their coherence is created by the formal law of the mind of the movement. The optically perceived surface becomes a figuration of figures. As an example, in the early Christian nave, any unity disappears in the interior, there is no longer an organic coherence between the parts. Modern art is a Far vision according to Riegl. The Kunstwollen here is an expression of causality and thought, that unites all the figures into one whole.

The basic expression of art, the relationship of form to surface for Riegl becomes a relationship between figure and ground, whereas the ground may be the Neutral or a figuration in itself. The figure is specifically formulated, which is understood contextually: in its accentuation, in contrast to or in harmony, in any case, as part of a composition.

The Kunstwollen as the will to power to art   On which of Riegl's thoughts does Hilberseimer really build and how does he further develop them? Direct, explicit citations and references like about the Kunstwollen in *The architecture of the Large City*[47] are scarce. But in the early articles which Hilberseimer wrote from the perspective of an art critic, one can find text passages clearly derived from Riegl's understanding of art. The article *creation and development*[48] can here be taken as Hilberseimer's key text of his art-critical phase[49].

Analogous to Riegl, Hilberseimer rests his approach on an equality between styles. Cultures exist side by side and not in an evolutionary sequence. "Styles are not hierarchically graded, with increasing complexity, as an expression of increasing complexity civilizational; the cultures of the Middle Ages and the Orient alongside those of classical antiquity"[50]. Later Hilberseimer will describe the history of the city as a juxtaposition of geometric and organic order[51]. Thereby the orders are put on an equal footing. This position is fundamentally different from the argumentation of Le Corbusier's for the formal interposition of a city. As Le Corbusier is in favor of the geometric organization, by polemizing the organic city as "the donkeys path", he built on an evolutionary understanding of the city[52]. Here the city is not a composition of exposed methods, but a purely figurative opposition to the ground of history. Against this background, Hilberseimer's design of the Vertical-City also should be interpreted as a criticism regarding Corbusier's geometrical order.

72   The Mereological City: a reading of the works of Ludwig Hilberseimer

Figure 3.5: Sarcophagus of Alexander Severus and Julia Mammaea, n.D. in: Riegl 1901

Another point that Hilberseimer takes over from Riegl is the definition of the Kunstwollen as opposed to the material. Hilberseimer takes literally Riegl's definition of a work of art as "a being put to harmony ratio of tension"[53]. But while Riegl sees the value of a work of art in the mediation of the natural motive within the meaning of the relevant artistic will, Hilberseimer valued a work of art more directly through the correlation between artistic will and material. Since Hilberseimer is not only an observing art historian but also a producing architect, the Kunstwollen becomes a evaluation criterion, the creating force of the design process. When the intentions of a culture vary, the material will be edited in a new manner. If the material varies, while material in the broad sense refers to the circumstances of a culture (environment, territory, economy, technology, etc.), the Kunstwollen manifests itself in a different form. New forms of art will therefore first be perceived as dissonant, due to a new tension between a new material or a new expression of will, which is different from the old. A style therefore reaches its climax when material and Kunstwollen have placed no more resistance and they are in accordance. Hilberseimer compares the different styles to the image of a "Mountains, springing up all the many peaks (cultures), which reached heights are absolutely"[54]. If we remember Riegl's analysis in *questions of style*, the Kunstwollen was made visible in the geometric works of "primitive", ie primal cultures. The nature motive here is transformed the most pristine in its strong abstraction. So Riegl connects the Kunstwollen with authenticity, just to formulate a counter-argument for evolutionary materialism. Hilberseimer will draw the conclusion, that if Kunstwollen and form should be more closely short circuited, a throwback to original shapes, geometric figures and operations is obvious.

3.1.2 The Dionysian and the Apollonian

In addition to the concept of Kunstwollen Hilberseimer borrowed much of his theoretical basis from Friedrich Nietzsche[55]. In addition to the attention-grabbing adoption of the opposition "Dionysian" as "the creative from the unconscious" and "Apollonian" as "the consequence of skill"[56], there is a large number of takeovers of Nietzsche's keywords. Analogous to Nietzsche's call for the revaluation of all values, Hilberseimer calls for the "revaluation in Art"[57]. Hilberseimer reformulates the "will to power" as "The will to architecture"[58]. He follows Nietzsche's definition of style and quoted Nietzsche's famous passage: "Over the chaos being Lord, that what one is; force his chaos to become form: logical, simple, unambiguous, mathematics, law to be – that is the big ambition"[59] as: "the measure becomes Lord, forced the chaos to become form: logical, simple, unambiguous, mathematics, law"[60]. Since Hilberseimer himself describes the art as the embodiment of the will[61], I would like to align my interpretation especially to Martin Heidegger's lecture: *The Will to Power as Art*[62] Heidegger's interpretation – the revaluation of all values as perspectival character of all living things – is certainly the most fertile review Nietzsche's for a mereological approach.

The "Dionysian" and "Apollonian" Friedrich Nietzsche introduces in his first publication *The Birth of Tragedy*[63]. With the introduction of the two terms Nietzsche took off an avalanche. In spite of great rejections from his old-philological colleagues, the contrasting pair was an active inclusion in the literature and artistic circles of the outgoing 19th century[64]. Although the two terms terms became popular with Nietzsche, the contrast appeared already in the writings of Schelling and Hölderlin[65]. On the other hand, for Nietzsche the terms are under constant change[66]. For these reasons, the terms are difficult to grasp, partly because of their mystical origin.

The Dionysian represents the frenzyness "in whose increasing the Subjective dissolves into complete self-forgetfulness."[67] It is therefore the absorption of the Many in the One. As pure will, the Dionysian stems itself against existing, is also destructive, cruel, form-busting creative urge, thus, the early Nietzsche. From the service of a Sole will, the later Nietzsche form "the Dionysian in the service of the eternal recurrence of the same"[68][69].

The Apollonian is the vision, the illusory world of dreams. The Apollonian creates a pictorial world. It strives for order and tangible terms. It designs form. It is the merging of the One in the Many. Individuation is an accomplished separation and distinction from the previously One, highlights the different aspects of existence. Thus, the Apollonian is shine[70]. In this, Nietzsche emphasizes that the Apollonian shine immediately also includes awareness, the dream becomes knowledge. The Apollonian, the dream and the Dionysian, the frenzy, are in contrast, but complementary compared to eachother, Because the Dionysian is first unpictorial and needs the vision of the Apollonian to represent. In the chorus in Greek tragedy, so the music[71], the union of the two forces is expressed, ie the Apollonian picturing the Dionysian. Without the Apollonian, the Dionysian would be "expressionless pain-pleasure"[72]. Thus, the Dionysian depends on the Apollonian to be experienced. Only the designed distinction of a One, which is a reduction, ie a perspectivization and the preference of certain aspects of being, brings the Dionysian to appearance[73]. Thus, the appearance of the artwork is the stimulant of life.

In the absolutizing of the Apollonian principle of the mind, the Platonic idea of the supernatural, Nietzsche sees the cause of the downfall of Western civilization. A fusion of the Dionysian with the Apollonian Nietzsche calls an ideal state, the birth of a new culture. The prototype he finds in Greek tragedy, the play between Dionysian chorus and Apollonian world of images[74]. The Dionysian is thus the overcoming of the structured everyday world through the mind. In an analogous way Hilberseimer summarizes the *Birth of Tragedy*:

"Then the young Nietzsche discovered the Dionysismus of Greek art. The entire so well informed aesthetics collapsed. He drew in place of the so overrated Apollonian side of Greek art attention on the so disregarded Dionysian. [. . .] One realized at once the high value of the primitive as opposed to reproductive, which rose in routined mastery of the material, the will died and in the development of skills, the work of art saw salvation"[75].

From the dialectic of life and shine or from the Being and the essence will the Apollonian will be completely subordinate to the Dionysian in the late Nietzsche[76] and becomes an aesthetic basic state: the frenzy[77].

The great style: Essential for the frenzy is a sense of power increase, which is a super-yourself-beyond-capacity and also a feeling of fullness, which means: an impoundment of internal events. Frenzy is thus a feeling and thus bodily. Heidegger speaks of "a bodily attunement, [...] as a way of bodyment, tuned standing for the being as a whole." This is the perspective point of view, the advancement of Schopenhauer's representation, the body-be is the Apollonian in late Nietzsche. In this, Nietzsche emphasizes, that the frenzy is not as something present-at-hand in the body (form) and soul (content). For this reason, Nietzsche later formulated the Dionysian and the Apollonian not as opposites, but merges both in a sensual physicality. The frenzy so is bound physiologically, a feeling that the Dionysian passion which is bodily, so expresses itself Apollonian.

For architecture, Hilberseimer concludes from this that: "The art the Will" here comes before any science[78]. Therefore laws are formed according to the art, and art (or architecture) is not derived from science. The New can not be assessed on the existing criteria. Ideas are always absolutely for Hilberseimer. "Evolutionary is only the mastery of the material, the skill"[79]. The frenzy, the will, becomes science that is the law and will therefore be bound physiologically.

The form by Nietzsche: The zone of content: At what does frenzy aim? To this end, Heidegger analyzes the definition of beauty in Nietzsche. Building on Kant, Nietzsche says: "The beauty exists any more than the good, the true" (that is transcendental) determines Nietzsche's beauty as that what pleases. What we like is what we "worship as a role model of our being", subsequently the beauty that what is "us and our behavior and capability determines". Thus, the Beautiful reveals in a frenzy and is so to speak in the qualification the frenzy[80]. The question of the nature of creation is "the ecstatic making of of beauty in the works"[81]. In order to produce a representational thing from a feeling, you have to idealize this feeling, that is "a driving out the main features". A representational thing Nietzsche calls a form[82], "a specific and circumscribed region where the frenzy as such is possible". And where there is frenzy, form rules "as the supreme simplicity of the richest legality"[83]. Nietzsche uses frenzy thus equal to law. An equivalent between form and content is therefore the only real form. It is thus clear, that any frenzy in its own physicality is a separate law. The form is not a hull, not a formal in the sense of covering, but the zone of frenzy, of the contents. The edge is simply a break of the contents, but no limit. The form cannot be thought of as a container, which means content can not be absorbed in the form to be hidden. When the material corresponds to the content, consequently the content which is provided in the form however remains unformed, nothingness, Any and the void. This is Nietzsche's concept of form in contrary to previously presented concept of form as a contour. Form does not limit the contents, but the materiality, the frenzy itself.

Let us talk about one of the most cited, because easily formally interpretable, quotes of Nietzsche on the great style:

"To be form: logical, simple, unambiguous, mathematics, to be law."[84]

With this Nietzsche does not mean that art is only logic and mathematics[85]. If the logical basic emotions are the delight of "subordinates, including concise, Limited, the repetition", then this means to have sense for order. Heidegger goes on to state that having sense of order in its fundamental nature is nothing else but the delight of all organic beings in relation to the hazards of their location or severity of their feeding. Therefore, logical, mathematical feelings are a kind of assessment and consideration of one's own life operation. The form-legality is thus again focused on the life conditionality. The pleasure of Orderly is thus a basic condition of the bodily life and thus closes the circle, because life is again life enhancement, frenzy[86]. For Nietzsche this means, that art is legislation and at the same time the subject of frenzy. The logic and mathematics of the form indicates the aspired purity of the translation of frenzy into the form and back again. Hilberseimer interpreted this passage as follows:

"Architecture stems from the Geometric. When geometrical figures becomes proportioned bodies, architecture evolves. Multiformity at highest unity. Details subordinate to the generating mainline. In front of the decisive cubic structure details completely withdraw. Important remains the general organization of the masses. The imposed law of proportion. The most heterogeneous material masses require an equally valid formal law for each element. Therefore, reducing the types to the bare essentials. Common. Simplest. Unambiguous. Suppression of many-kind-ness. Shaping by a general law of form."[87]

As one can see, at least in his early texts Hilberseimer puts Nietzsche's call for a logical geometric law of form directly into shape. In early designs of Hilberseimer this is also visible. His design for a factory building of 1923[88] builds on purely proportional laws of form. In the ratio 1 : 3 : 4 stand four buildings, inscribed in a cube. The building length is equal to three times the body depth. The building length and the depth of the aligned component, results in four depth units for four buildings, arranged in a quadrangle. The building depth corresponds to the lowest component height, three floors. Clockwise, the height of the parts, so three storeys, is increased by one unit of depth at a window dividing the depth length into three, which results in a vertical staggering in the shape of a square of three by three window units. The highest building has the proportion of 1: 3: 4. It is noticeable that Hilberseimer this design only presented by isolated drawings. In *The will to architecture*[89] we find only a perspective drawing, in *Large City Buildings*[90] we find also a proportional layout

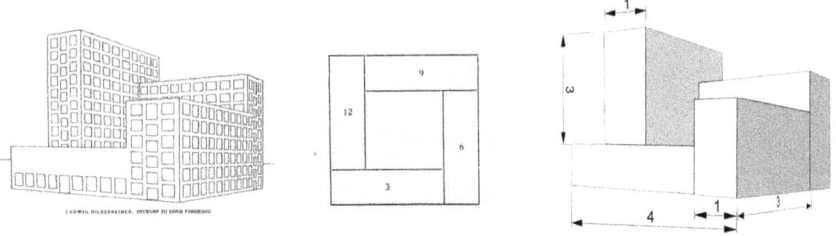

Figure 3.6: Hilberseimer draft of a factory building in 1923

scheme. It is questionable whether a functional floor plan or section was ever made. Furthermore, the design itself is not described in the text. The drawing is a mere supplement to the text. In other designs to housing, of which today only perspective views remain[91], in review of perspective construction it becomes clear, that the division of the figurative building structure perspectively is not possible. Compositional effects were obtained from the displacement of the vanishing points. Also the houses are known to us only through their perspective views. Detailed descriptions, plans or sections of the titled houses are unknown.

Hilberseimer concentrates on the geometric configuration of the form. Here the influence of Riegl's *questions of style* is noticeable. In the interweaving of Nietzsche and Riegl's argument, Hilberseimer in the early works of "primitive", sees the "unbroken purity of the will", ie the Dionysian and makes the works to his formal model[92]. In the closure of the circle life itself can be art. But art is created in a hierarchy and does not mean every life, but the over-yourself-beyond-capability of life when frenzy and Beauty condition are one. This names the great style by Nietzsche "the unity of the reference change of frenzy and beauty, of creating, receiving, and form to be understood as the great style."[93] Nietzsche refers to the Dionysian and Apollonian, frenzy and law as a unit in art, as under one yoke. Law is abstraction of frenzy through empathy. Accordingly the great style does not designate a form of style in a formal sense, but an abandoned thing, an aspired correlation, for Heidegger: the basic way of existence itself[94]. For Hilberseimer: the method of design itself[95].

In the interrelationship of frenzy and form, a contrast dissolves in the statements of Nietzsche on the art: On the one hand, the art is the counter movement to nihilism, in its broadest the transcendental[96]. Second, the art is object of physiological aesthetics – because the art, the form is frenzy: sensual[97]. For Hilberseimer form therefore is Eerollment of an idea into a material medium. As an idea is always absolute, the form also is a unique totality. "Works of art are demarcations of the factual"[98]. Their

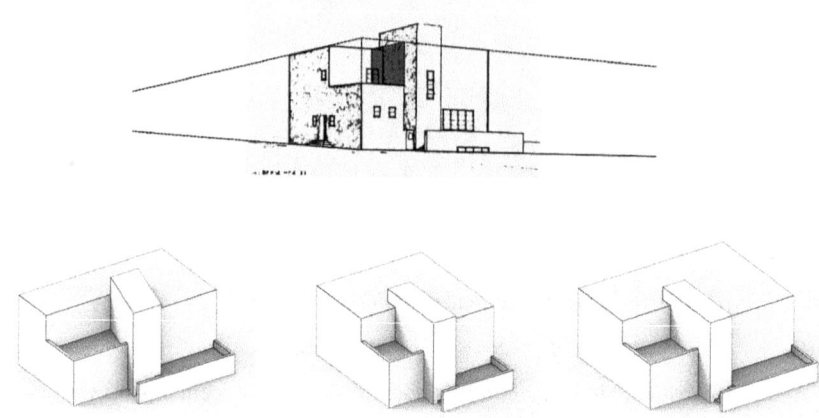

Figure 3.7: Hilberseimer, living house 1, before 1925; the perspective is ambiguous, it is based on aesthetic consideration of volumetric proportions; bottom: geometric reconstructions left: drawn cubatur in axonometric view; middle: cubatur projecting front proportions; right: cubatur projecting back proportions

bounding makes them graspable, writable. A form is used to separate different ideas of the factual. The form becomes a statement. "Through the form content is brought to consciousness to us"[99]. The form is secluded in time and space and only assessable based on its own relation between idea and material. The form of the demarcation is thus not defined as the distinction between One and the other, as happens for the concept of form as a contour, but by the multiplicity of singularities of individual self-contained elements.

The reversal of the dialectic The great style Nietzsche develops against nihilism, for the reversal of all values. By this he means the Platonic philosophy, as the root of Western thought and the Christian religion: the transcendental. For Nietzsche, the art as the highest sensual, plays a key role here, as it is in Plato, as imitation, subordinated to the idea of the transcendental[100]. In Plato the idea is the truth, unreachable and transcendental. The artist just through mimesis creates Many from the One and it is this relationship that essentially should be reversed. But for reversing it is not enough to replace Sensual and Transcendentual in the ranking, but a "turning out" from the hierarchy, to merge Sensual and Transcendentual into one object. This is what Nietzsche means with "upturned Platonism"[101]. For this, Nietzsche defines truth as the sensual, the scientific cognification. And here it is where art and truth meet and design the sensuous by creating and cognition[102]. The sensual-bodily, as defined region of the form, is separated from everything by cessation of the self. A recognition can only be done from out of the bodily. Heidegger quotes Nietzsche: "The essence of organic beings is a new interpretation of events. The perspective inner multiplicity, which is itself an event"[103]. The detection of a bodily is therefore an interpretation, a perspective on others. According to Heidegger, Nietzsche develops an image in that at first a work of art results from a backlinked interaction of frenzy, beauty, creativity and cognition and form. The form of something surrounding becomes something spatial. Recognizing means resistance to something else bodily. Recognizing means resistance the physicality of something else. The interpretation of othersfrom out of their own physicality is an interpretation and is done with a sense of order: in shaping.

Hilberseimer does something similar and accepts Nietzsche's perspectivism and transmits it to the art styles. This repeals thoughts of evolutionary development and equals all art styles. Hilberseimer formulates:

"The recognition of the equivalences, equality of cultures [...] All cultures are differentiations of the same. As such, all original and independent. The so-called lower are not precursors of the so-called higher."[104]

3.2 GROSZSTADT ARCHITECTURE

In Hilberseimer's early texts the boundary between reference, quote and his own thesis blurs. The texts are collaged with text blocks from art history and philosophy. Without direct indication of the source, but mostly obvious like in the word play of the title: "The will to architecture" as Nietzsche's "Will to Power".

Hilberseimer's reference also quotes his own work. Formally, his main work *Large City Architecture*[105] is largely a summary of previous essays, especially Hilberseimer's first book *Large City Buildings*[106]. The introductory essay *The Large City*, is a revised version of chapter one from Large City Buildings: *Large City and urban design*. In essence, its key points are also included in his first manuscript:*Architecture of the Large City*[107]. Hilberseimer takes over passages from further texts: from *The highrise*[108], *The will to architecture*[109],*creation and development*[110], *About the typification of the apartment house*[111]. All illustrated own designs in *Large City Architecture* have been published before. Only the design *Schema of a Vertical-City*[112] has been revised. The perspective drawings were detailed, a plan schema and a textual description created complementary. The constant resumption of his own subjects and their reconfiguration in the fifties will result in the publication of *The Nature of Cities*[113]. In the general review, this work is considered an edited re-release of *The New City*[114]. Hilberseimer himself described *The Nature of Cities* itself as a milestone in his development with a completely different weighting[115]. The example illustrates that for Hilberseimer it is important to present his exempted methodologies in increasingly complex mutual relatedness. Like in a collage or composition, new representations are created only by a reconfiguration them.

As an art critic, above all for the magazine *Socialist monthly booklets*[116] Hilberseimer writes reviews about artists, book publications and exhibitions. Without giving up the role of the architect, Hilberseimer never forgets to attach his own critique based on his design intention to the artcritical descriptions.. A few examples: an eulogy on the poetry of Paul Scheerbart and his influence on architecture turns into a warning "against the lack of imagination as an intention to realize the phantasies"[117] and the requirement for "unfolding, visualization of an idea". The description of African art turns into a desire for the "creation out of primordial awareness"[118]. An article about J.J.P. Oud's apartment buildings[119] starts with an introduction to J.J.P. Oud's general requirements for the apartment building and ends with the demand of Oud and much more Hilberseimer's: the design of the development "the organic grouping of the basic elements of the architecture". The report of the exhibition "Danish architecture"[120] does not refer to the exhibition but compares Danish with German classicism. In comparison, Hilberseimer finds arguments for the inadequacy of classicism and its method. Similarly, the review of an exhibition of American architecture[121]: Hilberseimer exemplary describes American buildings, none of his chosen examples discussed was part of the exhibition. Hilberseimer's criticism is not negative but is understood to be a reversing into an own solution. The criticism is operational[122]. The real issues are a pretext to promote his own project.

Another aspect is, that Hilberseimer in this way achieved to link himself with the projects of the avant-garde. About two-thirds of his main work *Large City Architecture* Hilberseimer dedicated to the representation of exemplary large city buildings. His own designs for a residential settlement, a boarding house and a train station, are placed inbetween the most-realized, avant-garde architectural projects. The photographic material was published before. The architecture examples were part of the exhibition*International plan- and model exhibition of new architecture*[123]. Curated by Hilberseimer, the exhibition was part of the Werkbund Exhibition *the apartment*[124] in 1927,of which today the most famous part is the *Weissenhofsiedlung*[125].

3.2.1 The abstraction as a discursive experiment

Used to work with references, in the communication of an architectural idea Hilberseimer differs considerably from the work of his contemporaries. Instead of emphasizing the difference, innovation and originality of his own work, Hilberseimer understood to integrate it into the discourse on the large city. The projects are part of solutions and collage-like contributions to a coherent discussion. Thus, the often criticized holistic approach of a self-contained experiment becomes an argument on which conclusions are provided in their purity for an architectural synthesis. The abstract project representations are therefore not related as inhuman, hygienically cleaned cities, but as complementary contributions to the large city. Hilberseimer himself describes his architectural representations again and again as "schema, purely theoretical, without any design intent to realize."[126], as "diagrams, [. . .] a framework, [. . .] abstractions only"[127]; Christine Mengin comes to a similar conclusion: For Hilberseimer, his designs as theoretical plans with demonstrative character, are the only possible way to counter today's metropolis. Hilberseimer starts from the real needs and develops general, generic rules that may later be applied to specific situations.[128]

In his projects, Hilberseimer also binds to planning guidelines of his predecessors. Here is an example: His large city projects are based on Martin Maechler's plan for Great-Berlin in 1919, the monofunctional proposal of a business city[129] based on an assumption of Mächler's specifications. In Hilberseimer project, the city consists of autonomous city blocks. Each satellite town, city block, includes a city. As a pure detailing of the Vertical-City schema, the *Proposal for City buildings* would also need to include living. Hilberseimer but accepts the functional separation by Mächler's plan and demonstrates, that it is the combination and weighting of solutions, which leads to the figure.

The Chicago Tribune: A schema of the representation of the American skyscraper One of Hilberseimer's most famous designs is the not submitted, high-rise design for the competition of the Chicago Tribune Tower from 1922[130]. The design is known for its clear, geometric-abstract language. But how did Hilberseimer develop the building? In several articles Hilberseimer described and criticized the American skyscraper[131], although the topic of the American skyscraper for Hilberseimer is interesting for several reasons: Firstly, it is a new type, derived from the properties of the large city. The skyscraper is the characteristic of the existing American metropolis. On the other hand, by treating it as an original row house and the resulting defects in the density of a neighborhood, the American highrise shows, that

82   The Mereological City: a reading of the works of Ludwig Hilberseimer

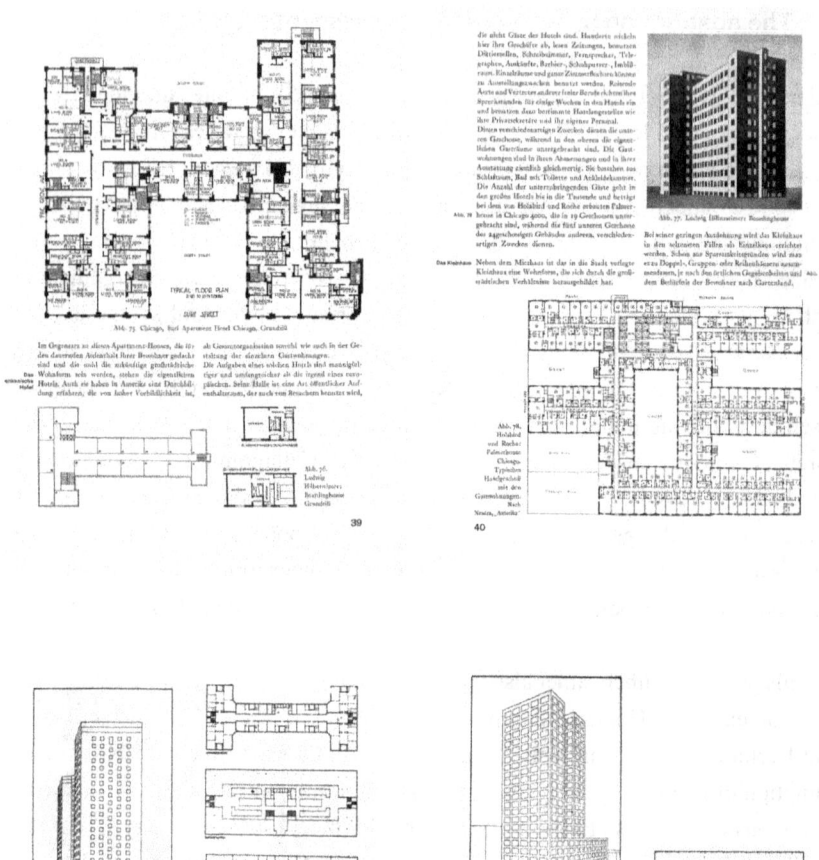

Figure 3.8: Hilberseimer develops his high-rise building typology by the abstraction of the American "Alphabet tower"; top: description of his own Boardinghouse with a direct comparison to the American skyscraper, Chicago, bottom: high-rise designs

The Large City   83

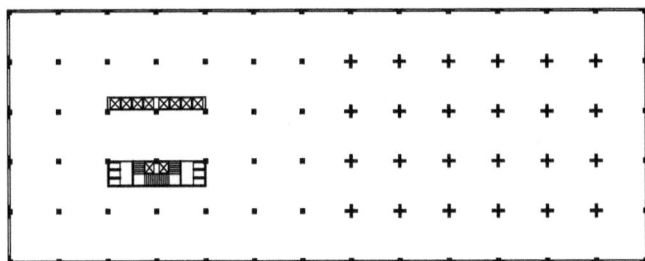

1. - 8. floor

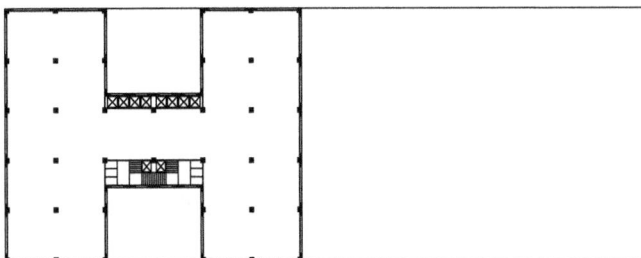

9. - 24. floor

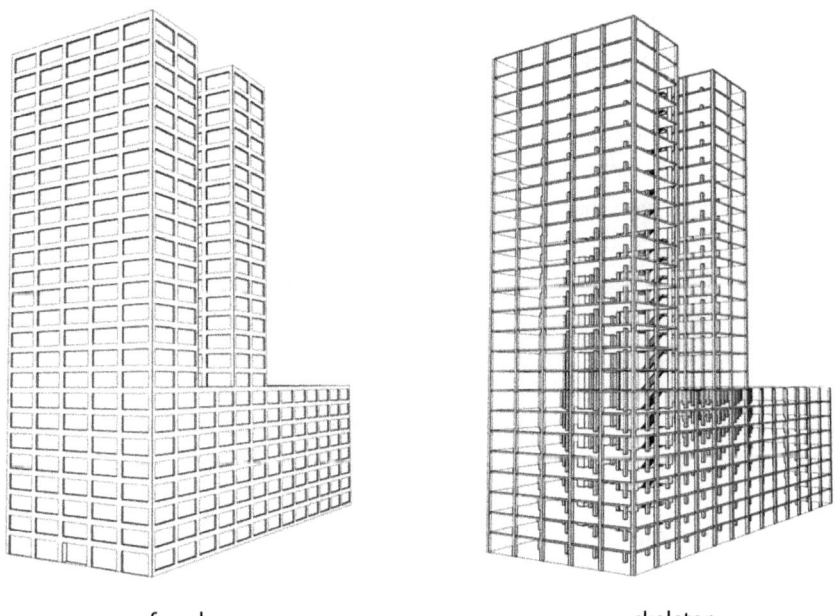

facade   skeleton

Figure 3.9: Hilberseimer, Chicago Tribune Tower, 1922

the large city cannot be developed only based on a purely horizontal plan. Hilberseimer takes for his own high-rise designs the American high-rise organization as a model. The outgoing stitch corridors from a center core formulate a character of a building, which will later be recognized by Stephen Holl as *Alphabetical City*[132]. Hilberseimer himself puts the American high-rise reference in relation to its own designs in his book *Large City Architecture*[133]. Here he holds up two existing floor plans of American skyscrapers with his own design of a boarding house. Due to the referential entanglement and coherence of cubature, Hilberseimer's own design does not appear as a formal difference to the above, but due to the lack of details and the even divisions of the facade as an abstraction of the existing: a schema. The plastic formulation of the building structure of the Chicago Tribune is caused by the reflection and abstraction of the already existing American skyscraper. Congruent to Alois Riegl's theory of art is for Hilberseimer the existing high rise is a nature-motif. The uniform subdivision of the facade corresponds to an offset of the inner construction. The window measurements vertically results as the distance between two structural supports and horizontally as the closure of floor and ceiling. Congruent to Nietzsche's definition of a form as zone of content, the facade for Hilberseimer is an extension and completion of the internal structural composition. When not understood as a hull, the facade is liberated from the dialectical communication of an outside and an inside. So the facade from an outside, without knowledge of the internal composition is withdrawn. The description of the facade exhausts itself being logical, simple, purely geometric, abstract.

As Hays[134] pointed out, it is this method of instrumentation, which characterizes the "Neue Sachlichkeit". Through the combination of biological, social, economic issues and actions with their own idea of architectural form, action is absorbed by form, as to say: punctualized. From the humanist concept of total causality of an outside, Hilberseimer so consequently reaches a mode of simulation. In the concept of form there is no dialogue between object and subject, context, history and subjective experience; the architectural figure emerges without an external, humanistic review. While the humanistic figured itself is asserted, the external ground here is speculatively absorbed into the configuration of the figure. The placeholder turns into an architectural position.

3.2.2 The large city as an elemental task

"The modern large city has been a product of the greed for profit of individuals, chaotic, with miserable living conditions. A city from the interests of individuals is speculative and thus an artificial product. It lacks the necessity"[135]. In this way

Hilberseimer describes the features of the existing city as an accumulation of disparate elements. The physical picture of the large city corresponds to the arbitrariness of economic speculation. In reversal of the equation a physically ordered city could transform the city to an analogy of a proper organism. In this way the socially ordered city is linked to the product of a material order. Therefore, city designs within the meaning of such reversal equation do not presuppose a tabula rasa, but consider themselves as the final product of a constant transformation of the already internationally constituted metropolis. Therefore, a physical projection, which would be based on a reality of a yet to be developed social order, is to be created. The work

Figure 3.10: The city as a democracy of the architectural elements; left: perspective Vertical-City, right: architecture examples in: Hilberseimer 1927b

of the architect becomes constitutive for drafting the law. A counter-position to the existing large city can so be only theoretical and developed as purely abstract, fundamental principle. Generally applicable rules should be designed, which allow to solve specific tasks. Only an abstraction can show, how the elements of the city can be brought into an evocative order. Idea and form are interlinked and influence each other through the formal laws of the material. In Alois Riegl's sense, the Kunstwollen will challenge the material factors and production processes and in reverse will be affected the Kunstwollen by new technical developments. In Nietzsche's sense, the frenzy is bound and is represented by the sensual-physical. "By union of the two moments in a single form arises Architecture"[136]. Or else, in Nietzsche's sense: the great style, as reciprocal relation of creation, receiving, and form.

Hilberseimer makes it clear, that his point is to examine how the elements of the city are related to each other in general. The new city should be built on the basis of its elements, so instead of a mere juxtaposition of elements, on a series of the needs of the elements. But what are the problems and needs of a city? How is "city" transferred into an architectural problem? What defines architectural elements and their relationship to each other? These are the core issues that Hilberseimer is trying to answer in *Large City Architecture*.

Figure 3.11: Hilberseimer, Vertical-City, North-South Street Perspective, left: drawing 1924; right: drawing 1927

Figure 3.12: Hilberseimer, Vertical-City, East-West Street Perspective, left: drawing 1924; right: drawing 1927

Hilberseimer identified two problems: At first, the housing grievances. From this Hilberseimer developed demands to be complied for minimum standards. Even the smallest apartment will have sufficient living space in relation to the number of its inhabitants. The room should be provided with sufficient air and light, resulting on an architectural scale in minimum proportional relations between building height and building distance. For the construction of the city Hilberseimer recommends the satellite-town-system, in which the city consists of several self-contained neighborhoods-satellites.

The second major problem of the City Hilberseimer recognizes in the speed of motorized traffic. As walking distances are not an issue, the large city for the first time in history is not physically, territorially bound. Thus, the new means of transport permit indeed new urban systems like the satellite city system, but also lead to places of extreme compaction. The American high rise emerged as a result of the fast infrastructure and shows that without the vertical dimension of a city the city cannot be planned anymore.

3.2.3 The Vertical-City as vertical composition

The harmonization of the existing city From this insight Hilberseimer developed the Vertical-City in response to Le Corbusier's plan of a city of 3 million inhabitants. The design presented by Le Corbusier is an inversion of the historic city. Le Corbusier's plan promises a higher population density than in the historic city and at the same time amples open spaces: A city in the countryside. But Hilberseimer notes, that Le Corbusier's raise in density by increasing the open spaces is based on an incorrect comparison: Corbusier compares the residential density of an existing city to the occupation density of commercial buildings of his city. Hilberseimer calculates that, designed as a pure residential development, the vertical design of Corbusier would only have a density comparable to existing cities. Furthermore, the open spaces obtained between the tower blocks would be drastically reduced once the consequences of a functionally separate city showed: The tower blocks are office buildings and at equal working hours, the simultaneous commuting would lead to a significant increase of the traffic infrastructure. The parking areas would turn into parking lots and little would be left. The gained advantages thus turn out not to be any. The only thing that Le Corbusier's design provides, is a successful reorganization of the existing chaotic city. For Hilberseimer, Le Corbusier's city design is a pure harmonization of the existing city however, no fundamental solution to the problem of the large city. Also and especially because Corbusier is not taken into account the vertical implication of the large city. With the large distance between the high-rise crosses, Le Corbusier does not deal with the actual city problem.

The vertical solution of the large city problem The vertical solution Hilberseimer presents in terms of the City Schema of the Vertical-City. The name of the literally tall-house-city represents the vertical organization principle of the city, less the metric height. The main ingredient of the design is the textual description, accompanied by two perspectives and a plan scheme. First the textual description[137]: Here Hilberseimer explicitly emphasizes, that the representations are without any design intention. It is a scheme, not an absolute architectural representation.

The high-rise city for Hilberseimer is the implementation of the satellite town concept with a vertical structure. He explicitly makes demands for a clear and con-

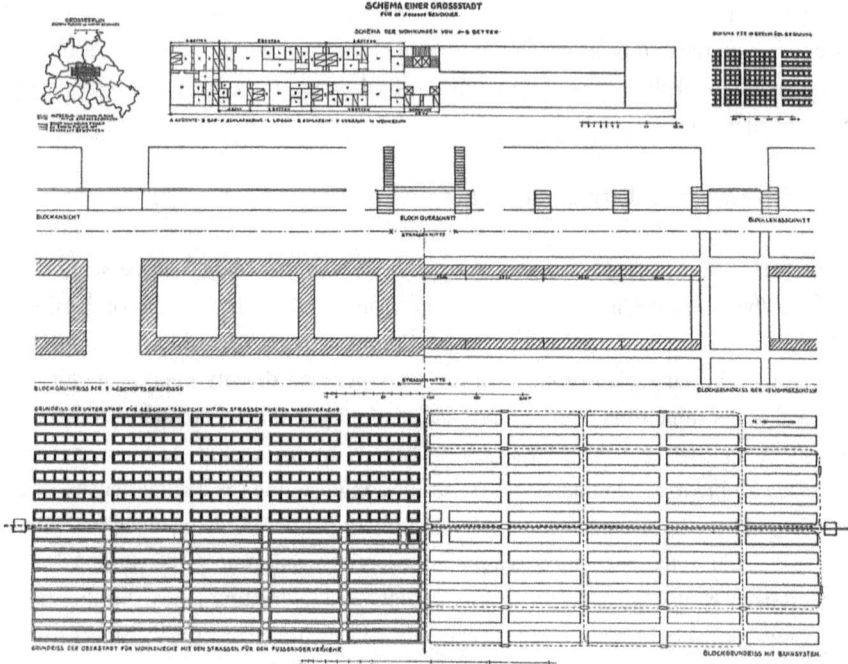

Figure 3.13: Hilberseimer, Schema of a Vertical-City, city plan, 1927

cise city plan, for healthy apartments without enclosed courtyards. Building height and space should be in equal proportions to each other. The shown high-rise city has twenty storeys. The buildings are divided vertically by a separation of function. The lower five floors of a city-block contain the business city, the top fifteen the residential city. The business city consists of workshops and workplaces, just like in the *proposal to City-development*[138], Hilberseimer will differ between commercial and office. Covered Courtyards becomes covered exhibition halls. The entrances to the apartment house circulations, shops and various communal facilities are on the first floor of the residential city. Apartments of different sizes are located on the upper 14 floors.

Living and working are vertically linked, each resident can and should live above his working place. With this Hilberseimer wants to continue the morphology of the single house of the medieval city. There, the size of the house has also complied to the size of a craft establishment: On the ground floor the business and working spaces, overlying the living rooms. The medieval single house in the Vertical-City is the collective community house, the city-block, according to the development from craft

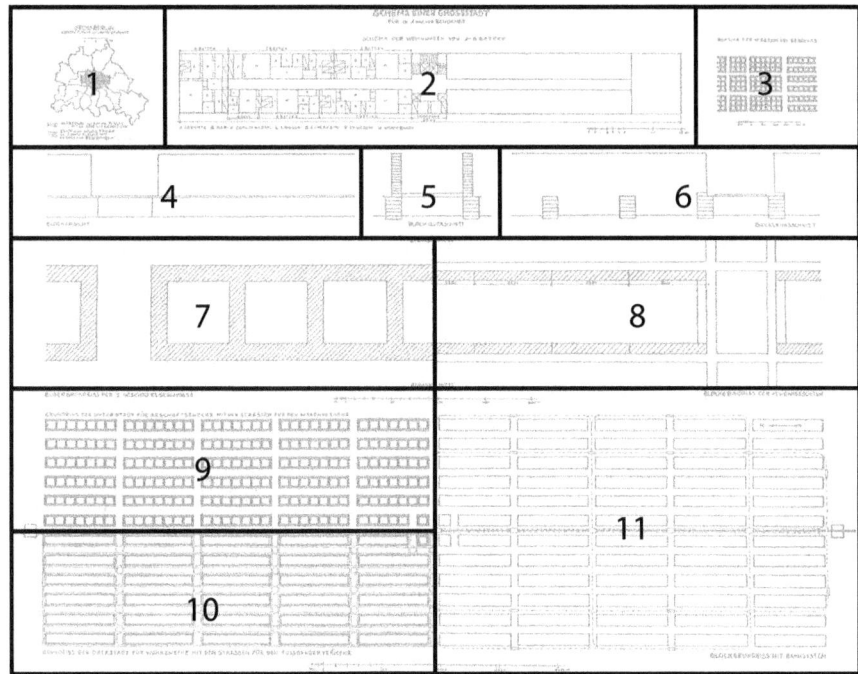

Figure 3.14: Hilberseimer's schema of a high-rise city, city plan, 1927; No 1: schematic of land use compared with Berlin; No 2: schema of apartment layouts, 6 modules 1-6 beds; No 3: comparison of the usual Berlin block construction, interior courtyards, with the morphology of the Vertical-City; No 4: block elevation; No 5: block cross-section; No 6: block longitudinal section. No 7: block plan of the 5 office floors; No 8: Block plan of the 15 residential floors; No 9: city plan of the floors 1-5; No 10: city plan of the floors 6-20; No 11: city schema with railway system

to industry. Hilberseimer here did not accomplish a morphological transformation like Corbusier, based on geometric properties, but a topological transformation based on the inner links the city elements.

The length of a city block corresponds to the distance between two underground stations. In the text and plan, the self-contained blocks are described by a width of 100 meters and a length of 600 meters. The layout of the city system and thus the street network is determined by the orientation towards the sun. The traffic is also organized vertically separated into functions. Sidewalks are separated from vehicular traffic to avoid risk to pedestrians[139]. Not part of the plan representation only described in the text, points Hilberseimer out that the concentration of Vertical-City is a reduction of the built area at the same time. The Vertical-City should not be endless. The free- and park spaces outside the Vertical-City include schools, hospitals and sports facilities, entirely analogous to later in the Settlement Unit. In contrast to Le Corbusier Hilberseimer not mentions museums, theaters and places of public assembly as public institutions. Public institutions are not part of the urban schema. But a city block should contain in addition to apartments, workshops and offices everything else necessary for life. The combination of many apartments into one unit is preferred, because this will allow institutions through the pure amount of the apartments, which would otherwise be uneconomical. The mass of apartments allows so one the one side technical innovations, such as central heating, which lowers rental costs, to the other community facilities, such as washing and cooking kitchens, which liberate women from being a housekeeper. Social demand for the individual can be realized through the mass of architectural elements in a composition according to Hilberseimer. The apartment itself is supposed to be for the purposes of industrial relations, a typed object. But that does not mean that the apartments will all be uniform. A model set should allow variation and expression. The apartments are functionally organized, possess separate rooms according to their purpose. Living room, kitchen, hallway, loggia and a certain number of bedrooms. The furniture is an integral part of the apartment. Position and measurements of the furniture determines the room size and its figure. The model of the apartment is no longer the single house, but the hotel. The relocation is done with only a suitcase, no longer with a moving van. Here the room becomes static, the inhabitants flexible. Thus, the apartment is not tailored to the needs of the inhabitants, but the occupant selects from a specific deterministic but differentiated range of apartments. The purposefulness of a room refers so to the organization of its architectural elements, and not to the living behavior of its inhabitants.

Let us consider in more detail the drawings for the high rise area. The plan schema[140] is difficult to read and, typical of Hilberseimer, a superposition of several representations in one drawing. The plan scheme consists of a total of eleven different drawings in five different scales.

The limit of the Vertical-City The upper left *drawing No 1* compares the land use of the Vertical-City to the existing area of Greater Berlin. The contour of Greater Berlin is aligned to the north, according to the coarse scale of a map, while the city plan of a city element was placed rotated by 90 degrees counterclockwise. The rotation of the city plan and marked area is to be considered for a projection of the city plan to the schema. The illustrated city plan for an urban element is aligned to 1 million inhabitants, but the schema refers to the design of a city of 4 million inhabitants.

The Large City 91

One possibility now is to quadruple the block number of a city element in order to reach a city plan for 4 million inhabitants. This however, results in an area that is far too small and would accupy only a third of the labeled size comparison area. It is correct, to place the city element vertically aligned and quadruple it for comparison to Greater Berlin. This results in the right proportion of height in Hilberseimer's schema, but not yet in width. In the textual description Hilberseimer also speaks of free space outside the city element as crucial part of the schema. This space is part of the planning, for example Hilberseimer speaks of the arrangement of public facilities in the open space. If you now take an empty place holder as open space, the same extent of the city element along the longitudinal sides provides the disposition of four city elements and the attached empty spaces provide a congruent proportion and size, as the area marked in drawing no. 1. Instead of an endless sequence of city blocks, the Vertical-City consists of a specific layout of urban elements and their open spaces. As the block of apartments and the city element consist of blocks, the schema of the city consist of city elements. Many argue, that the Vertical-City as a symbol of the urbanization, consists of infinitely repetitive slabs. This is contradicted by the construction of the Vertical-City from city elements, which in size are discrete determined analogous to the city block, by the span between two intercity railway stations on the ends of the city element. The point symmetry of the plan of a city-element is another compositional aspect, that contradicts an infinite sequence. The construction of Vertical-City from city elements so is compositionally congruent to Hilberseimer's later regional planning of the city made from settlement units.

The city block as overlapping of architectural parts The upper center *drawing No 2* shows a schema of a possible apartment layout. Hilberseimer shows six different residential units, which vary in size and room allocation by number of beds, between one to six. Each apartment has an entrance hall, a kitchen, a bathroom, a balcony, a living area and a specific number of bedrooms. The spatial organization of the apartments is mereologically equal. Hilberseimer does not make absolute specification of the location of the apartments towards each other. The scheme shows six possible apartments varying in size and their mereological overlap with a staircase and a corridor[141]. A relation between the apartments except the common partition wall is missing. The location of the apartments along the corridor is variable. The modularity of the rooms and the apartments are multiples of each other. Only the location of the staircase and corridor is determined. As a result of recombining apartment cells within the span of two staircases is possible.

In a mereological representation[142], it is apparent that Hilberseimer only defined a house as the distance between two staircases. The distance forms a contour within

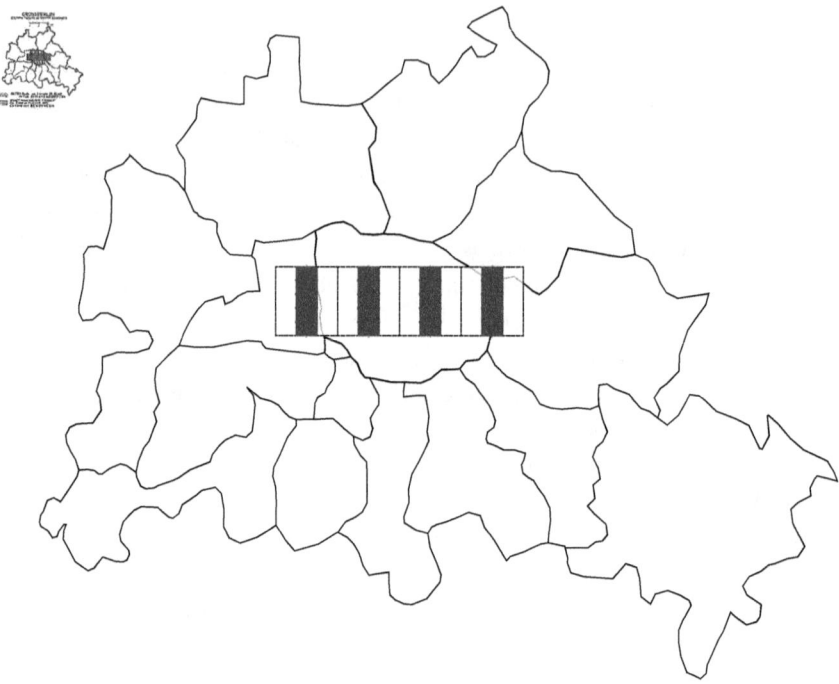

Figure 3.15: drawing No 1: city for 4 million inhabitants, size comparison with Greater Berlin; the dotted zones mark the open spaces associated with city elements

which the composition of the apartments remains undetermined. In this way, a free space is created, that allows variation by arrangement and combination. In the urban schema, the house is described with only one partial aspect – not as a whole – even to allow a specific architectural formulation. According to the textual description a city block is characterized in a similar way.

Drawing No 3 on the left side shows the schematic urban morphology of Berlin's existing city blocks, blocks with the other courtyards lined up behine and on the right, the schematic urban morphology of high-rise city without trapped courtyards.

Drawing No 4 to 6 in elevation and section provide the block cubature. Not as usually for elevations, a possible unwinding of the height is represented by a circular arc. Through this, the minimum sunlight is fixed through the proportional relationship between the height of the blocks and the width of the streets. According to Hilberseimer's distance regulation of slabs depending on the slab height, slab to slab would be equally spaced. But the lines of a block are closer to each other. An unwinding makes clear, that the distance rule within a block only counts for the residential slab.

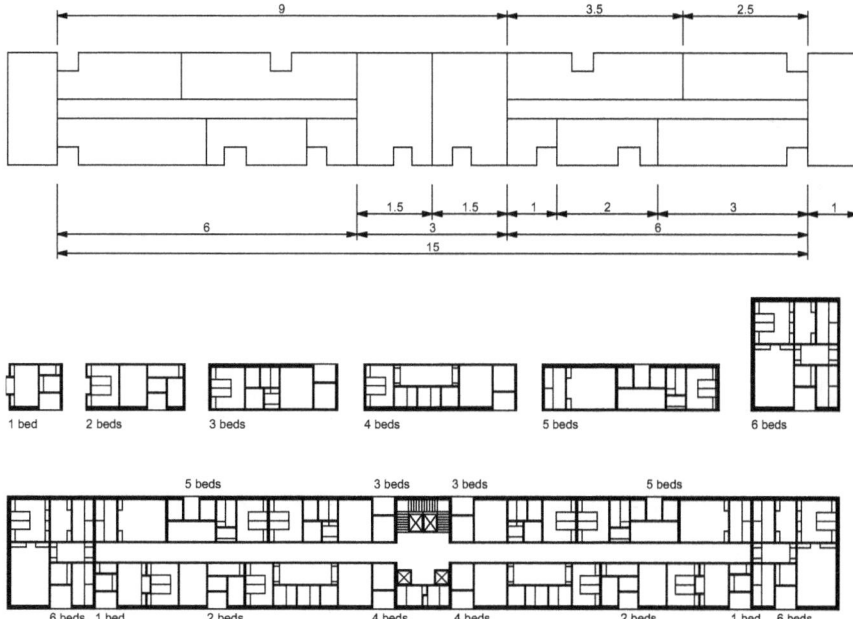

Figure 3.16: drawing No 2: plan schema, different residential units; the units are mereologically congruent to the varying number of bedrooms

Between the blocks the full height of the block is measured as the distance. The commercial or lower city seems to differentiate qualitatively from the residential city. But precise details relating to the commercial city are missing.

Drawing No 7 shows the floor plan through the building mass of the commercial city. Each block is divided by transverse tracts into seven courtyards. In the text Hilberseimer speaks of exhibition halls, but the lack of representation in longitudinal section, drawing No 6, does not speak for a roof.

Drawing No 8 shows the floor plan through the building mass of the residential city. The slab is divided into 7 equal portions. The residential slabs are even to the block center of the commercial city. The free roof portion is a pedestrian street and the individual blocks are connected through bridges. At the top of the blocks shops are located, so that the walkways are always lined one-sided to the shops and community facilities.

Drawing No 9 shows the city layout of the commercial city, so the floors 1 to 5. The *Drawing No 10* shows the city layout of the residential city, so the floors 6 to 20.

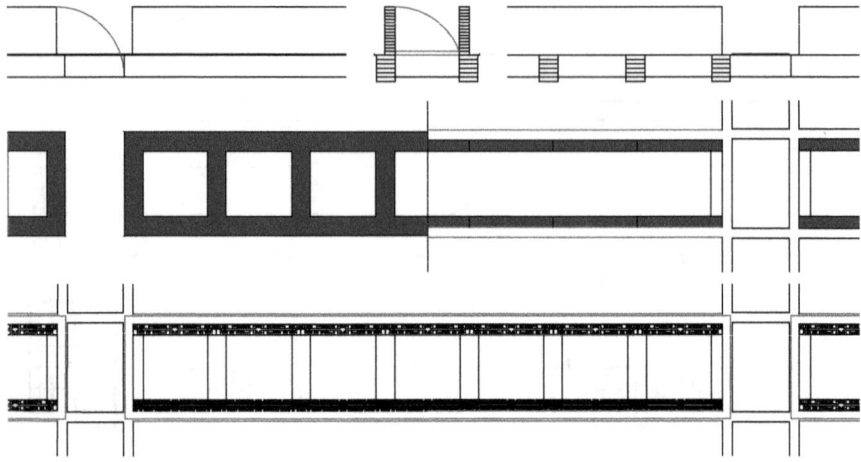

Figure 3.17: drawing No 4-8: Representation of the city block

Drawing No 11 represents the public transport infrastructure. The track routes are underground. The presentation is not a classic as a section through a geometry. It is not a horizontal section through a basement and no plan view of a city element. The blocks are shown in their outlines, the railway stations marked as framed units between the track route are drawn by dotted lines. When comparing the drawing to the textual description, it is noticeable that the drawing is not a geometric representation, but emphasizes the mereological elements which were textually brought into relation. In the text the distance of the railway station determines the block outline. A city block spans between two stations. The drawing emphasizes the mereological combination of block and stations. A block is formed by the overlap of two stations. For this reason, only blocks and stations are bound by their outlines. Block and station are separate elements, which are in relation to each other. As is clear from the drawing, the station is not a property of a block or otherwise.

The perspective views: Both perspectives on the level of the pedestrian street, look to the direction of the axis of one of the two main streets. Both are constructed to a central vanishing point. As Mark Kilian has pointed out[143], the perspectives are based on the construction of the perspectives of the previous residential city design. The perspective *East-West-Street* reveals little for a mereological analysis, since the cubature of the individual city blocks is not traceable. One detail is still striking: In contrast to the plan schema, at the end and in the axis of the East-West-Street, Hilberseimer placed a single building. This can be interpreted, as Kilian did, as a design expedient for the completion of the streetscape. On the other hand, the solitaire complementary matches the textual description. It could be a case of the required public facilities, which are planned to be located in the free space of the city elements. The placement of public facilities at the ends of the east-west streets would also be congruent to the previous design of the residential city[144]. There, on the tops of the east-west streets, Hilberseimer placed schools[145].

In the perspectives, the facades of the residential city are distinguished from the commercial city: The commercial city is divided by horizontal window strips, the residential city shown with a punctuated facade. Because Hilberseimer in general provides little information on the commercial city, here only the facade design of the residential city should be examined.

If one locates the point of view of the perspective North-South-Street in the plan schema, one can notice that the perspective wasconstructed extremely abbreviated. When seen, one expects an ordinary slab with an average length of 70 meters. But compared with the plan scheme, the proposed length of a city block is 600 meters. The extreme perspective shrinks the perceived distances. Thus, for example, the building at the end of the streetscape is 2,400 meters away. When constructing the block with the shown number of punctuations[146], it is clear that in relation a hole has a real length of approximately 15 meters. The distance between the punctuations, takes about 15 meters. As Hilberseimer himself already stated, the representation of the punctuated facades must be a schematic representation. The holes cannot display windows, not with the phenomenological length of a block of about 70 meters. In this case, opening and wall would be and at a distance of an ordinary skeleton grid, similar to the design of the Chicago Tribune Tower. The distorted perception of a much shorter block than in the plan drawing is supported by the construction of perspective. The distances between the blocks are much larger than in the scheduling scheme in perspective, which makes the block length appear smaller due to the shifted proportion.

The hole in the facade must stand for another signifier of an architectural element. As is apparent from the textual description, each apartment should have a loggia. If one now constructs a block with schematic apartment units from the plan scheme, a block-slab has 27 loggia openings on the West- and 56 loggia openings on the East side. Now turn the constructed block, which is accented with one loggia per apartment in the facade, to the perspective of North-South-Street and to the shape congruent with the original facade. One can then say that the punctuation in the perspective facade is the signifier of a loggia and thus a residential unit. As a schematic representation the facades of perspectives embody the structural logic of the underlying apartment cells. The representation is not an absolute of architectural aesthetics, but represents the structure of several apartment elements of living in a

Figure 3.18: Hilberseimer, Vertical-City, perspective East-West-Street, 1927. The building in the central streetscape indicates the planning of public buildings in the free space of the Vertical-City.

large form, the city block. The representation is mereological, the type of fabric is parts to a whole.

What would now be a possible architectural formulation of such a scheme? Considering the presented apartment floor plans, one cannot obtain a homogeneous partitioned facade. In each unit the position of the loggia is different, a uniform disposition would only be possible with a flat type per block per city. But Hilberseimer already proposes six types as examples. If one reads the schema as a mereological one, the perforation of the facade first of all means an overlap of the city block with a specific amount of housing units. From the plan scheme, drawing No 2, it becomes apparent that Hilberseimer establishes a specific intersection of flat and city block. The first overlap is the location of an apartment at a city-block corridor. The second overlap is the maximum distance of an apartment to a staircase. Both overlaps frame the order of units without determining absolute dispositions. The framing of the overlap produces an open space, which creates a certain amount of variation by combination. Assuming a steady, equal distance between two staircases in the scheme of the Vertical-City and using only the developed exemplary six types of apartments, the number of possible combinations of permutation while taking into account the absolute size of the untis is *182.681* possible variations. Follow the schematic representation a city block has 7 staircases, therefore 7 sections times 14 residential floors by 2 slabs per block by 10 by 12 blocks per city element time 4 City units, so the presented city for 4 million residents consists of *94.080* sections between two staircases. So the schematic structure of the basic plan-typologies already allows twice as many variation freedoms as with explicit situations. Especially in a frequently used example for the postmodern polemics of the fatuousness of modernism, we find the possibility of variation and difference. But of course, one difference to postmodern criticism: difference one does not find in the figure, but in figuration.

If we recall the textual description Hilberseimer's of the Vertical-City, each statement is a mereological parthood relation, as those analyzed by loggia-apartment-corridor-stair-city-block. Each statement describes the kind of mereological composition of parts without being absolutely determined. The city is described by a mesh of part-conditions. The more limited and reduced the statements are, the more freedom and variation they allow. The monotony of the Vertical-City renderings means a reduction in the planned framing on urban scale to create open space at the architectural scale.

On the one hand it is therefore possible for Hilberseimer to describe a city only through determination of parthood relations. The image of the city is empty because it only represents its deterministic aspects. It is a scheme, an image in the making. The schema of the parthood relation as contour creates open space. But on the other hand the schema as a contour frames the space. The definition of an outer frame will always limit the set of possible compositions. In the Vertical-City each design will always be a kind of tessellation of the schema. Perhaps Hilberseimer was confident of this fact, as he later called his scheme of a metropolis a necropolis.

98   The Mereological City: a reading of the works of Ludwig Hilberseimer

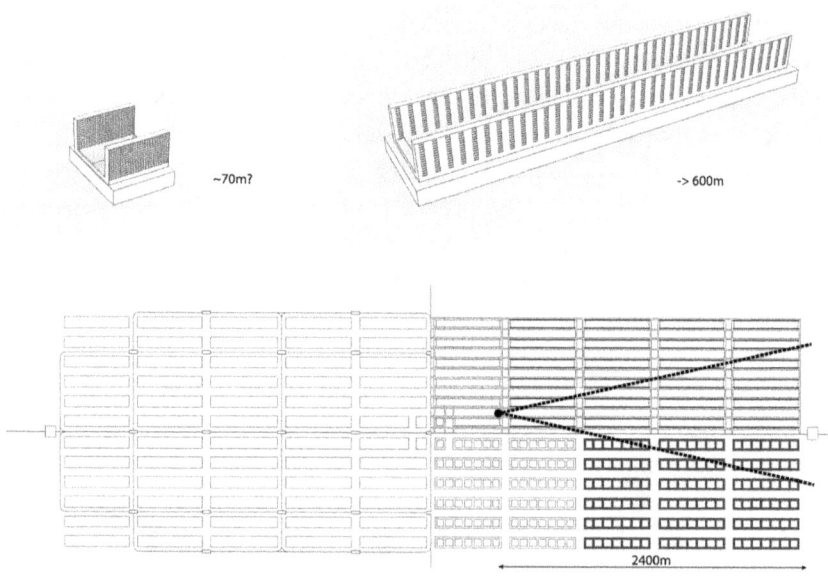

Figure 3.19: Hilberseimer, Vertical-City, perspective North-South-Street, 1927; bottom: Localizing the point of view in the plan scheme; center left: expected proportion of the city block; center right: true length of the city block; facade allocation pursuant perspective, 35 punctuations per floor

The Large City 99

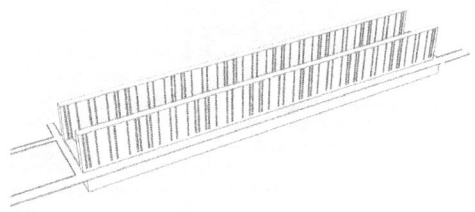

Figure 3.20: top: perspectively constructed collage with loggia openings, without windows, middle, bottom: city-block with accentuated loggia allocation by Hilberseimer's plan scheme

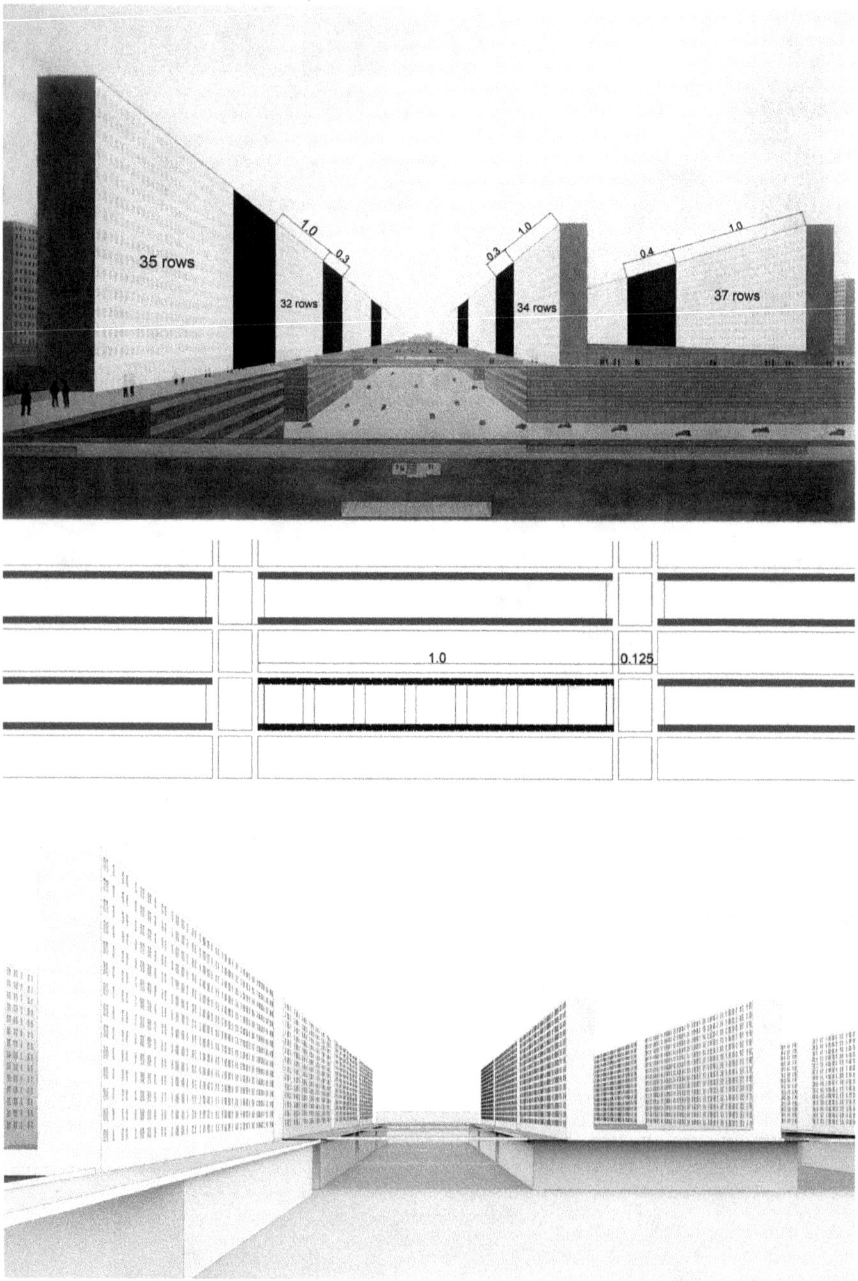

100 The Mereological City: a reading of the works of Ludwig Hilberseimer

Figure 3.21: Hilberseimer, Vertical-City, perspective North-South-Street, 1927; top: comparison of proportional spacings between perspective and plan scheme; bottom: rebuilt perspective according to the proportions of the plan scheme

Figure 3.22: Vertical-City rebuilt, top: perspective North-South-Street; possible division of the facades; bottom: perspective of an exemplary city-block, color coding of the different units

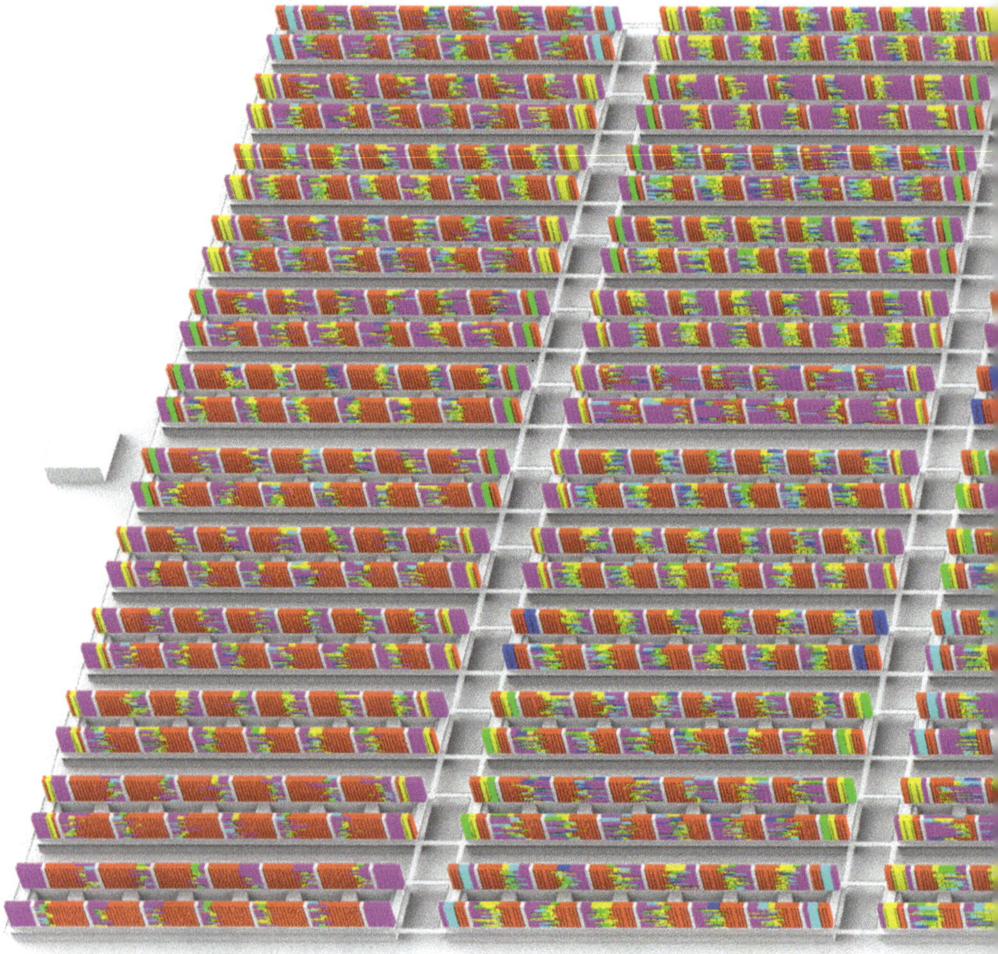

Figure 3.23: Vertical-City, axonometric of one city element, color coding of the different units

The Large City   103

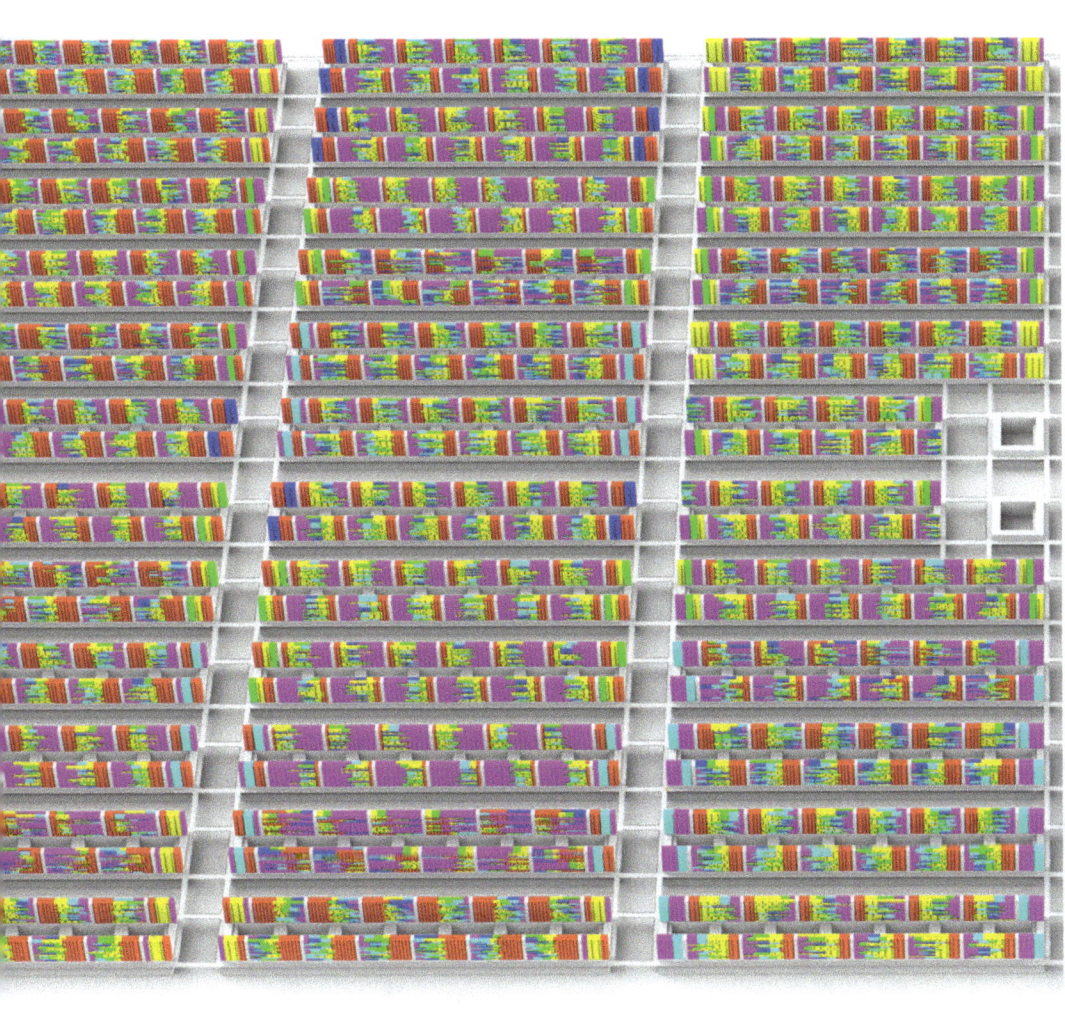

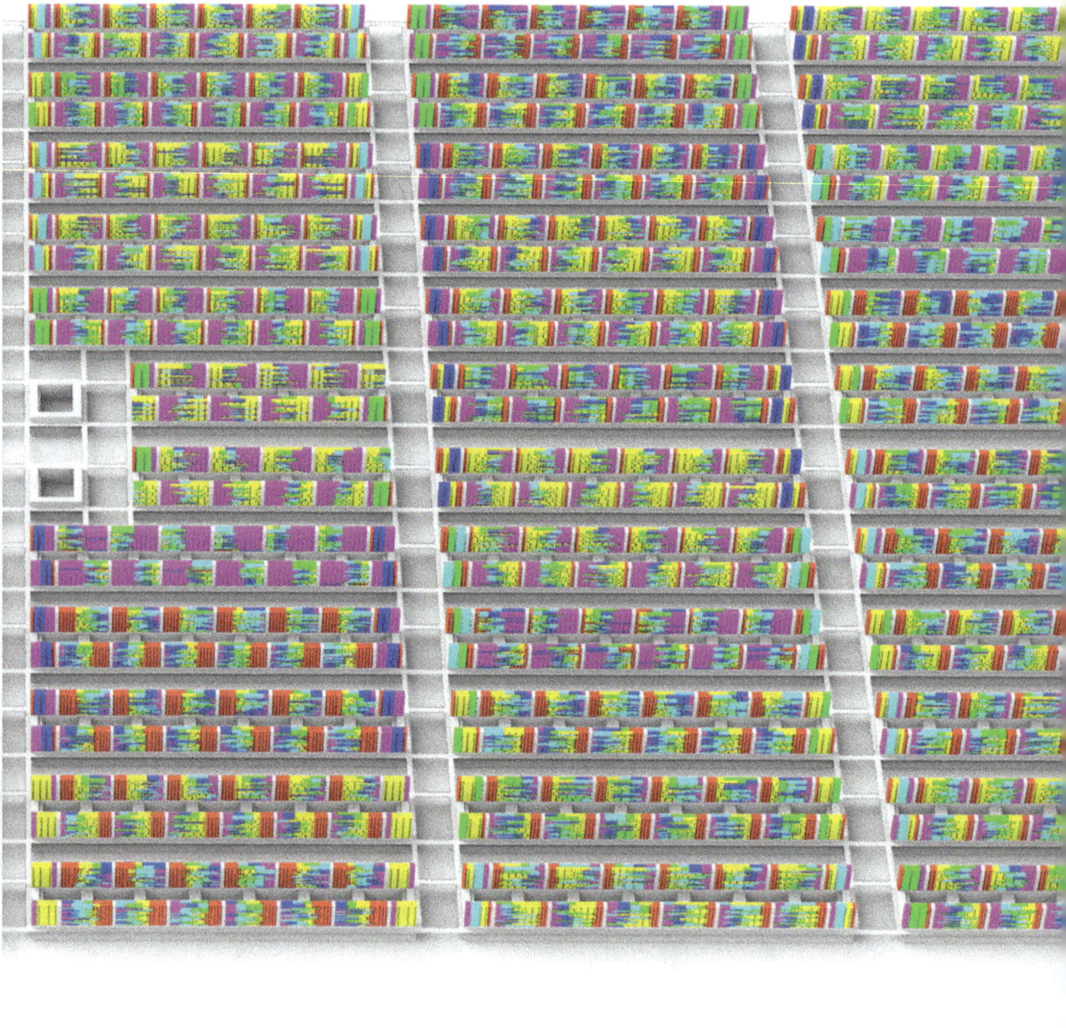

104   The Mereological City: a reading of the works of Ludwig Hilberseimer

The Large City 105

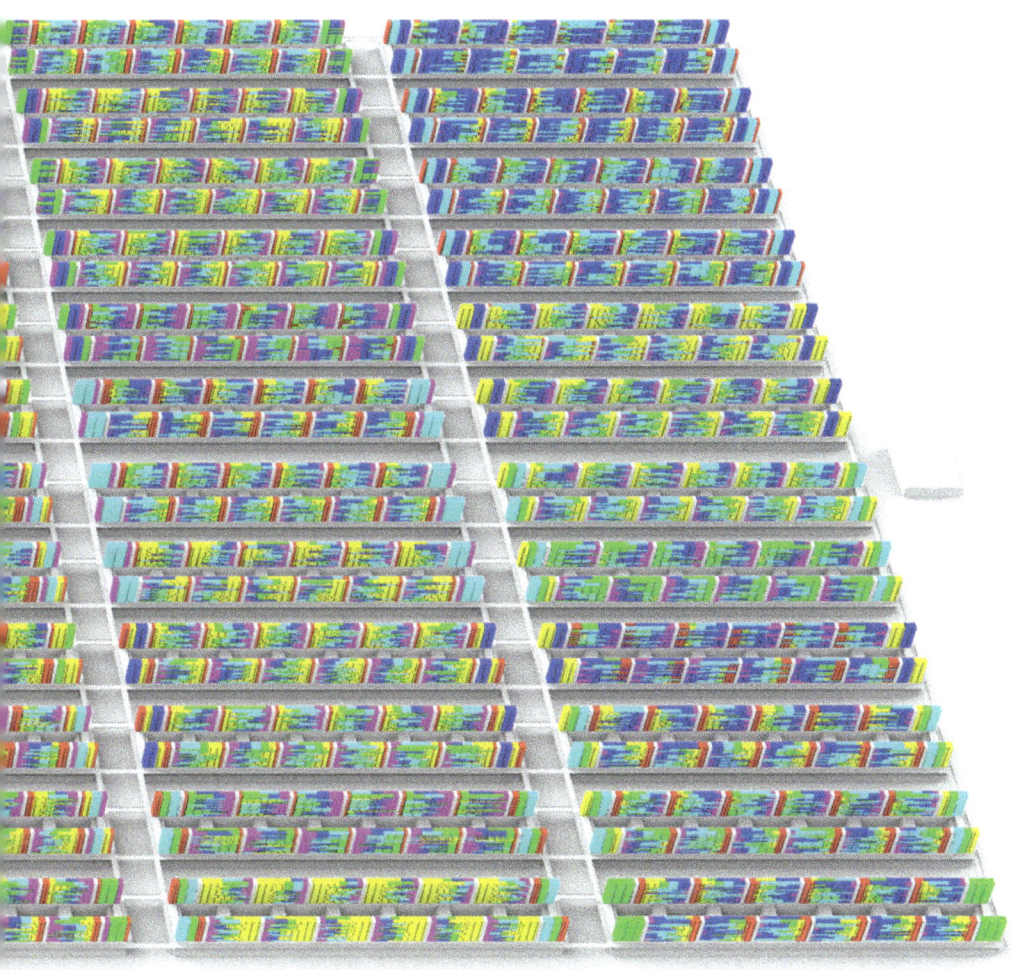

106   The Mereological City: a reading of the works of Ludwig Hilberseimer

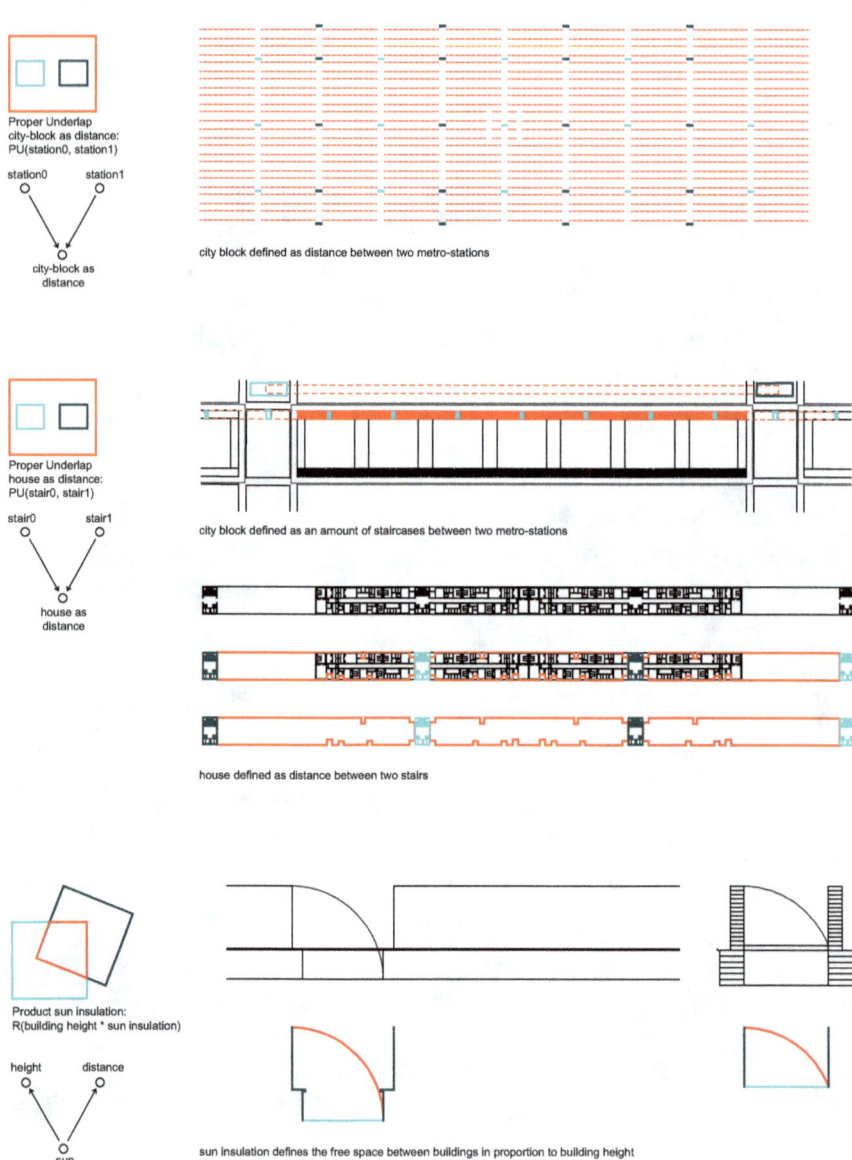

Figure 3.24: mereological analysis of the Vertical-City; top: mereological proper underlap relation, the city block as intersection of two underground stations or the house as intersection of two staircases; bottom: mereological product relation: sunlight, the minimum insulation is fixed in the proportion of building height to street width

The Large City 107

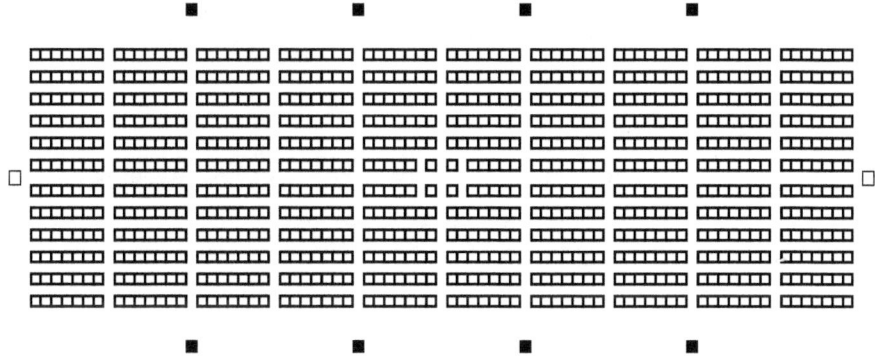

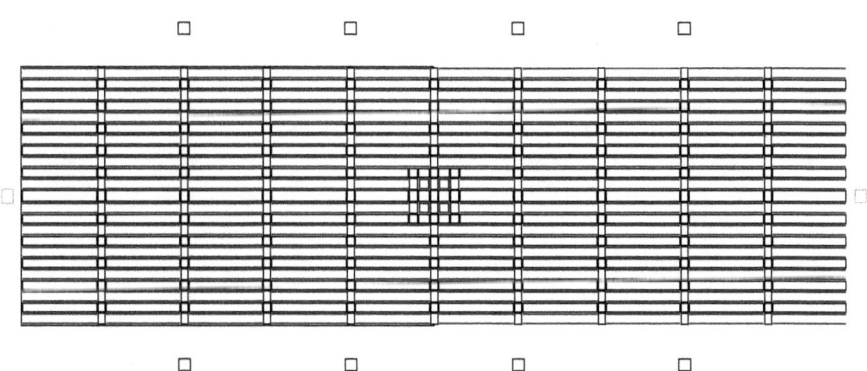

Figure 3.25: Hilberseimer, Vertical-City, 1927, top: drawing No. 11: block floor plan with rail system; midle: drawing No 9: city plan of the commercial city, floors 1-5; bottom: drawing No 10: city plan of the residential city, floors 6-20

108   The Mereological City: a reading of the works of Ludwig Hilberseimer

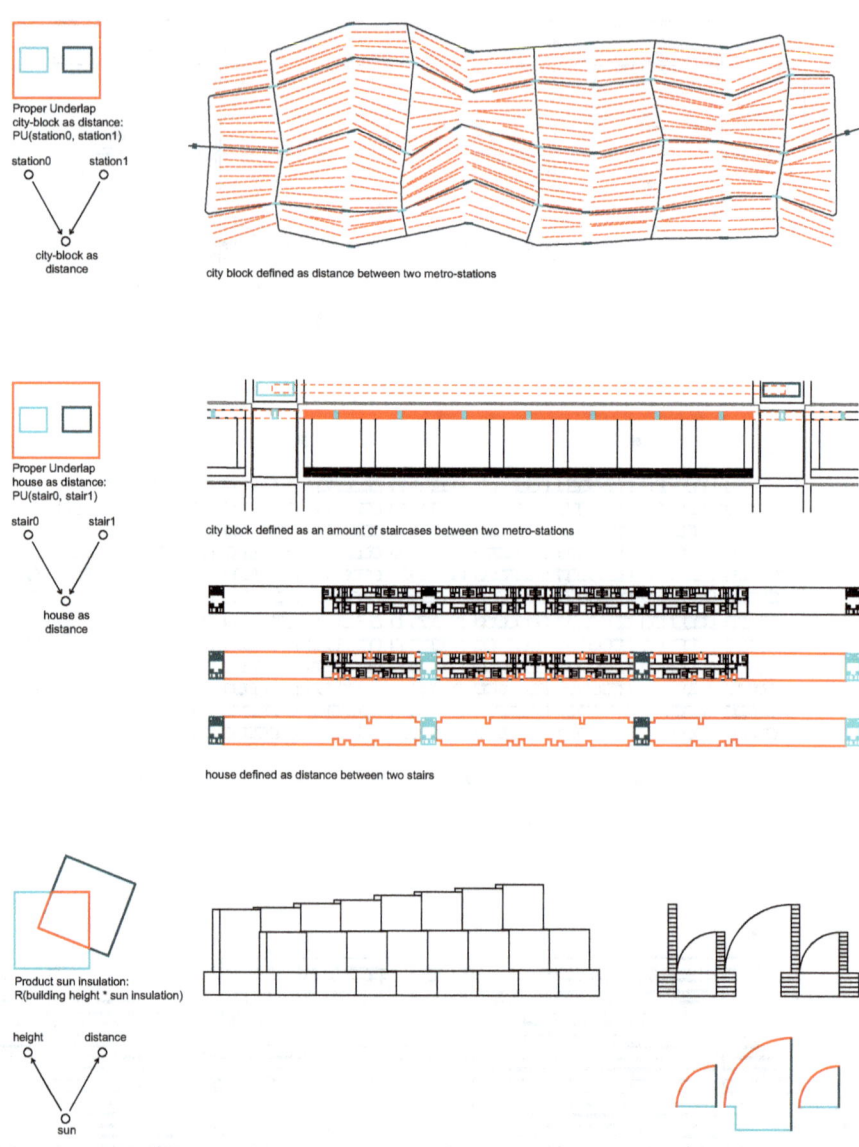

Figure 3.26: mereological composition (A) according to the schema of the Vertical-City; top: Proper-Underlap-Relation, the city-block as underlap of two metro-stations or the house as underlap of two staircases; bottom: Product: sun-insolation, the minimum of sun-insolation if fixed in the proportion between building height and building distance

The Large City 109

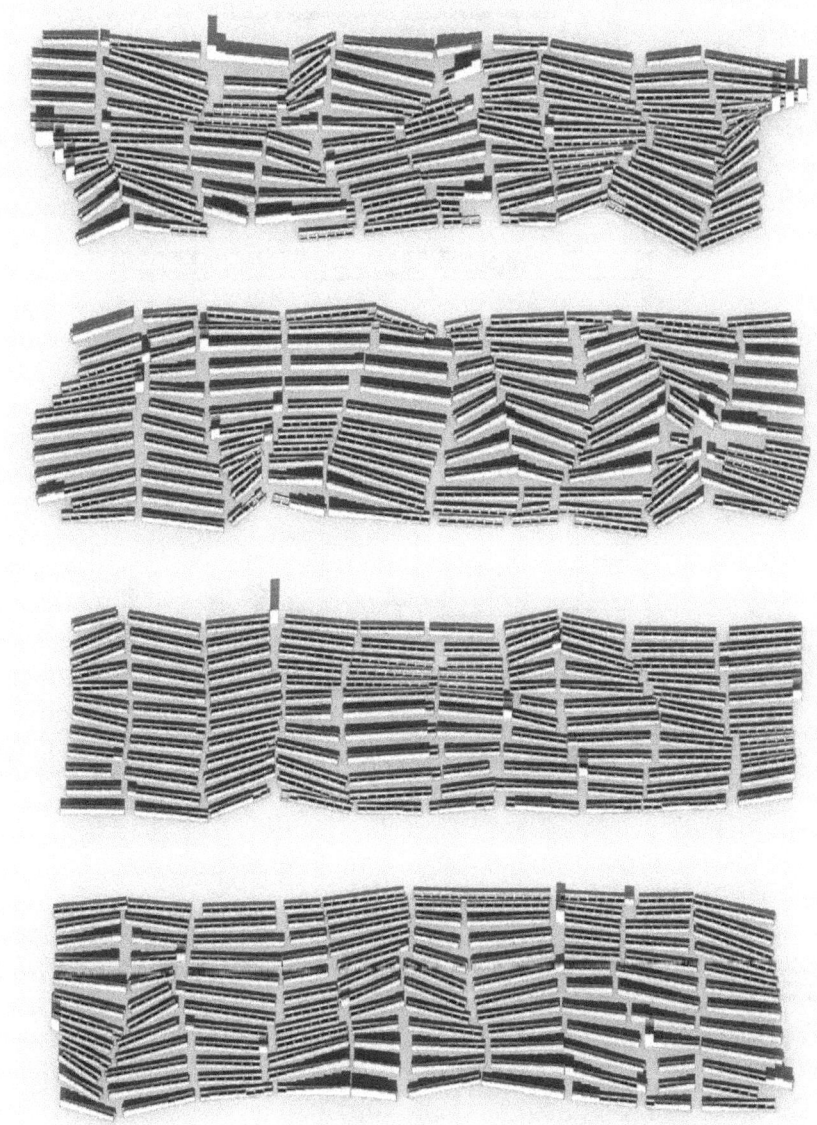

Figure 3.27: mereological composition (A) according to the schema of the Vertical-City; four possible variations of a city-element

110 The Mereological City: a reading of the works of Ludwig Hilberseimer

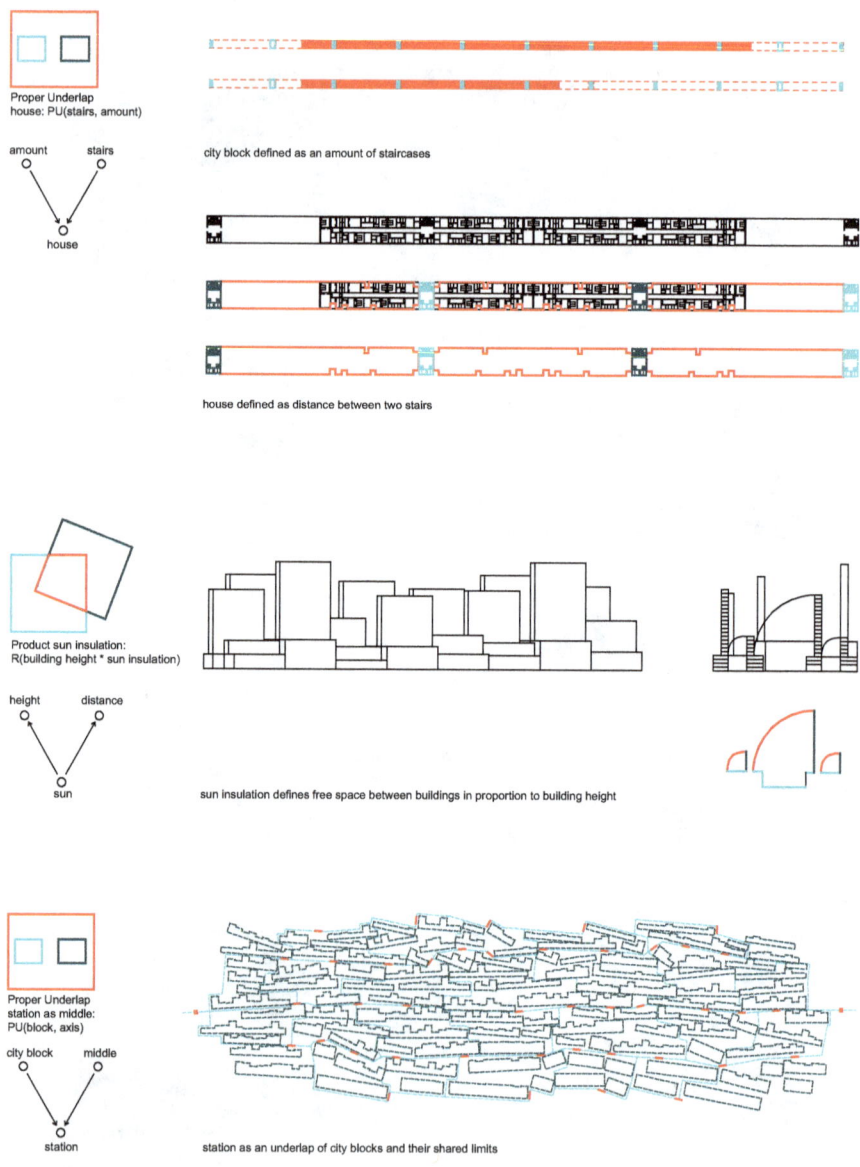

Figure 3.28: mereological composition (B) according to the schema of the Vertical-City; top: Proper Underlap: city block defined as an amount of staircases and the house defined as distance between two stairs; middle: Product: sun insulation defines free space between buildings in proportion to building height; bottom: Proper Underlap: station as an underlap of city blocks and their shared walking limits

The Large City   111

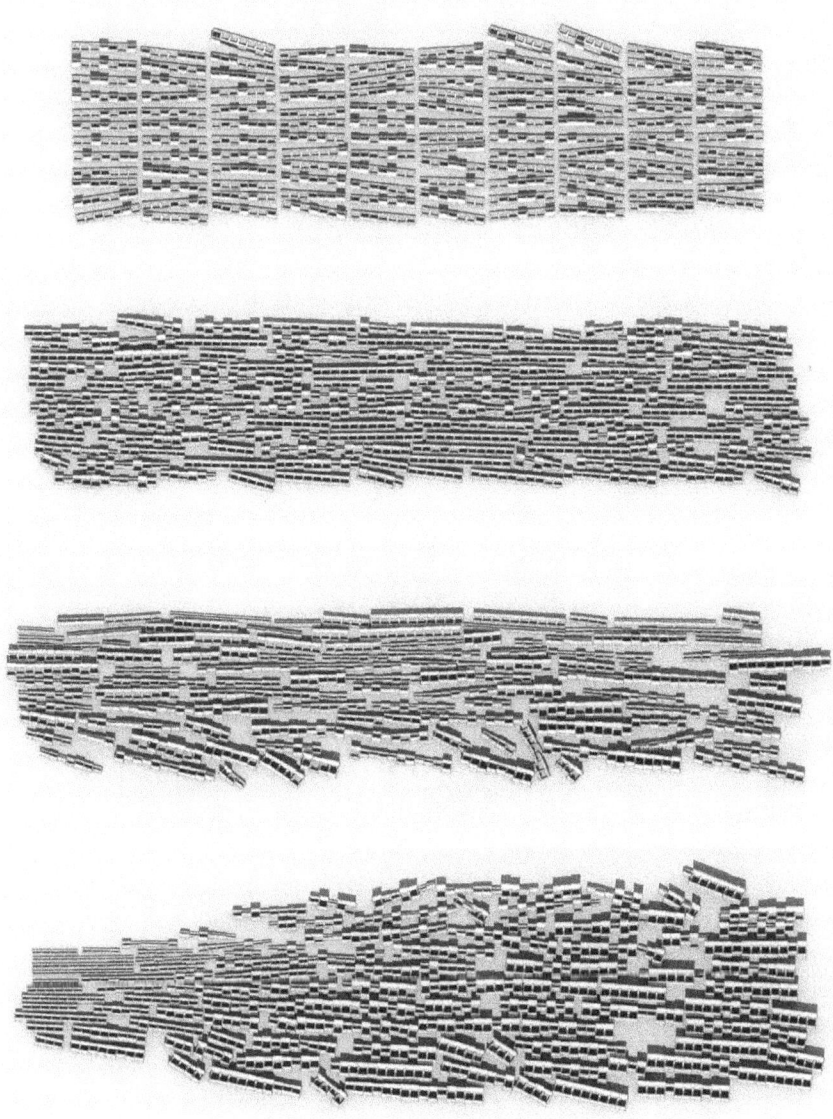

Figure 3.29: mereological composition (B) according to the schema of the Vertical-City; four possible variations of a city-element

112 The Mereological City: a reading of the works of Ludwig Hilberseimer

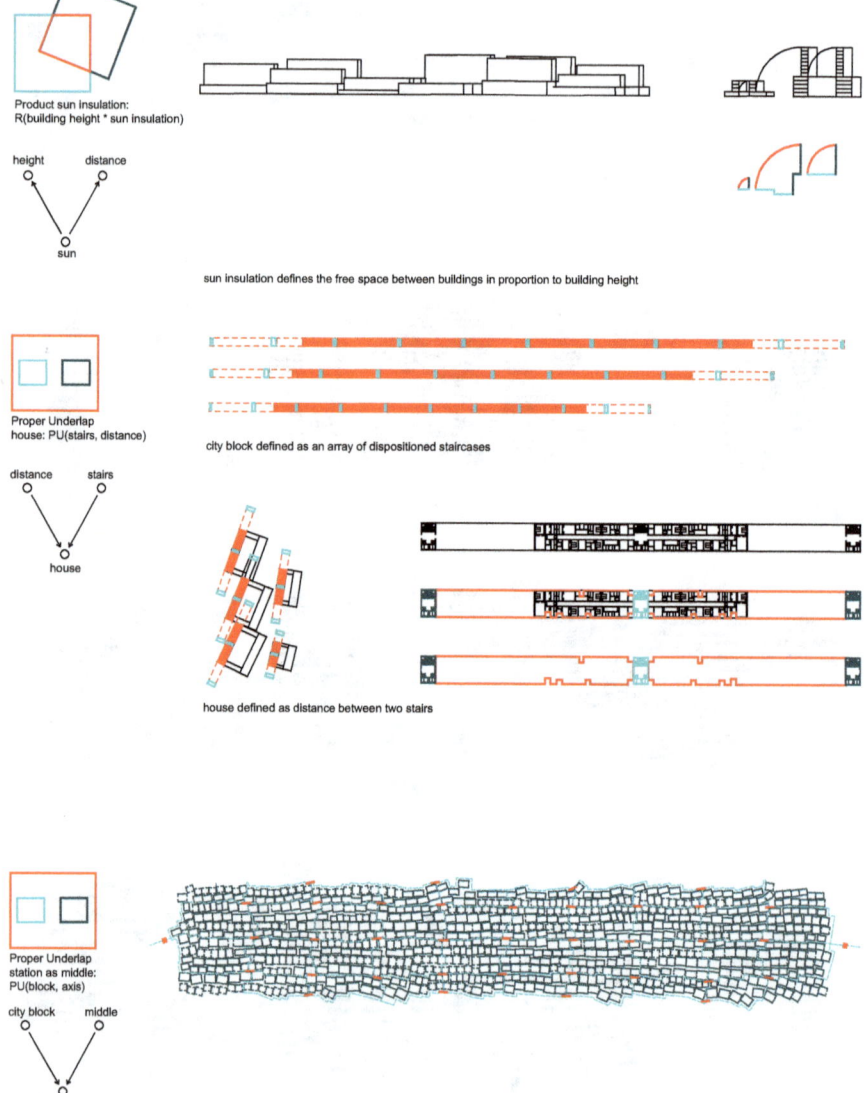

Figure 3.30: mereological composition (C) according to the schema of the Vertical-City, mereological schema, drawing by author; top: Product: sun insulation defines free space between buildings in proportion to building height; middle: Proper Underlap: the city block defined as an array of dispositioned staircases and the house defined as distance between two stairs; bottom:: Proper Underlap: the station as an underlap of city blocks and their shared walking limits

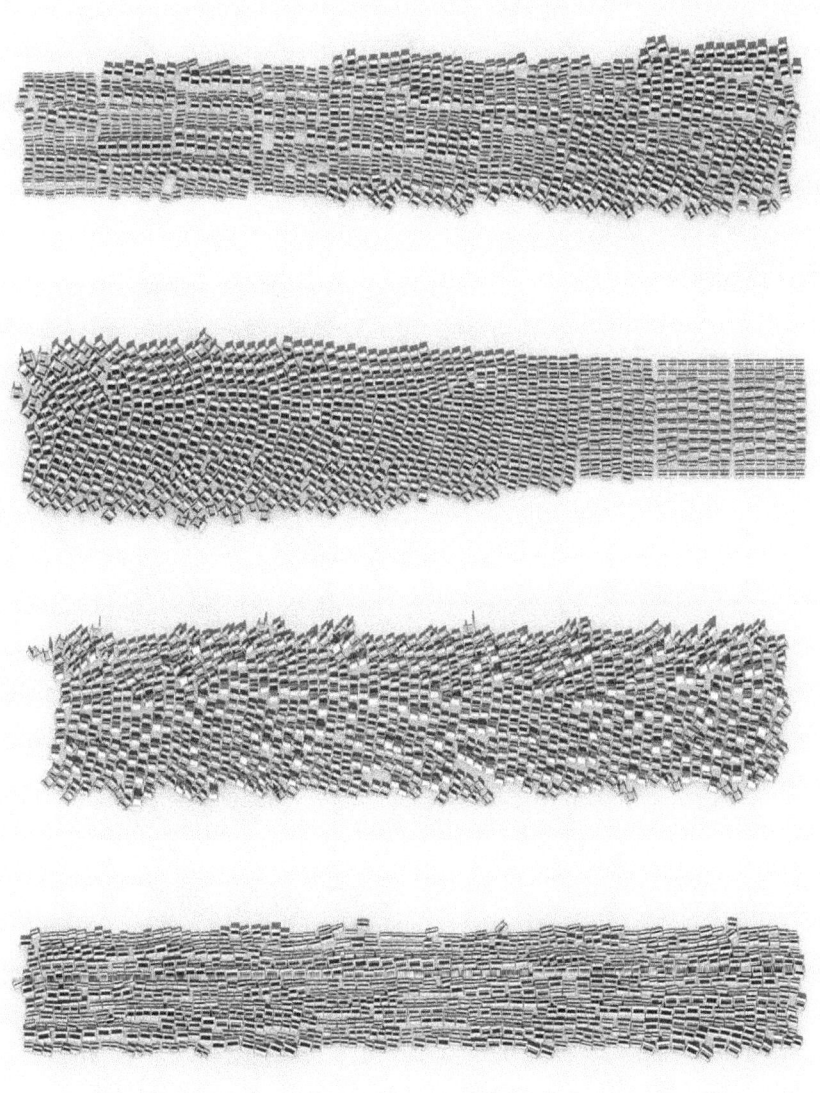

Figure 3.31: mereological composition (C) according to the schema of the Vertical-City; four possible variations of a city-element

114 The Mereological City: a reading of the works of Ludwig Hilberseimer

Figure 3.32: selection of three possible mereological compositions inherent in the schema of the Vertical-City

The Large City 115

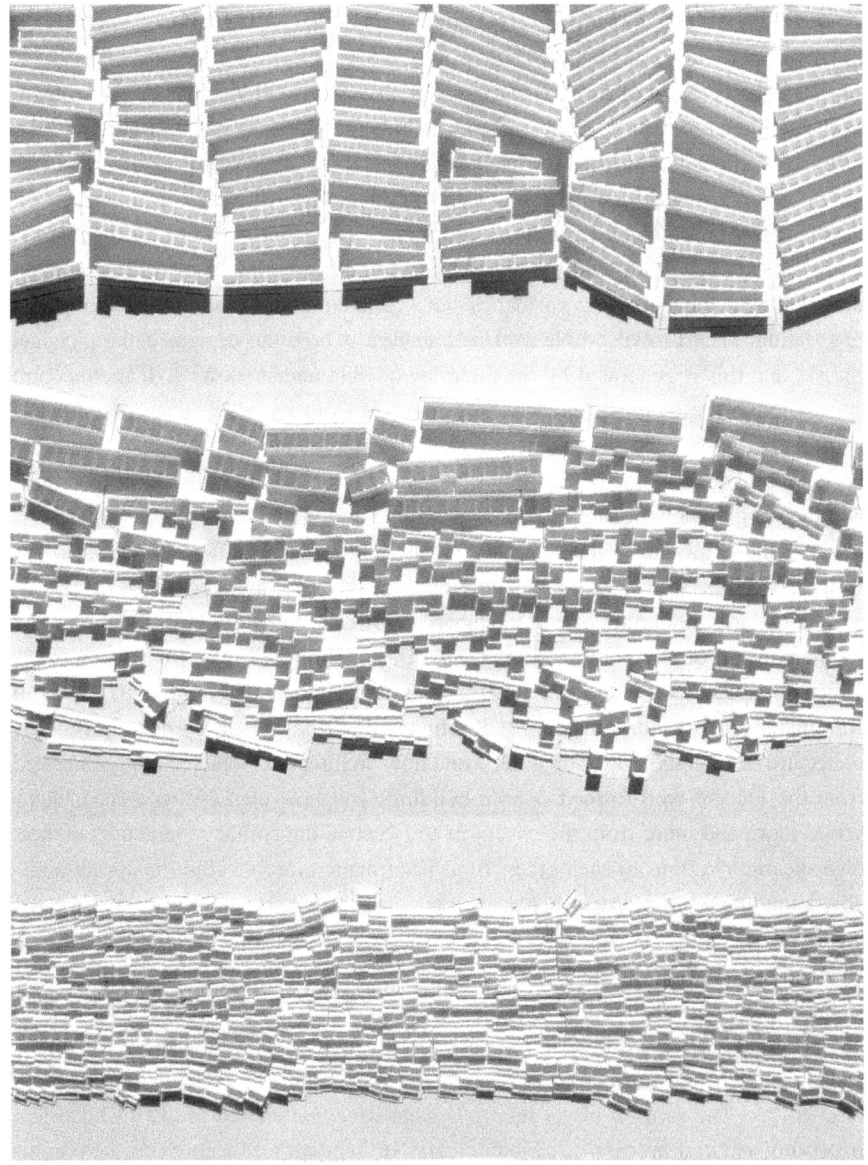

Figure 3.33: model foto of three mereological compositions inherent in the schema of the Vertical-City

3.3 TOWARDS AN AUTONOMOUS ARCHITECTURE

Through the creation of a room instead of a shell, the clothing, the symbolic layer of the architecture, vanishes. This allows architecture "only in itself, relying on their primordial elements, only out of itself be designed."[147] According to Hilberseimer, the pursuit of architectural logic will lead to uniformity. All works, despite their diversity, must be obtained from a uniform mind. But what is meant by that all the works emerge according to the same architectural design principles? The unification does not mean the uniformity of shapes, but a coherent understanding and knowledge of creating. The formal problem of architecture is now the design of the physical masses and this is generated by the interplay of light and shadow[148]. If architecture can no longer be clothing and will be developed from its inner coherence, the design of the masses and their light and shadow effects must be carried out with the basic architectural elements: Volumes, surfaces, color, windows and door openings and their organic relationship to determine the expression of large city architecture. Without the symbolic syntax, architecture is only left to itself. In a retrospective from 1964 Hilberseimer also looks back and describes the architecture of the 20s as a trend towards autonomy of architecture[149]. However, what did Hilberseimer mean by the concept of autonomy and his time? Here, a hint of Detlef Mertins helps[150], which pointed out parallels between Hilberseimer's concept of autonomous and Emil Kaufmann's architectural history[151]. Kaufmann describes the development of the architecture of Ledoux to Le Corbusier's and how architecture is increasingly liberated from the idea of well-formed, whole buildings and how elements detached themselves more and more from the ensemble to freestanding solitaires to establish their own specific relations to each other. Emil Kaufmann as architectural historian probably knew the work of Alois Riegl, who is considered to be one of the founders of Art History. In any case Kaufmann's continuously considers a development which Riegl already fronted in the *late Roman art industry*. In Riegl's context, at the end of the 19th century, Konrad Fiedler together with Adolf von Hildbrand developed an understanding of the work of art, which revealed in the interplay of the autonomous world of forms, the form of existence and the position of the observation, the form of effect[152]. The form of effect finally is what Riegl elaborated to the art historical method of cultural perception. Fiedler's and Hildebrand's concept with the combination of form of existence and effect attempted to apply Kant's concept of a priori form to art. As cultural historian, Helmut Müller-Severs[153] based on Kant's concept of a-priori form shows former new insights in biology, instead of relying on a theory of pre-formation, ie on a theory that all variation is based on original creations. During this time a scientific version of Aristotle's theory of entelechy evolved, which indicated that new organisms gradually formulate themselves under the guidance of

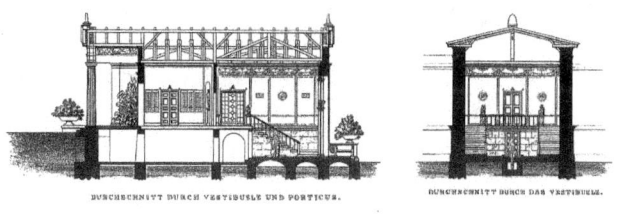

Figure 3.34: Karl Friedrich Schinkel: Schloss Charlottenhof, Potsdam, 1822; the autonomous form of architecture responds to the topography of the place in the reorganization of its internal circulation

a building power. Kant's a-priori category of knowledge then based on a theory of self-organization of organisms[154]. Resting on this supports, the building in the architecture detached from the ensemble. More relevant in the architecture of Ledoux's or for Berlin architects: In architecture, Schinkel's building takes on the form of an autonomous block[155], whereas autonomy does not mean a form closed in itself, but rather a form with a specific individual will. A careful examination of the relationship between house and landscape in Schinkel's works[156] makes it noticeable, that Schinkel's buildings specifically develop from an inner order but also respond to the landscape. In the most extreme case, such as in the residence Charlottenhof[157], a shift in the landscape can also cause the reorganization of the house in the logic of autonomous order. On Schinkels heritage also based Friedrich Ostendorffs teaching and the organic planning principles of his student Ludwig Hilberseimer. If architecture is a self-contained element, Hilberseimer then concludes in the words of Mondrian:

"Architecture as an art could be realized only with a multiplicity of buildings, with the city itself."[158]

Autonomy will only be visible to the means of diplomacy. Only in variety the individual reaches autonomous form expression. Architecture as the diplomacy of autonomous elements means an architecture as a strategy to mereological composition by disposition of architectural elements. What remains is the design of the large city by the determination of its elements through co-location and their disposition.

3.3.1 The definition of the smallest architectural element

The figure of city is dependent on the ratio of two factors: the single cell of the single room and the entire urban organism. Hilberseimer regularly used this metaphor in his texts. However, it is not clearly defined for which architectura element cell and organism stand. Only the size comparison remains. For the first time Hilberseimer mentioned the ratio cell to organism in 1922 in his essay *The high rise*[159]. Here, the cell is the single house and the organism the state. One year later in *The will to architecture*, the single room is the cell and the city layout the organism[160]. In the description of the Vertical-City[161] the cell alternately is the room, the apartment or the city-block. The city element or the whole metropolis stands for an organism, which is in turn part of a global economy[162]. The contrast between cell and organism referred to in Hilberseimer, is scale-independent, the relationship between the part and the whole. The smallest architectural unit which Hilberseimer ever defined in his texts is the single room as a compositional element. The smallest architectural parts are the designed objects that define the room through their composition. The room is a product of its producing basic elements: walls, floors, ceilings, windows, doors and furniture. Hilberseimer forecasts that these industrially manufactured elements in the future will be pressed. Furniture and windows so become self-contained design objects and are no longer a part of a compositional design process. The single room is the first composed unit and thus the smallest architectural element. The room quality results from completely fulfilled requirements by the formal unity of space proportion, incidence of light and color. The space is not intended as a boundary or envelope but as a zone. This is Hilberseimer's architectural implementation of Nietzsche's great style. Architecture is the logical, legitimate composition of discrete and designed – this is purposeful for Hilberseimer – objects.

Figure 3.35: Hilberseimer, residential city, Interior perspective views of apartment, 1925

3.3.2 The city as a new compositional task

One repeating aspect of Hilberseimer's design-series *Groszstadtbauten*[163] (Large City Buildings) is the merging of small-scale plots to provide housing collectives. Property is not defined by individual floor plots per house, but first as a consolidated common property. As a whole, the urban organism *Large City Architecture* refers to the consolidation of plots, its impact on the size of the resulting "Großform" (large form) and the independence from land-speculation. The sheer quantity leads to an obvious withdrawal of the city-block from its context. Exposed the single room-type an inaccessible vitality of the thing, here the massiveness de-celerated the effect and turns into the object's isolation from context and control. Largeness withdraws as it becomes indescribable through the plot.

The room is a part of a single house, the apartments are drawn together in city-blocks. The appearance of the city-block is the design factor of the city layout. Thus the single room is related transitively to the entire city. According to Hilberseimer, this ordering ratio should be visible in the cubic mass of the city-block. The means for this is firstly the purposeful organization of the plan, on the other hand the division and aperture in the building surfaces[164] with openings. The architectural task is to organically develop pro- and backtrusions, recesses out of the building. The contrast between the combined surfaces and the breaking through of the dark recesses determines the rhythm of the building figure. The ratio of the single cell to the organism of the city is represented by the ratio of the form to the light[165]. This is a transfer of the analysis of the question "how" of a work of art: the basic means of expression of the Kunstwollen: the relationship of form to surface. The large quantity of parts has an impact on the consideration of the part, the single cell. Using the example of the window[166], Hilberseimer shows how the part-to-whole relationship changes through the increase in quantity. Historically, windows were used to place accents or determine the axes. A perfectly placed architectural element, such as a window, could provide harmony, beauty, and a complete order to the whole, classically described by Alberti as Concinnitas. In contrast, due to the quantity of windows in a combined city-block or high-rise, the emphasis is on rhythm. The window is part of the surface itself. Finally, the mass of windows produces the effect of a grid, an effect what Michael Hays identified as mass ornament[167]. The grid is not an object in the first place, but the result of the assembly of windows. The quantity of windows absorbs the facade as a whole to a mereological condition for the part. The possibility of assembly, in modern sense typically the array, is contained within the single window, the single cell. The whole is a part of the cell, for the cell as whole. More general: The whole becomes a part for the part as whole. In a discourse about things this effect is well described as mereological isolation. Here the concept of withdrawal not only occurs between isolated objects, which leads to a form of inaccessible vitality of things, but also it occurs within them. As Peter Wolfendale mentions this "involves the mutual withdrawal between parts, but as well the withdrawal of parts from the wholes they compose, and wholes from the parts they contain."[168]

Of course in Hilberseimer's example, the windows are parts of the facade and parts of a grid. But vice versa the windows are distinct from each other, they can not be comprehended by a grid and produce the facade as their effect. Mereological conditions isolate things from each other. This necessarily leads to compositional gaps and the possibility to re-orientate the technical object through the reshaping and repurposing of the mereological conditions between the parts of the modern and well-prehended wholes, as the grid of a curtain wall or latent in Hilberseimer's project the city as such. With Large City Architecture Hilberseimer means new architectural methods, which allow to design in the tension between one and many, form and surface, mass and masses. Large City Architecture is finally a new architectural methodology.

4 The unfolding of a planning idea

> Added elements can be well organized, but never become an organism.
>
> LUDWIG HILBERSEIMER. SCHÖPFUNG UND ENTWICKLUNG

4.1 FROM VERTICAL-CITY TO FLAT-BUILDING

A year after the release of *Large City Architecture* in 1928, Ludwig Hilberseimer was appointed to the Bauhaus by Hannes Meyer. The year of the appointment also marks a design driven reorientation of Hilberseimer. Instead of high-rise building typologies, Hilberseimer at the Bauhaus now develops flat buildings and their settlements. Within the academic framework so far new to him, Hilberseimer begins to develop his proposals. Hilberseimer together with his students gradually investigates aspects of density, sun insolation, infrastructure and functional arrangement.

Two urban studies conducted between 1926-1930, accompany the changes from high- to flat buildings. The first design is the *Wellfare-City*, a study of possible housing types at different densities. The second design is the *Proposal to City-building*, an office- and commercial city study in the center of Berlin.

4.1.1 The Welfare City

In May 1926, in Düsseldorf Hilberseimer presents on the *exhibition of the free welfare care* a city-model. The exhibition, conceived as a study for a city of 500,000 inhabitants, should identify possible strategies to create non-profit housing and improved quality of life[1]. The city model does not represent a suggestion for a city development. The model is a schema. It shows possible forms of public welfare institutions in the city at different densities[2]. Formally, the study follows Le Corbusier's city of 3 million inhabitants. In a radial instead of linear arrangement, the building heights

124 The Mereological City: a reading of the works of Ludwig Hilberseimer

Figure 4.1: Photo, "exhibition of the free welfare care", Stuttgart, 1927

are graded in this study as well. Starting from 15-storey comb-houses, to 4-storey slabs to solitary point houses, the density decreases from the inside to the outside. The typologies used reflect previous studies of Hilberseimer: The comb structure of the high-rise buildings reflects the folding of the corridor circulation of an American Highrise. Like in the existing buildings, Hilberseimer can increase the density with minimal circulation and similar sun exposures. The slabs are recognizable as the city block of his designed residential city from 1923. With their cubic articulation the point houses remind of Hilberseimer's early designs of homes.

The model is typologically differentiated, unlike the Vertical-City, which is based on the repetition of a single type. But as a scheme, the Vertical-City represents the kind of a type and not an Absolute. As mentioned above, the type of Vertical-City's city-block reflects on a medieval town house. However, amongst them Hilberseimer does not see the scale of the figure of the medieval house, but the scale of what it creates: the house creates a common unit, a place of working, the power and life. These characteristics in terms of what creates the building in relation to its inhabitants, Hilberseimer develops to courtyard-buildings for commercial and office, capped by a shopping street located above with slabs for apartments. Considering the slab-groupings developed for the residential city, here Hilberseimer designed a similar type. East-west oriented slabs are flanked by single-storey low-rise buildings in the south-north direction. Together they form a group around a courtyard. While the slabs are designed as residential buildings, the single-storey buildings are considered for businesses. What is stacked on one another in the city-block of Vertical-City, is grouped side by side in the Residential City. The density is 1/5 of the high-rise city, per grouping 1,800 inhabitants[3]. The distances and dimensions are not explicitly limited. The slab-grouping of Residential-City can be read mereologically congruent to the city-block of Vertical-City.

For different densities Hilberseimer designed typologically different urban units. Both types of cities however provide comparable neighborhoods. In Hilberseimer, the density affected the formal organization of the city unit crucially. Differences in the density lead to typological fractures to generate coherent "Leistungsformen".

In low density at the typology of the point houses, Hilberseimer cannot yet offer a model for a settlement or neighborhood as a congruent scaling of a medieval house. One argument for Hilberseimer to turn to the flat building also is, that settlements are much more difficult to plan at low density than the city blocks at high density and a solution for an organically structured settlement is still pending.

4.1.2 The Proposal to City-Building

1929 Hilberseimer for the first time publishes the study *Proposal to City-Building*[45]. According to his own statement, this study adds to the Vertical-City from 1924. The reason for this proposal is the Berlin debate on new policies for Highrise Buildings in connection to the replanning of Berlin. As with the Vertical-City, Hilberseimer here emphasizes the abstraction of a specific case for obtaining general rules to bring the Large City in evocative order[6]. While the Vertical-City, like a tabula rasa, was a new planning of Great-Berlin, the *Proposal to City-Building* is a plan to a specific territory. Taking up the existing street grid and the same density, Hilberseimer replaced the existing buildings with three-times three city-blocks, constructed analogously to the Vertical-City. The form of the blocks is formulated by the ratio of distance between the buildings to building height, the separation of pedestrian- and car- and public transport. However, in contrast to the Vertical-City, the city blocks are mono-functional: Hilberseimer is planning a purely commercial city. With the following Hilberseimer refers to real conditions of the territory: the city model of the Regional Plan of Berlin developed by Martin Wagner.

Michael Hays points out[7], that the repetition of the shape of the Vertical-City as thoroughly mixed, functional city and the city-building as mono-functional quarters, an indication is that for the "Neue Sachlichkeit" functionalism is ultimately a fiction. To Hays architecture does not correspond although with the real functional conditions of the city, but the city translates it from the socio-economic system of signs in the connotation of architecture. Form here represented function, in which function was previously interpreted as a way of form. In Conclusion, according to Hays, Hilberseimer creates a sign system for architecture as a translation for an external network of socio-economic and historical forces. In the last phase of the Weimar Republic, represents Hilberseimer a project as a logical unfolding of the modern idea, the totalitarian planning of the public. With this, so Hays, Hilberseimer prophesies himself and unintentionally the crisis of modernity with the elements of architecture[8].

Hays interpretation may perhaps be a little extreme in its conclusion, but several aspects of the study should take developments in urban design of the 20th century ahead. The *Proposal to City-Building* is the first known urban study of an office- and commercial city. If previous urban designers like Nicolas Ledoux in France or Robert Owen in England were able to show, that conditions in the emerging industry generate their own form of the city, Hilberseimer shows such as trade and administration formulates into the form of the Large City of the 20th century. And this form of the city is the large form.

Based on the building development of the Wertheim department store at Leipziger Platz, Hilberseimer shows that the type of department store was created by the constant expansion of one shop over a number of individual houses. Therefore, Hilberseimer concludes that the store should be designed directly as large form, such as the department store Tietz at Alexanderplatz. The same applies to the office building. Here Hilberseimer terms the office building of the Scherl magazine complex, which also gained its current size by extensions. From the large form, the desire of the mass for mass, there are further implications for architecture. As Hilberseimer cites in *The new commercial street*[9], with size and the need for sun-exposure, the architectural task of the facade design disappears[10]. The size of the store as an exhibition of products leads to "the city itself tends to be permanent exhibition"[11]. The function of the shop window is transferred through the size of the store ultimately to the interior itself. The facade loses as a contour, its task as a signifier of an interior and is the closure of a zone, in line with Nietzsche's definition of form as a zone of content.

In the further development of the city-block of the Vertical-City, in the City-Building Hilberseimer covered the courtyards of the lower-/commercial city. Thus, the courts becomes spacious halls. The halls become permanent exhibitions, accompanied by shops and small workshops, located in the building masses[12]. The city becomes an interior, new colonnades for the mass from the economic demands of their time and furthermore a foreshadowing of the future shopping malls.

Hilberseimer's interest in hall buildings as places of public assembly finally culminates in the publication *hall buildings*[13].

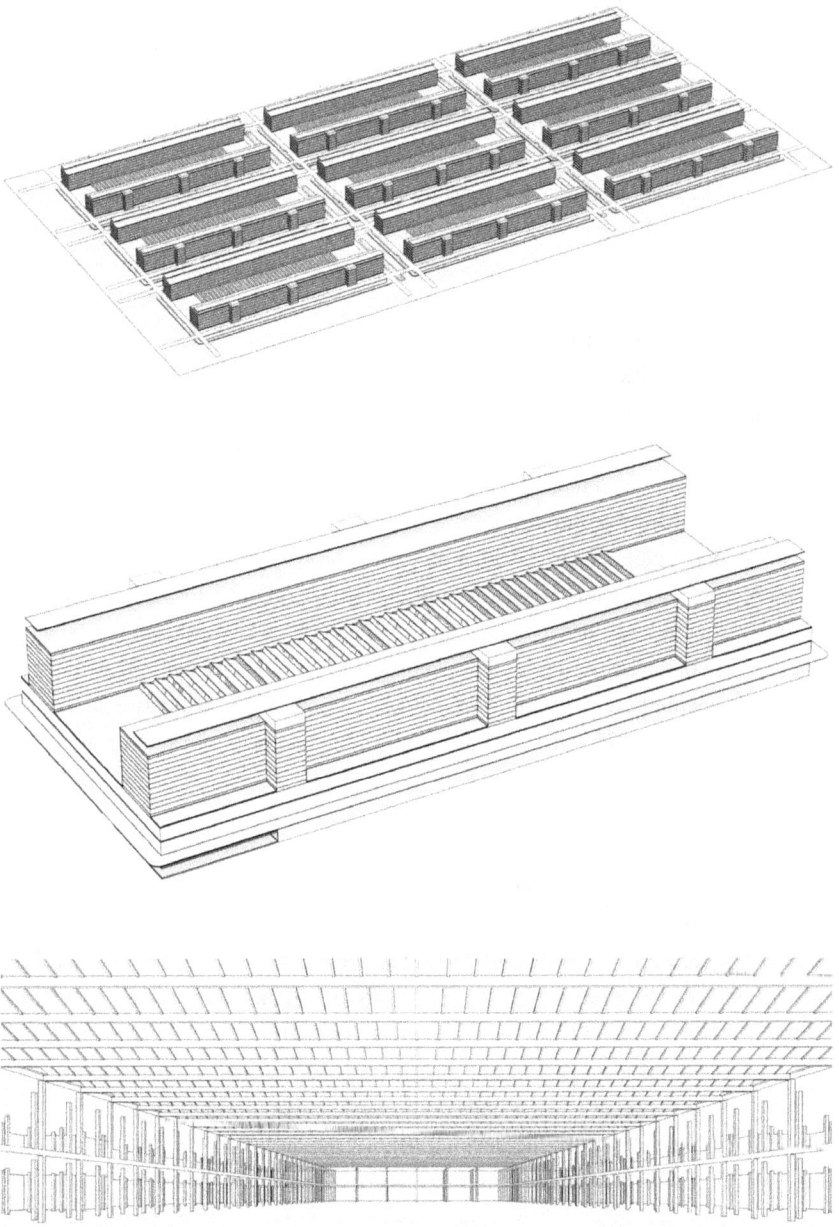

Figure 4.2: Hilberseimer, Proposal to City-Building, top: axonometry, middle: axonometry city-block, bottom: perspective of the hall between the commercial slabs

The large form is the result of the analysis and careful consideration of possible consequences of economic factors. The shape here is understood as the speculative development of economic factors of a territory. In the final analysis Hilberseimer points out, that the new economic conditions of trade and administration can be resolved only through a complete transformation of the urban plan[14].

In a comparison of the block cubatures the first mass study published in *Das Kunstblatt*[15] with the drawings created about one year later and published in *Die Form*[16] it is apparent that in the early mass study, the cubature is shorter by about one staircase circulation. The size of a building is not an absolute dimension for Hilberseimer. The whole is an organizational principle, a relative overlap between organizational conditions.

The City-building is Hilberseimer's last developed design of administrative and commercial buildings. The typology of administration seems to be solved for Hilberseimer. In upcoming urban studies Hilberseimer uses similar cubatures as a placeholder for administrative buildings. The concept of an administrative building on a podium appears again as part of other studies. The Commercial Super-block holds such mereological parallels[17]. Office buildings on a podium with business halls we also find in sketches for the reorganization of the North and West Loop in Chicago[18]. In the further course Hilberseimer will from now on focus on flat-buildings. Detailed, ie in an architectural scale, it will from now on only develop housing typologies. The cell or the territory of the individual as the unfolding element of a settlement.

4.1.3 Flat buildings

In the Bauhaus courses Hilberseimer begins with studies of single-family houses and their arrangements to settlements as a logical development of large urban form. As the model of the welfare state shows, for Hilberseimer the city has different densities. For high density Hilberseimer developed a vertical organization by the stacking of building typologies, as in the Chicago Tribune Tower and as a city in the Vertical-City. For the large form of the mid-rise density Hilberseimer in the Residential-City suggests the merger of two slabs with two flat side wings before. In both city plans Hilberseimer describes the development of the large form by the merger of its parts: mostly the residential apartments, a body consisting of cells. But in both the large form dominates, the cells disappear behind the cubic geometry, the relationship between part and whole tilts in favor of the large form.

At low density, by definition the single form dominates. For Hilberseimer this raises the task of a settlement as a large form to be created from the conditioning requirements of single parts. Crucial here is the ratio of the form of the single-family home to the surface of the settlement.

During the second half of the twenties, Hilberseimer more and more turns to flat buildings[19]. His texts are changing from art criticism and theoretical considerations to specific building problems. From 1924 on Hilberseimer writes specifically about architectural projects. The chapter *comments* in *Large City Building* is dedicated to housing. In 1927, in *The apartment as a commodity*, Hilberseimer describes the apartment as web of relationships from everyday programmatic and social factors[20]. Two years later and after a year as appointed teacher at the Bauhaus, Hilberseimer finally released his first study on low-rise buildings in *Large urban micro flats*[21].

Teaching at the Bauhaus In 1928 Hilberseimer was appointed as teacher at the Bauhaus, lead by Hannes Meyer. Hannes Meyer is usually classified as a functionalist in the history of architecture. Meyer did not understand architecture as an aesthetic object, not as an harmonic whole so as fictitious organization within the meaning of Alberti's concinnitas[22]. For Meyer, architecture was a communication system[23], a program, a set of procedures. Therefore Mayer is also considered by many to be a functionalist. But for Meyer himself architecture was as a program and an apparatus for the production of psychological effects. Architecture for Meyer was created only by the subjective perception and interpretation of the building: Therefore, the building as an event and production facility of events. So the method of design could be liberated from historical reference or individual, artistic expression and dedicated to the shape of social, functional-economic factors[24]. The will of architecture without historical reference and individual expression as a representation of a society by the composition of things we too found in Hilberseimers work. The urban design approach of Hilberseimer was a complementary addition to Hannes Meyer's Architecture program.

In the implementation of his project in the teaching at the Bauhaus, Hannes Meyer removed the workshops as the basis of artistic development from the center of the curriculum. They became only a complementary part of systematic studies of technology and materials. In addition, natural sciences, theories of psychology and perception, supplemented by Hilberseimer's urban design, were offered. These studies provided the basis to the individual design work in the advanced study[25]. Thus, the focus of the Bauhaus changed from the production of products to more planning work. The Bauabteilung, building department, moved to the center. Although on a small basis, the goal of the teaching was aimed at the construction and building department[26].

Whether through the direct influence of Hannes Meyer or by the possibility as appointed professor to research, Hilberseimer designed his courses systematically as an academic work. With the help of the Bauhaus courses and the student work, Hilberseimer began to research on typological problems in the intersection between housing and urban design[27]. The publications of this period are based on the student material of the Bauhaus era. There are exemplary research reports but also abstract studies to urban planning. Hilberseimer refined his studies as a research-led teaching, based on the same methodology, consisting of four components: (1) an introductory task leads to (2) a systematic typology problem. The type is understood as (3) complex disposition of rooms, with which finally it (4) can be designed structurally[28]. Through the introductory task a real condition was abstracted to its essentials, the type restricted and became the principle of relevant design factors. Abstraction became a means to narrow the task to a few straightforward conditions[29]. However, the abstraction of the real situation also means the specific selection of design-related factors and their inscription in architectural objects.

A weekly correction was carried out under four aspects[30]: (1) The house as order of rooms is determined by the functions of life and the criterion of maximum sunlight. (2) The apartment, the house and grounds are subject to an economy. This means they are valued by the urban context. Relevant here is the relationship between house-structure, circulation and open space. (3) A rational method of production. (4) Design and optimization is done by considering the relevant parameters.

Flat as the theme of the 20s Hilberseimer was not the only architect who devoted himself to single storey houses in the mid 20s. One realizes that proposals such as the Vertical-City were difficult to implement from economic aspects. The desired large form, whether as an urban block or slab, could ultimately be realized only by a major investor. Thus, the new typologies are based on the same economic model as already the housing estates of the industry Patriarchs of the 19th century[31]. If the modern forms of housing, in addition to functionally enabled economic and social flexibility, required a local urban form per housing unit to be financially viable. The single family house with a separate ground for each housing unit seems to resolve the problem. After the modern apartment, tailored to the needs of a bio-political large city family, was considered as solved, many architects tried to transfer the aspects of the apartment to the single house.

In this framework, Hilberseimer's interest in low-rise buildings can be seen. Surely, Hilberseimer would have known the works of his friend Hugo Häring. Häring already in 1923 developed settlements with garden houses, anticipating the later carpet buildings[32]. In 1928 presents Häring a L-house settlement[33]. One can safely say that the first drafts of the L-house based on studies of Hugo Häring. Hilberseimer has also pointed directly to Häring's studies and emphasized that "the L-shaped plan

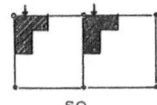 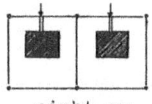

Figure 4.3: Hugo Häring: L-House Schema, 1934

arrangement goes back to him"[34]. The publication *The growing house*[35] by Martin Wagner gives a good overview of similar low-rise houses. All have in common that they are based on organic principles of organization.

4.2 FLAT-BUILDING AND CITY SPACE

After a year of teaching at the Bauhaus in 1929, Hilberseimer published the first Bauhaus work[36][37], studies on small apartments and thus preliminary studies of the later Settlement-Unit. A small apartment means a room arrangement according to the life needs of the individuals placed therein. The apartment is declared by the most essential factors and it is not the area that determines the quality of a flat, but its partitioning which decides on its "utility value". The main value of a city for Hilberseimer is isolation, the ability of the individual to be themself. The apartment is the space of isolation, the relaxant for the individual, which is exposed in the large city extraordinary stimuli. The free space of the city is in contrast with the impenetrable apartment. The classical distinction between the urban space and mass[38] in Hilberseimer is a distinction between the collective space of the city and the individual room of the apartment. The reallocation to the individual produces a crucial difference: the room is not neutral but embodies the life claim of an individual. The individual apartment is not transparent to the collective, a specific commodity formed for its residents. In order to create an object from the initial space and mass, Hilberseimer designs schemes on the basis of minimum requirements, not to restrict the living space to essentials, but to show the planning boundaries under which an apartment still has a utility value. The establishment of a minimum draws a line that defines the smallest possible free space. The free space becomes so the physical entity of the utility value. The minimum requirement allows for a reflection located outside of the designed object. The minimum is external to the practice of design, it is not a direct definition of a standard. It is the description of an extreme condition, the smallest possible proportion between mass and free space of the to be designed residential type.

Although the studies concentrate only on the living area of a settlement, Hilberseimer later says that the planning principles developed can be applied to any type of urban planning, regardless of the function[39]. The studies are, as Hilberseimer repeatedly emphasized[40], theoretical studies. It is important to understand that the presented studies develop a kind of planning and still are not planned, explicit cities. Hilberseimer was aware of the apparent fracture of his work and incorporated his

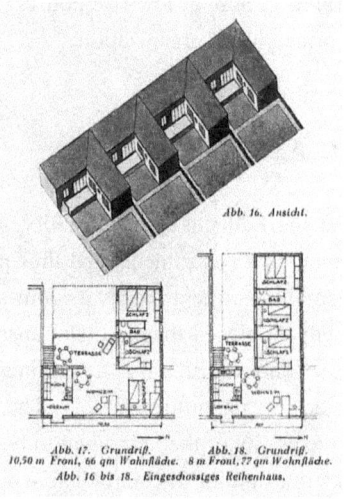

Figure 4.4: Ludwig Hilberseimer: one-storey row house, 1929; first published L-Shape house study; both plans refer to the same axonometric view

studies on the flat-buildings and the small apartment in a number of previous articles. Another example for his systematic and progressive research on one idea of urban design, Hilberseimer based on the following results[41]:

The spatial planning demand for the reorganization of the industrial city: *On urban design problems of the Large City*[42]: The Large City is a new type of city, brought forth by the economic conditions of global capitalism. The resulting large cities are no longer more specific and embody the physiognomy of a country or rulers[43]. Cities are alike, so that one can speak of an internationality. However, the existing large city was planned in the understanding of previous economic models. This anachronistic planning of the city is the cause of the shortcomings of large city. For this reason, Hilberseimer calls for a reorganization of the large city. A new material order will also be able to produce a new spiritual order. The nature of the city will be able to change the nature of society.

The urbanistic conclusion of the political-economic demand is an object- instead of ground-speculation in *building industry and housing construction*[44]: If the shortcomings of the city are of economic and political origin, the aspect in the planning process must be considered, where politics and the impact on architecture affect economy. Hilberseimer recognizes, that the former housing promotion politics puts grounds and building mass in relation to an interest rate policy. The individual apartment itself is not addressed. This means that the quality of living is excluded from the interplay of politics, architecture and economy. One solution is to translate politics and economics not through the speculation of ground and mass, but through the shift of speculation to the part of ground and mass: the apartments as an economic product itself. An increase in the planning quality would be coupled directly with the earnings. In urban terms, Hilberseimer first calls for the combination of small-scale plots to provide housing collectives. The mass is decoupled from the ground through the generalization of parcels. Due to the high number of residences in this way communal facilities could be profitable. The quality of each apartment would be increased. The housekeeping as a relict from medieval structures would disappear. The woman will be emancipated from the apartment. The apartment itself will be designed according to the requirements of living. The rooms are separated by the functions, the areas will be structured by the appropriate space requirement. The number of bedrooms depends on the number and sex of children and one bedroom will be for the parents. The room and the furniture are to be made with architectural sensibility. Formally, the room should form a unit by means of proportions, the type of light incidence and color. The apartment types are distinguished by bio-political contexts: apartments for families or single persons. The properly and appropriately designed apartments will save space and thus costs. The combination of building industry and industry can lead to new methods of construction. Through the use of new materials and prefabricated components, other costs may be saved.

If architecture is to be an economical product, it must also be evaluated as such in: *Room Design*[45]. The room is understood as a commodity and is determined by its intended use[46].

Urbanism as a political tool sets the framework for economy in:*City- and residential construction*[47]: City and building plan condition each other. That means the arrangement of a city determines the quality of individual apartments and needs of flats affect the plan of a city. The city becomes the organism, thew apartment becomes the cell. Urbanism will be the relationship of part to whole and the whole to its parts. Part and whole interact with each other. The transport system should be sized and oriented according to the functions. Residential and commercial streets should be functionally distinguished based on the direction. The street and block dimensions are determined by the building heights. The width of the streets and the distance between the blocks should be at least equal to the height of the building. The buildings should be oriented towards the sun. Transverse buildings should be omitted to allow urban ventilation. The apartments are designed to provide cross ventilation. Through the integrated treatment of the house and city, settlements emerge. The large city will be no longer individually extended house by house, but by means of satellites. These settlements are limited in size, allowing an interaction between the free space and the city. In the free space, the public facilities are located: hospitals, sanatoriums and schools. The individual satellites can be linked to supra-regional transport networks. The city becomes hierarchically structured.

If the economic product is architecturally designed, it is a composition of parts: *Large City Buildings*[48]: The individual rooms should be oriented according to their purpose with respect to the direction of the sun.

If economy is oriented towards humans, the smallest product is the room of an individual: *Large City Architecture*[49]: The furniture should be part of the apartment and installed permanently. So room and furniture can be matched. The design is done by means of the room itself. According to their function, as a commodity furniture, walls, floor, ceiling, doors and windows can be formed. Hilberseimer recognizes that architecture itself deals with the composition of designed objects. The economic and technical conditions will lead to a model kit by normalizing all elements. The task of architecture are its variation and expression[50].

Economic and political demands are placed in relation to each other by three urban aspects in: *Berlin and its building problems*[51]: What will be built is decided by the urban arrangement of the apartments, the building density and the type of floor plan.

All the requirements enumerated so far are Hilberseimer's own references, upon which he explicitly begins his research on flat buildings at the Bauhaus. Back to the original article: In *Large Cities micro apartments* Hilberseimer gives an overview on different residential building typologies he developed. Their planning quality above all is characterized by their combination and expansion options. Each typology, whether apartment or L-house, first is based on a minimal flat consisting of: circulation, access, entrance hall, kitchen, bathroom, living room, balcony and a minimum number of bedrooms. The number of bedrooms is determined by the family constellation of the inhabitants: An apartment has at least one bedroom[52], for one person. An L-house has at least three bedrooms: one for the parent[53] and two for children, one per possible gender. Each housing type can be expanded by adding bedrooms. Thus, according to Hilberseimer's demand an apartment is suitable for a couple as well as for a family. The sizes of all presented houses are described by their number of beds. The size of the living room is relative to the number of bedrooms. The house, so the apartment or row house as a pack of apartments, is defined by specific combinatorics of several apartments. The collective house affects the kind of combination and the possible variation of the apartments as follows: by a structural grid; the distance of the stairs; the determination of closed walls to the sequence or the front length, which has an impact on the overall depth and thus the layout design.

In several studies Hilberseimer combines the presented residential building typologies and generates schemata of settlements with different densities. The shown axonometries have no border-edge, no adjustment to a territory or specific conditions. They are formal expressions of textual requirements for a settlement. When considering the arrangement of the houses with respect to the orientation towards the sun, no apartment is oriented to the north. Between the buildings there is at least a distance of the height of the building. Streets are differentiated according to residential and traffic roads. The resulting combinations Hilberseimer referred as *Mixed-Settlement*: the spatial structure of a city arrangement "directly from their needs". The endless city, Hilberseimer does not oppose the limit, the exception but its rhythm, eternally recurring, designed "by a general law of form"[54].

The rhythm of the city   In the following, it is no longer the individual house or the settlement that Hilberseimer designs, but the interaction between the house and settlement. Hilberseimer explicitly emphasizes:

"In addition to designing the floor plan of the housing cell is the correlation between the individual housing cells crucial. It causes major urban differences by that an apartment is located in a single house, in an ordinary level house or in a high-rise building."[55]

In his article *Flat building and city space*[56] Hilberseimer compares housing typologies in their arrangement in urban space. There are investigations on the density at constant demands for the sun exposure of individual apartments. The scheme of settlement results from the requirement for an apartment and its possible disposition. A change in the floor plan, the addition of a room, the orientation of the garden. Accessibility to the house changes its disposition and influences the plan of the settlement as a multiple of a house. According to Hilberseimer's theoretical requirement, building- and city plan are placed here are placed in a line to the extreme. There are far more than just theoretical studies on density. The bird-perspectives show the studies as a city interwoven with the landscape. Far from the arrays of the site plan the single

136 The Mereological City: a reading of the works of Ludwig Hilberseimer

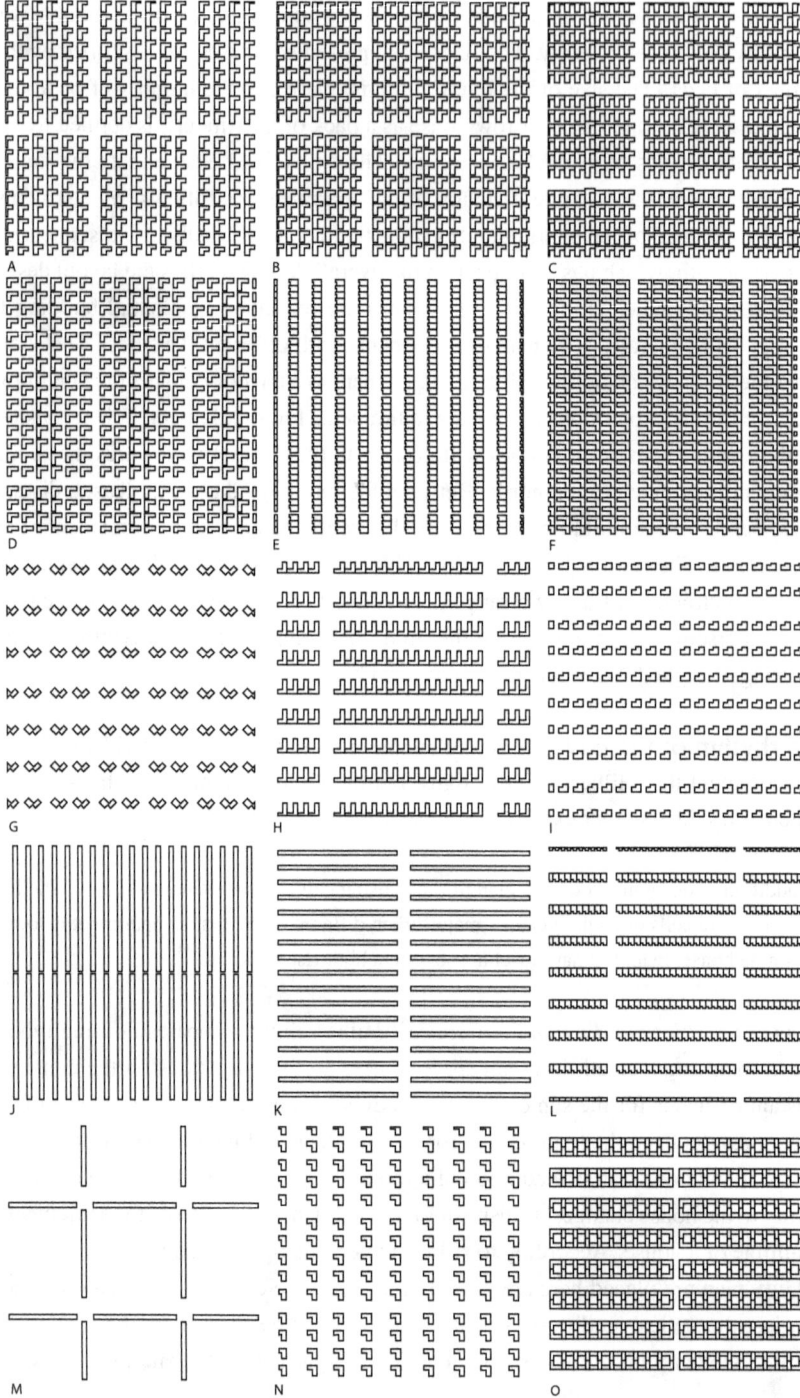

Figure 4.5: Mixed-Building ratio form to surface

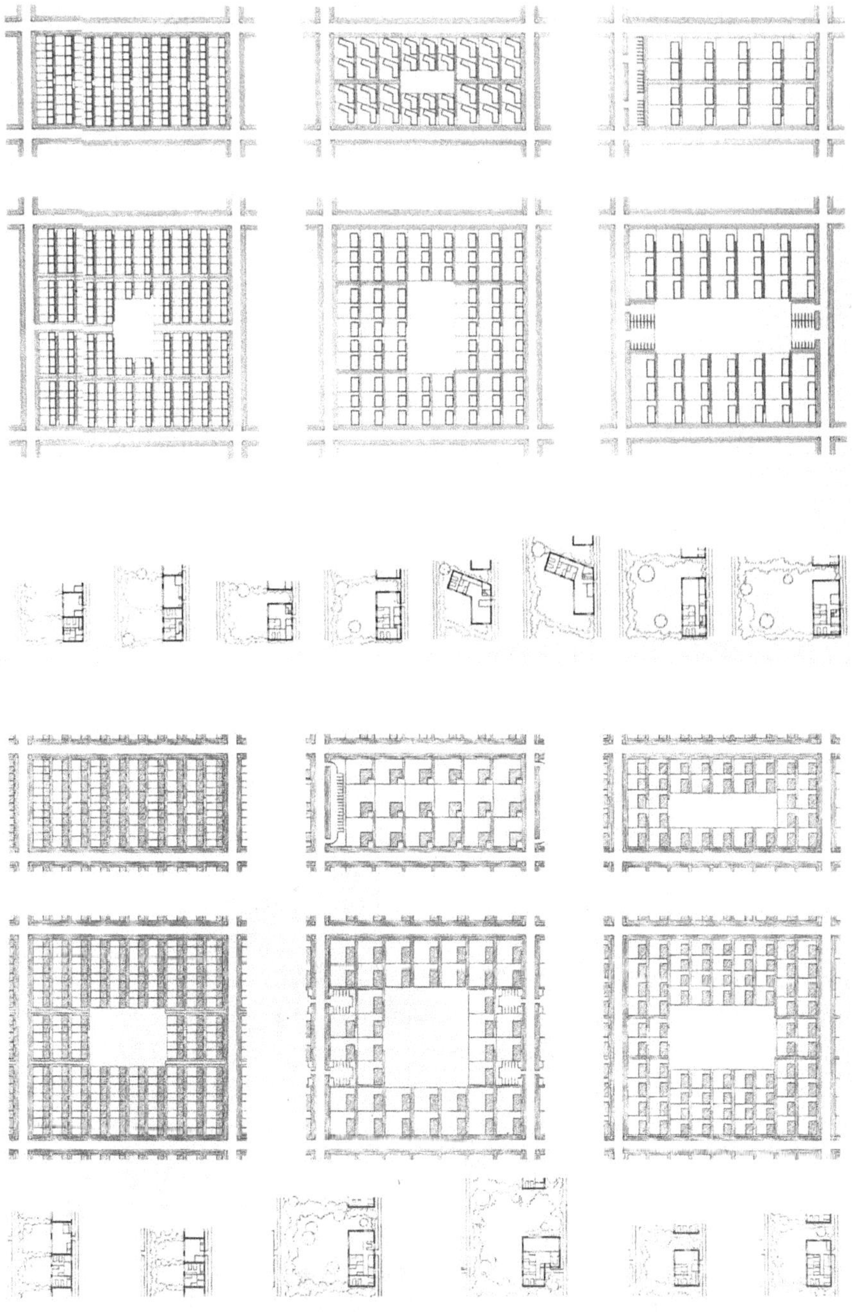

Figure 4.6: IIT course: City Planning 201, supervisor Ludwig Hilberseimer, studies, 1948; dependence of house plan on settlement layout and vice versa

houses blur into each other, also by the superposition with nature. It is not the precise image, the contour as a boundary which Hilberseimer plans here, but its topological fabric. The form of the city is determined by a rhythm: the ratio of the forms of the houses to the area of the settlement.

The Linear: the representation of the open Poché Here the type of presentation of the drawing itself is interesting. The new perspectives differ in the representation of Hilberseimer's earlier drafts. The presentation of the early twenties expressed simple geometric masses. The figure was drawn together by large shadings. The individual elements were combined, windows disappeared in the rhythm of the grid and ultimately in the geometry of the cube. With the interplay of monotonous, uniform surfaces he succeeded bringing together a group of individual elements, the apartments, to form one figure. The technique of uniform shading enabled Hilberseimer to present form as one body and its contour.

This technique is one of the classic techniques of representation of architecture and finds its origin in the "Ecole des Beaux Arts" of the classicist France: the *Poché*. The Poché indicates the exposition of a figuration through a comprehensive shading, the composition becomes a uniform figure contrasted to a ground. This technique is normally used to mark figurations in section or plan as an element, such as the construction of a ceiling or a wall. The form in this is marked as a contour, as a border line and then is infilled to a surface. There is no allocation to either figure or ground, for example through the figuration's own density, but based to an outside referencing. In this case, a judgment is made about figure or ground and also through the one or the other. A Poché-presentation is therefore unable to visualize a specific *constitution* of the parts of an element. With the technique of Poché it is not possible to show the One as the Many. As a Cartesian contrast medium, the Poché allows to set figures against a background. But what if a ground should only arise from the figuration itself? How to mark an apartment if its economic value is not created by the specific property on a ground, but by its disposition in a figuration[57]?

At that point, Hilberseimer switches for the Linear[58] as representation technique. The figure is indeed characterized by its contour, by a boundary, so it differs from an Other but at the same time it remains transparent as a composition from parts. The figure is figuration and is only described by the complexity of the settlement as a shimmering rhythm consisting of landscape, houses, windows, roofs and gardens. The figure is produced in the space between the lines as a limitation of the parts. The surface quality of a Poché is replaced by directions and changes of direction distances; sequences of parts of forms in the visual field of the surface of the settlement as a ground. The rhythm of the single houses is articulated by alternating housing types.

The surface of the row and L-houses is broken by the placement of apartment blocks. So the concept of Mixed-Building obtains a compositional meaning and architectural intention.

The interplay between the organization of the house and its disposition in the settlement becomes Hilberseimer's main exercise in teaching. The tasks in the Bauhaus seminar are continuous modifications of the design of a specific house and its plurality in one settlement. The presentation is carried out in three drawings: the plan of the house to represent the spatial organization of single rooms; a site plan-schema as the multiplication of the individual house and third: perspectives to evaluate its urban and architectural form.

Hilberseimer will later emphasize that the problems of urban design can only be solved,

"when plans for the whole city and plans for the houses in it are both taken into consideration. Only then will it be possible to meet the social, economic, psychological, and hygienic requirements of good human living [. . .]. The plan of a house must relate each room to the other rooms and to the house as a whole."[59]

However, in the article *Flat-buildings and cityspace* the figures are set in such a way that the house types, perspective and settlement plan are difficult assignable. Only with a reordering, like here in figure 4.14 to 4.16 becomes apparent how the designed "cityspaces" are based on the same methodology and evaluation. With this insight, the article can be understood as the description of Hilberseimer's city planning methodology. Hilberseimer refined in other Bauhaus seminars this basic interplay of house and settlement. In subsequent student work of the Bauseminar this scheme was enhanced with additional topics. The work of Pius Pahl (figure 4.17) is exemplarily for investigating the relation between house and garden. The role of the garden on the one hand as self-supporter garden and on the other hand as private recreation area affects the figure of the house, possible extensions and its disposition in the settlement. The size of the self-supporter garden leads to the inversion of the L-house figure remaining the same mereological schema. At the other extreme, the relatively small recreation area leads to the merger of L-houses to chains, urban major figures. The work of student Heinz Neuy examined the tension between house orientation and settlement density. The organization of the floor plan and thereby changing conditions of ambient lighting imply new settlement patterns. These are evaluated by the sum of housing units on an equal area. Such and similar studies of the Bauseminar became part of Hilberseimer's later study Raumdurchsonnung.

In the subsequent article *flat-building and flat house types*[60] Hilberseimer evaluates additional cost of construction and costs of infrastructure. The article mainly shows variations of row- and L-houses. Each type is presented in various sizes, expressed by the number of beds. A new requirement is the isolation to the neighbor.

The methodology Hilberseimer's to describe the settlement as speculative part of the house, can enhance our understanding of typology in the age of digital representation. In architecture, we are accustomed to describe a typology by means of an equation between content and form: On the one hand we comprehend content with its figure, e.g. the patio-house, or on the other hand we comprehend the figure with its program, e.g. the Single-family-house. Robert Venturi addressed these both sides ironically as the duck and the shed, half century ago. Whereas here the mereological condition describes the architectural type of the house by means of a circular relationship between the elements of the building as a possible disposition in a settlement. The architectural type is on the one hand not treated through the hierarchization of content or on the other hand as material expression.

A similar problem confronts us today in digital models as representation of buildings and cities, known as building information modelling (BIM). The digital representation of an object is based on an object-oriented approach to software development. Here, "objects" in first place are data structres that contain data, often known as attributes and procedures. An object's procedures can access and modify the data fields of the object with which they are associated. Objects have a notion of "this" or "self"[61]. This concept unfolds its strength in plurality. In object-oriented programming, computer programs are designed by making them out of objects that interact with one another. Therefore the OOP-paradigm is twofolded: on the one hand one deals with the internal organization of an object, on the other hand with external stimuli and the multitude of an environment. In a BIM model, the building is distinguished as an object between an internal management of geometric and constructive aspects and attributes for an external evaluation and disposition[62]. The attributes for an external prepresentation are meassures, like weight, transmission coefficient, price, etc.. As a consequence such models allow change and improvement of the meassure, but not allow compositional refigurations, any design as such. Here Hilberseimer's methodology of city planning demonstrates, how the internal managed compositional aspects can be addressed indirectly by the incorporation of the whole as a part for the part as a whole. Figure 4.19 - 4.22 are the results of digital physics simulations, based on Hilberseimer's textual demands on a flat building type. Each house of the resulting settlement patterns acts autonomously. The clusters are drawn together by the demand of the shortest walking distance to the outside for every house. The parthood condition of Room-Insolation stimulates the specific figurations of the settlement. Changes in the composition of rooms lead to their reorientation or the house as such. Specific densities of houses and their figuration lead to specific self-shadowing properties, which in return specific characteristics of the settlement layout provoke. A mereological schema provokes self-similar settlement layouts, without to determine Cartesian properties. Each mereological schema incorporates a specific settlement layout.

4.2.1 In the shadow of Mies

When Mies van der Rohe took over the Bauhaus as director, Hilberseimer's influence grew, too. Mies kept the curriculum designed by Hannes Meyer to a great extent. In addition, the school became even more focused on architecture. Basis of the education was the impart of technical knowledge. The balance was the Bauseminar, which was conducted in two parts in the architecture by Mies and city planning by Hilberseimer. Despite Mies as executive Hilberseimer evolved "to a gray cardinal that held together the Bauseminar. This seminar consisted not only of a dominant Mies, but out of Mies and Hilberseimer in equal parts"[63]. In the absence of Mies Hilberseimer even acted as Mies' substitute[64].

Mies exercise in the Bauseminar was to design a courtyard- or single-storey house. Christian Wolsdorff already pointed out that Mies' exercise of the courtyard house leaned on Hilberseimer's flat buildings and their urban environment. Mies' practice itself had no specific commission for a courtyard house at this time. The courtyard house was an abstract task, designed as a teaching and research instrument. The works produced in the seminars are usually associated with either Mies or Hilberseimer as teachers. While the stand-alone courtyard houses associated with Mies define complex spatial structures between an inside and outside[65], the houses with Hilberseimer associated are morphological studies, mostly simple spatial sequences, only understandable in the context of the settlement. The transitions between the two instructors are fluid. Despite differences in shape both sides of the Bauseminar are parts of a coherent research: both understand house or settlement as a composition. Mies on the scale of architecture, Hilberseimer on the scale of city planning.

The exercises of the student Heinz Neuy show that the house is understood as mereological schema. The relations between rooms and their sequencing are similar between the two subsequent studies, however size, proportion and quantity of parts differ. The idea of the identical and the problem of the uniform copy in modernism becomes revaluated, if one considers the type as mereological composition. In the site plan of student Ernst Hegel the settlement is arranged through arrays of the same house typ. However, each house is a specific actuality on the basis of its mereological

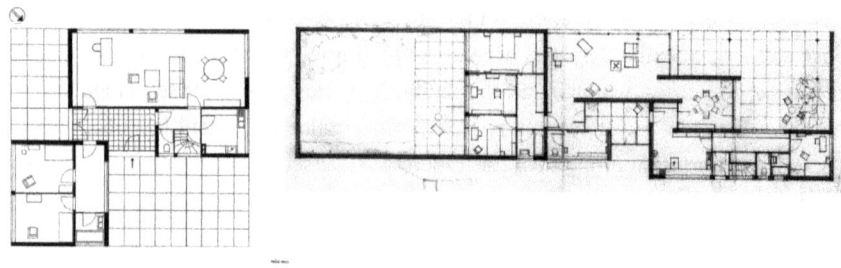

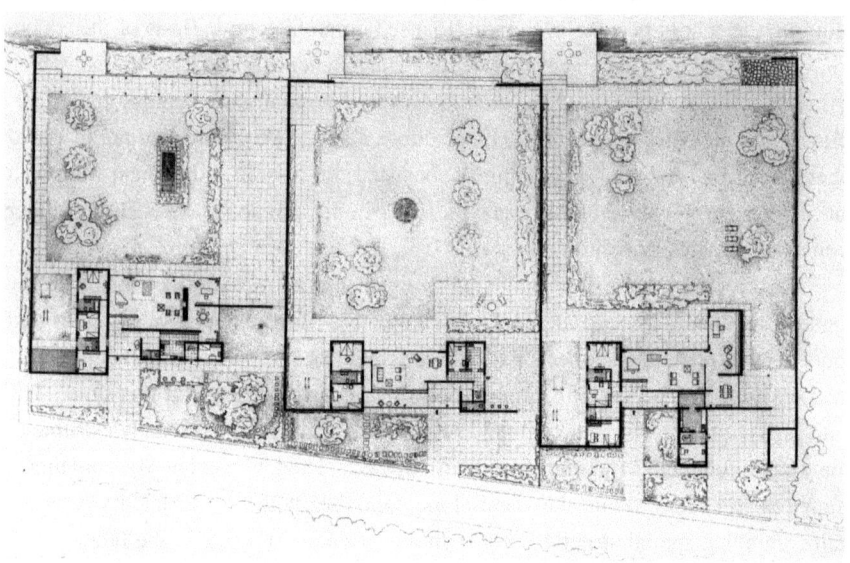

Figure 4.7: Student works at the Bauhaus, supervisor Mies van der Rohe; top: Heinz Neuy, one family house study, 1931; left: 3. exercise, right: 4. exercise; bottom: Ernst Hegel: 3 Einfamilienhäuser, 1933

schema. Analogously to the schema of the Vertical-City, Hilberseimer's L-shape-houses became placeholder for a subsequent architectural elaboration. As urbanist Hilberseimer worked on a negotiation between the house and the settlement. The important aspect of this work is to indicate the interactions and influences of the house and its context to the settlement.

In his practice Mies introduced the topic of the courtyard house several times. The house Lemke in Berlin built in 1932, also encloses L-shape-like a courtyard. Furthermore, the use of simple materials rather remind one of the studies of the Bauseminar. Two years later, Mies for Margarete Hubbe designed a courtyard house type, which however was not realized. The site plan is worth to be noticed: the plot Mies divided into 16 parcels. The various sketches and variations of the courtyard house type in this context are not to be interpreted as the search for an ideal house, but as morphological figure which was to be built in 16 variations[66]. That would be a direct parallel to the urban studies of L-house and its arrangement in the settlement.

When Mies later received the commission for the IIT campus he gave a part of the commission to Hilberseimer[67]. Hilberseimer proposes a courtyard house arrangement, which is strongly reminiscent to the density studies of L-houses. Despite the opportunity for realization, Hilberseimer's design remains a schema. The spatial complexity of Mies' flat buildings is not reached by the design, which probably is one of the reasons that the realization of the design was denied. Hilberseimer lost the contract to SOM. The apartment project is the first construction project, which SOM build for the new campus of IIT. In the following years SOM took on more and more parts of Mies' master plan until Mies finally lost the contract completely to SOM.

4.3 STUDIES ON ROOM INSOLATION

With the closing of the Bauhaus it is increasingly difficult for Hilberseimer to continue his work in Germany. His order situation is bad, but it is known that Hilberseimer at this time held private lessons and regularly met with a group of students. The draft of the Free University of Berlin is a known result of working with students. Forced into a niche for political reasons, Hilberseimer is able to publish only two articles until his departure for America[68]. These are probably his most technocratic articles, studies on the room insolation[69]. The studies were originally developed in the Bauhaus seminar: housing and city planning. Annotated with graphs and tables they describe, which parameters influence the insolation of houses and rooms. Extracted from the context, each parameter is considered separately evaluated and classified according to an optimum. Since his first plans the orientation and the influence of the sun played a major role in the design of settlements. Obtained bibliographies testify that he comprehensively addressed the international literature with this aspect[70]. New in these articles, probably out of political restraint, is the fragmented-schematic representation of the sun and house under different conditions and their evaluation in graphs.

The study is based on the observation that the sun insolation has therapeutic value to human health. Consequently, the room and the house are aligned towards the highest possible sun insolation. The rooms to be oriented are the bed- and living rooms. Solar insolation is measured throughout the day, with the on average best rated sun insolation in the morning[71], at a point of day for which one must assume that the inhabitants of an industrial town, are at work or school and not at home. The evaluation of sun exposure is independent of whether persons are staying in the room or not. Thus, the room is designed according to the condition of the therapeutic sun exposure, but not for the actual residents. The condition for humans is transferred to the room. Room and house are equated with man. The room here no longer is a hull for people but inherits the properties of its users, becomes a placeholder.

Mark Kilian indicates that the metaphysical significance of Room-Insolation, the combination of sun and room, can also have historical origins[72]. In many cultures the sun had a cultic significance. Buildings were aligned with the sun for centuries. The pyramids of the Incas, Mayans and Egyptians are oriented to specific sun constellations. Baroque residences such as the Versailles of the Roi Soleil are oriented to the south. Not only the residence but also entire baroque city facilities like Karlsruhe, Hilberseimer's hometown, were aligned with the sun. Here, in the study of Room-Insolation the room of the individual is aligned towards the sun. Divine myths or glorification of rulers will be replaced by the individual in the interplay of nature and culture. Kilian's insight I want to share only limited in its conclusion. In Hilberseimer's intervention of the Room-Insolation it is correct that the individual person becomes the new surrogate in the dialogue of the moderns. On the one hand, the individual becomes the representative of culture. But further, the inscription of the sun in the proportion between mass and open space means a translation of social collectivity in the collective of the settlement without addressing a symbolic reference. The physical reproduction of the social community here is done indirectly through the designed inscription as the demand for an interval, a spacing. While pyramids or baroque residences symbols were an expression of their society, the value of Room-Insolation represents the minimum requirement of an individual to a collective. This demand physically designs the settlement with its impact on the distance between buildings. The political representation of a better constitution of society is transmitted as a therapeutic effect of the individual to the single room in an idea of the arrangement of rooms and ultimately to the reorganization of the city. The political practice is expressed in the proportion. The raised claim means a transformation from partial aspects between the elements of the various collectives. In this manner the reference is uncoupled from reproduction. The structure of the reference takes place reciprocally through the term of the Gestalt of the settlement as an expression of the form of the settlement, without a direct bridge between the collectives as a symbol[73].

Through the inscription a shift takes place, which at first sight and depending on the view allows to collapse one of the two opposites in the other. On the one hand, cultural aspects represented by the individual seem to be expressible by nature. On the other hand, by definition incomprehensible nature becomes a design element, conceived as one element for the representatives of culture. If both are absorbed in constant change, what is the argument for even the preservation of one of the representatives? What succeeds here in an approach, is the composition of a real part without categorization with one of the two representatives[74]. For Hilberseimer, the sun in the room is the possibility to transform a vision of society in a conception of architecture. Later at the IIT, his students will celebrate the winter solstice as *Hilbs-Day*. December 21 is the day on which the sun shines again longer. In all objectivity the sun for Hilberseimer did not lose their cultic shine .

The placeholding or better inheritance is made mereological, through parthood-conditions. The evaluation of various room orientations with respect to their sun exposure takes place through explicit architectural elements: measured and drawn to the light-flooded prisms in the room. "The room size of the sun irradiated air prism and not the striked floor or wall surface is essential."[75] So, in Hilberseimer's type of the room the technical demand of sun insolation undergoes a translation into the tectonics of the architectural type itself. The light prism as void-volume is not considered as measurement, but becomes an explicit element of the room. As parthood relation the demand becomes the ratio between the volume of the room and the light prism.

As part of the room the environment becomes articulated as void, the zero placeholding the light or the slope. In a negative way you can read this *ecological gap* as zero defined by the absence of something, placeholding an external condition. But from a compositional point of view, an external condition can just be described as reaching out. In this way absence turns into an interest, a desire for something. Like arms stretching towards a desire[76], mereological conditions anticipate specific possibilities in an environment. As opposed to describing something discrete as merely something *that is*, parthood conditions also describe interiority as *what is has*, or by reaching out beyond it's exterior, to *what it does not have*. Describing *to have* in the

146   The Mereological City: a reading of the works of Ludwig Hilberseimer

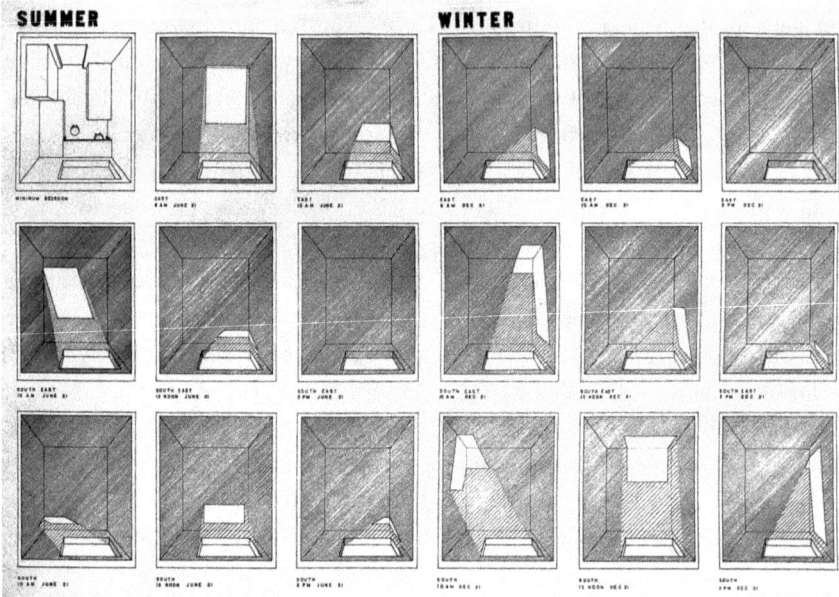

Figure 4.8: Anthony Clyde Lewis, sun penetration study, 1943; part of his Master-Thesis "Survey And Replanning Of Montreal" at the IIT by Ludwig Hilberseimer; the sunlit light prism is shown as a volume in space

opposition of *to be* has the advantage that in a reversible manner it defines both: who possesses, as well as that which is possessed.

The investigation of room orientation concludes that rooms facing south, southeast or south west are the most favorable. The orientation of the house affects the organization of the floor plan. The solar intensity is not considered.

For the determination of the minimum building spacing, several parameters must be calculated, first the sun angle. The sun angle is comprised of the angle of the sun's altitude and azimuth, both changing throughout the day and year. Therefore, studies at different seasons are necessary, to retrieve examples of the extremes of the solstices. The daily variation is superimposed and yields to the irradiated air prism, shaded differently based on the duration of the overlay. The sun angle is regionally depending on the latitude. Depending on the orientation of the rooms, the sun angle gives an interval unit that increases or decreases regarding the influence of the relief. The proximity unit is multiplied by the shade causing edge, which results from the difference between building height and lowest sill height. The result is the minimum distance between the buildings to allow a minimum quantity of room in-

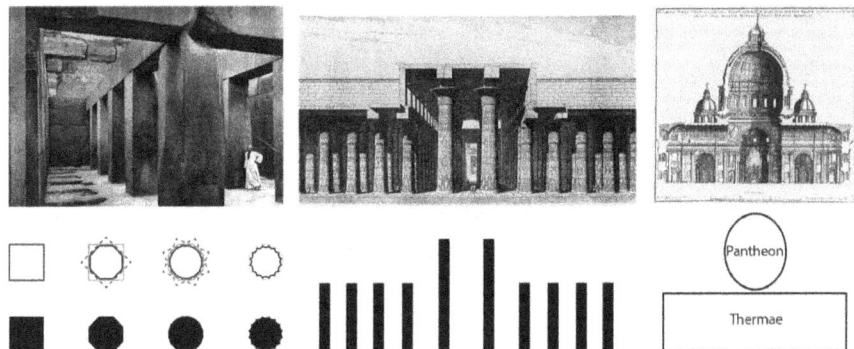

Figure 4.9: left: from pillar to column, middle: the differentiation of columns leads to a basilica, right: St. Peter's Basilica as typological pile

solation for all the apartments of a settlement. To calculate a maximum population density, Hilberseimer takes up the same space requirements for each resident. It is the space requirement of a person, as measured by the area of the floor plan organization, which is crucial. The following properties of the shape of the building have an influence on the distance and thus the maximum population density: At first the depth and the height of the buildings, second the height of ceilings, while a low height allows more storeys with the same height, third the roof form, while saddle roofs increase the shade causing edge and fourth the floor plan organization, which determines the space requirements of a person. An efficient floor plans allows a higher density with the same building spacing.

The theoretical study of the Room Insolation is based on the assumption of a minimum sunlight. To demonstrate its applicability, Hilberseimer applied his study to the metropolitan area of Berlin. For this he extracted area and demographic subdivision according to single or family householdsfrom the existing Berlin inhabitants. The demographic composition is assigned to different types of apartments and their building typology. The assumption of building typologies allows the extrapolation of the area required for the adoption of a minimum sun insolation. The extrapolation of the area needed for a city of the same population as Berlin coincides with the area of Berlin. The assumption is no utopian demand but an assumption for the reorganization of Berlin and other cities.

The historical inscription Hilberseimer as prior art critic takes the moment of inscription of Riegl: the shift of perception in the elements themselves. The inscription of an action first takes place by abstraction. Here we find a parallel to Alois

Riegl's view through abstraction. In the study of Room Insolation Hilberseimer abstracts a hygienic assumption into planning. In a similar manner Hilberseimer in a later, unpublished text: *Architecture, Structure and Form*[77] using historical examples shows, how inscription as a form of craft leads to an autonomy of the object. Hilberseimer describes the history of architecture as a pool of objects with complexity levels that build on each other through the development of architectural strategies, compositions of architectural elements[78]. Hilberseimer describes a column produced from a repeated section of a pillar. The concave shape of the Cannelure amplifies the absence of the material. The type of a basilica is caused by the different scaling of columns. The increased middle pillars lead to gradation, disruption of the roof. The element of the skylight is created. The space is differentiated between main and side aisle. The complex structure of the Vatican Basilica can be understood as a typological stacking of a pantheon on a basilica. With this kind of architectural history Hilberseimer establishes a hierarchy of complexity, in which an architectural element on each scale level is the result of architectural operations on architectural elements. An increasing complexity of the combination of elements forms new, third elements.

4.4 ELEMENTS OF CITY PLANNING

Two years after leaving Germany and teaching at the IIT, Hilberseimer published a city study based on the sequence of a single element, the *Settlement-Unit*. This prrobably is Hilberseimer's second most-famous design – after the Vertical-City. In the review of his work both designs are often contrasted for two different planning phases of Hilberseimer[79]. While the Vertical-City stands for the German period, the Settlement-Unit stands for the American phase of his work. Certainly, Hilberseimer contributed to this view. The identification of his person with the design of Vertical-City was so great, that he for the promotion of his later publication *The New City*, he himself condemned the design of Vertical-City with the famous words: the design is "More a Necropolis than a Metropolis"[80]. The New City and the Settlement-Unit in specific are different in shape, but the basic requirements of the Vertical-City can also be found in the Settlement-Unit. The Settlement-Unit is based on the scheme of the Vertical-City and can be compared to a city block of the Vertical-City.

The article *Elements of City Planning*[81] for the first time introduces the settlement unit and anticipates as a kind of outline, his four years later upcoming book *The New City*. In this article already all the essential aspects Hilberseimer's for planning decentralized cities are listed. Coherent to the framework of *Large City Architecture* the planning of the city is first based on historical facts: As also formulated in 1923[82],

Figure 4.10: Ludwig Hilberseimer: The City in the Landscape, 1940, first published perspective of a Settlement-Unit

the shortcomings of the existing industrial city are the result of a planning which is based on an assumed however no longer appropriate materiality of society. Urban planning shall now integrate the new epochal elements of the city, such as car. Which elements need to be changed is recognizable by historical consideration and classification. For the traffic in a city Hilberseimer shows, that historic cities were created centrally originated from the circumstances of the pedestrian. The new element of motorized traffic led to an expansion of the city beyond the natural boundaries of the pedestrian distance. The overstretched mass of city brought the centers to the collapse. Hilberseimer concludes that the contemporary city, with the insertion and speculation on the element of motorized transport, should no longer be oriented towards a center. As an alternative to the centralized city Hilberseimer offers the linear city. In Soria y Marta's *Ciudad Lineal* from 1883, Hilberseimer finds a precursor for a new type of transport system, the ribbon[83]. Without center, the traffic in the ribbon city is homogeneously distributed over the entire city. The ribbon is structured using the demand, that every entity should be reachable from the main axis in walking distance. Motor and pedestrian traffic become superimposed. Settlements in the radius of an acceptable walking distance, with all the elements needed to live, results in the so-called Settlement-Unit. Thus, the original ribbon-city is divided into settlement units. The shape firstly is determined in the expansion: the route between home and work should be a maximum of 15 to 20 minutes. On the other hand, Hilberseimer accepts a demand of the urbanist Raymond Unwin[84]: Paths of pedestrians and motorized traffic should never crossed in order to avoid accidents. To comply with this requirement, the crossing points with streets are reduced to a minimum. Reduction of walking times and street junctions ultimately leads to the herringbone shape of the street network of a Settlement-Unit. The transport network is organized hierarchically, from the Highway to the residential street. Passing traffic is limited, residential roads are generally dead end streets – cul de sacs. Public institutions like schools are placed between the settlement units to be accessible by foot, without the need to cross a street. The supra-regional transport system attaches to the street in the central axis of the Settlement-Unit. The street is the backbone of the settlement while the residential streets as just fishbones. Hilberseimer himself calls the transport network a "fishbone-structure". Pedestrian lanes lead from the residential streets, if possible only footpaths to the single houses. Each intersection represents a further folding of the neighborhood hierarchy[85]. It is also the transition from car to pedestrian. Both ends form a pair of opposites, the highway only for the car, the residential lane only for pedestrians.

Despite the detailed instructions to infrastructure, for Hilberseimer traffic results from the city planning. In several texts Hilberseimer mentioned that traffic and appropriate transport systems arise from the city planning[86]. The houses of the settlement are no subordinated components of a traffic system. On the contrary, careful consideration is aimed at making the required infrastructure in a city as superfluous as possible[87]. The Settlement-Unit results from the superposition of the rib structure with the studies of flat-buildings from the Bauhaus era. The studies on the flat-building focused on the design of a single house and its reciprocal effect on the settlement. The result was the so-called Mixed-Building, endless city-fields without contour, which are defined by their rhythm of masses. With the Settlement-Unit Hilberseimer in many ways defined the contour of rhythm: The field is limited. The size of a Settlement Unit depends on several factors and in depths determines the maximum walking distance between home and work. The number of inhabitants of a unit depends on the number of workers and employees in the coupled industrial and commercial zones. The number of employees and number of inhabitants should be in accordance. Hilberseimer assumes the fact, that the Settlement-Unit is a socially coherent whole. With this he stands in one row with early modernist urban planners like Robert Owen and the cooperative movement[88].

From the settlement to the region With the increasing complexity of the work, Hilberseimer begins to investigate not only the ratio of house and settlement or of architecture and city planning, but also of settlement to region, ie from city planning to spatial planning. Hilberseimer destined the following properties to a settlement in order to be able to disposition the settlement like the house: Settlement-Unit is

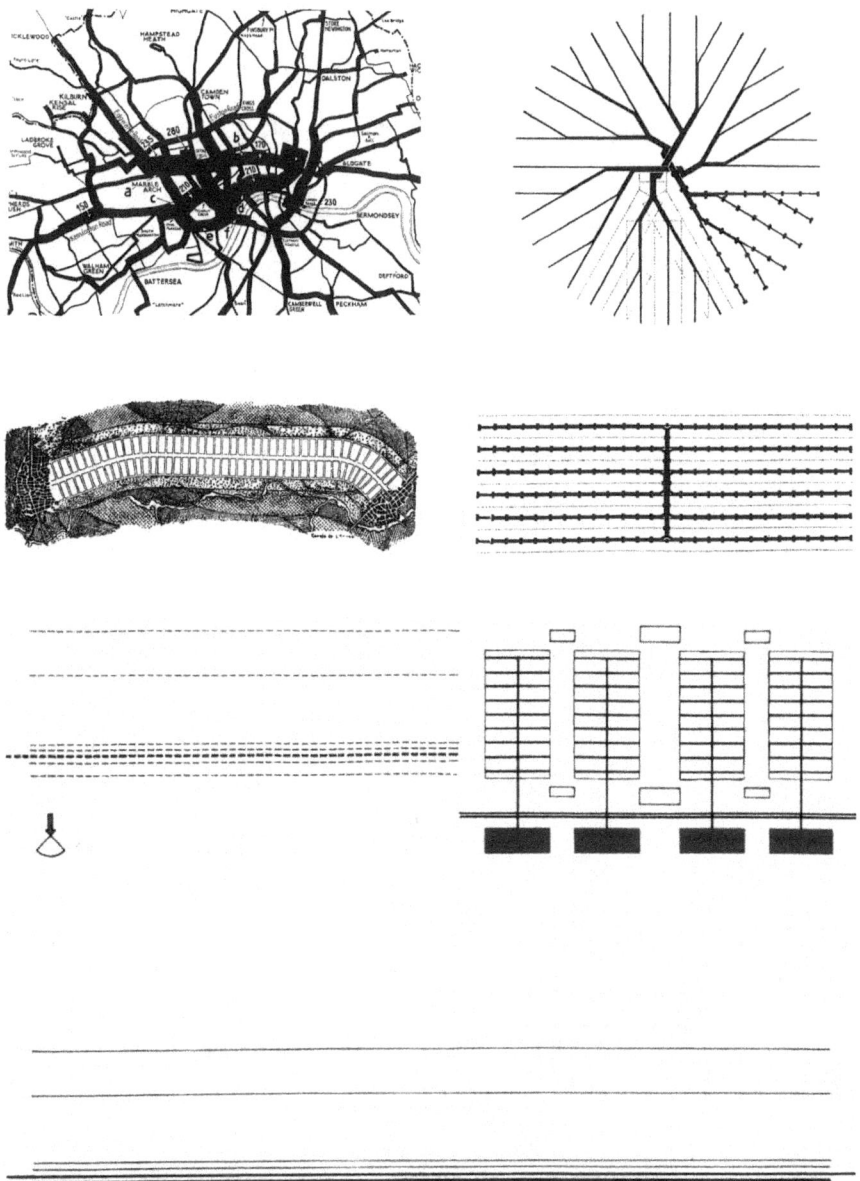

Figure 4.11: Ludwig Hilberseimer: study settlement and transport, 1940, top left: London traffic diagram; top right: Ludwig Sieverts: Centralized Traffic System; below left: Soria y Mata: La Ciudad Lineal; below right: Peter Friedrich: Traffic System in Ribbon Development; bottom: Ludwig Hilberseimer: linear stratification of transport; Schema of the subdivision

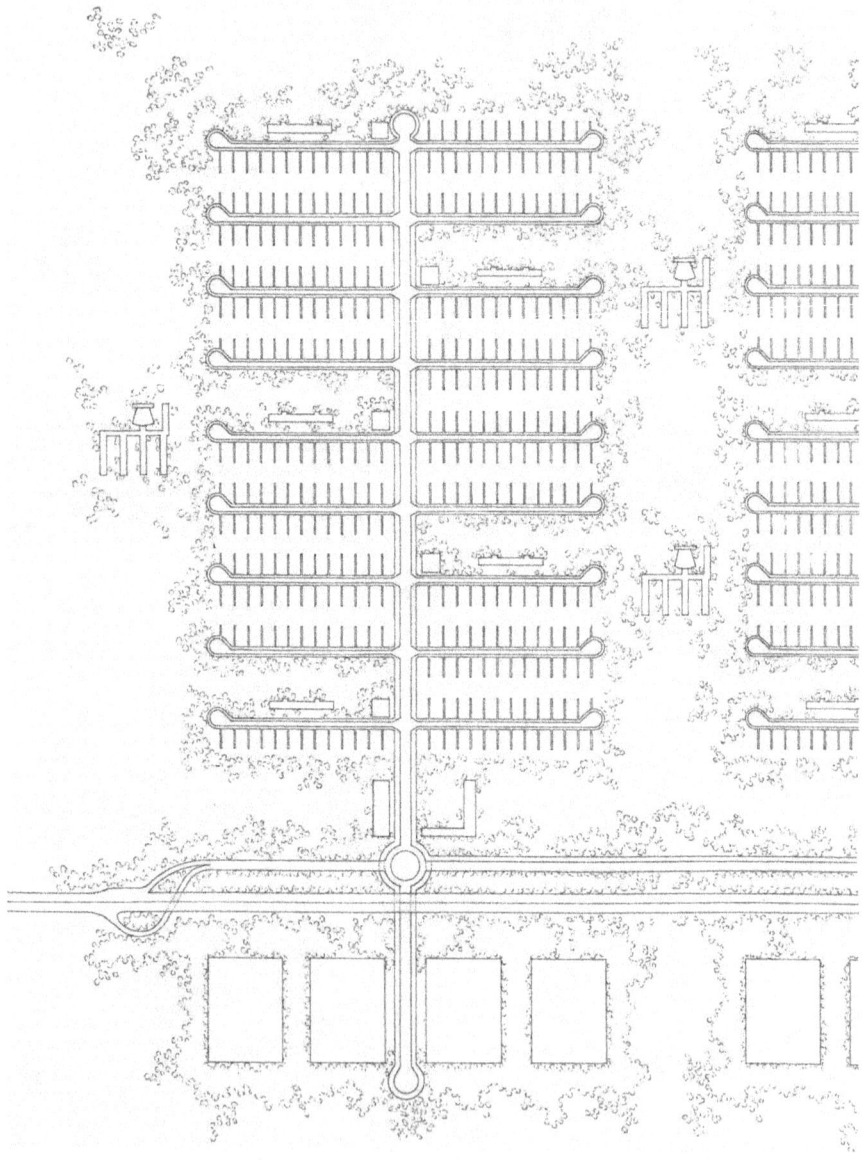

Figure 4.12: Ludwig Hilberseimer: Basic City Unit, 1940, this settlement unit is designed for 125,000 inhabitants; the settlement unit is the result of the overlap of the flat-building studies and the concept of infrastructure

functionally divided into parts: residential, industrial [89]. Position and form of the settlement elements to each other is determined by the prevailing regional wind direction and strength. Residential areas should never be in the lee of an industrial area and thus the industrial emissions. The wind shadow as shading of surface gives the industrial sector a specific area. Unshaded areas are the void for the living areas. The areas are oriented to each other. For complex wind situations of a region, the shading of an industrial region may also leave no void on either of its sides. In this case, the functional elements cannot be aligned with each other. The Settlement-Unit would not be a unit, residential and industrial sectors would have to be arranged separately[90].

The classic Settlement Unit is formed by the simplification of wind conditions. In the shown and well known diagram, the unit only works with a linear wind direction, with the national transport routes running between them. Therefore, the residential area, averted to the wind shadow, is loacted opposite to the industrial sector. Between both run the national transport routes. Between Highway and living area, a green stripe is arranged as a zone for administration and office space, shops, garages, hotels and government institutions. The residential area on the remaining three sides is surrounded by a park. This park explicitly is a free space. This zone should include community facilities, schools and kitchen gardens[91]. After the park an agricultural zone is located, which is measured by the personal use of the inhabitants of the settlement unit and according to the absorption of industrial gases. The area exposed to the exhaust gases is placed behind the industry sector. For Hilberseimer agricultural land is cultivated nature for people.

The illustrated Settlement Unit according to the textual description, is designed for 12,500 inhabitants, according to the drawing for a maximum of 9,000 inhabitants. Larger Cities, so called *City-Aggregates*[92], can be designed by the composition of further Settlement-Units. The size and shape of the individual units vary due to their specific characteristics. Thus, according to Hilberseimer, each city designed on the principle of the Settlement-Unit will be specific, by means of the variation and possible composition of the individual units. For the combination it helps, that the contour of a settlement unit is indeed determined by the parameter density, pedestrian distance, street length and the surrounding free spaces, however only in their area. The outline of the free area is defined only by the amount of empty space. The combination of Settlement-Units is not a sequence along discrete edges. The lack of outline allows a soft portion of the assembly, which ultimately will allow all sorts of aggregates[93].

The New City Throughout the following four years, after the article *Elements of City Planning*, Hilberseimer further developed the outline of the Settlement-Unit[94].

While in *Large City Architecture* the design of the Vertical-City was the central element, in *The New City* the reorganization of the city is argumented through the design of the Settlement-Unit. The requirements for room, house and settlement are more detailed. As new requirements are added: Each room should have a separate entrance from the corridor. The living room should be larger than necessary. Shape, size and arrangement of windows should let small rooms appear larger. Kitchens, bathrooms and stairs should be arranged in the north[95]. For summertime, sun protection can be provided by the positioning of trees or by structural elements such as roof overhangs or cantilevered floor slabs, balconies[96]. Studies point out which influence the contour of the possible form of the settlement unit area has on the cost of the infrastructure dependent on the length of streets. The orientation of the houses is influenced and influences the rotation of the streets. In this case, the rotation of main street, residential street or residential lane have a different effect on the shape of the settlement unit and the arrangement of the houses. The location of the grouped garages at the house or in public has an impact on the number and the width of streets, the density of the houses and types of accessibility.

Density Studies at the IIT   As a professor at the Illinois Institute of Technology (IIT) in Chicago, Hilberseimer in his seminars assigns the same task as in the Bauhaus Seminar: to design the reciprocal relation between the house and settlement. This examination of the balance between the individual and the Many becomes the basis of the higher architectural education. At IIT, this task was the basis for the fourth year of Architectural Education[97]. With this task architecture was introduced as art in architectural education at IIT. On the one hand, the students dealt with the design of complex organizational building under the direction of Mies van der Rohe. On the other hand, it was the design of the relationship between the house and settlement, under Ludwig Hilberseimer. The organic relationship between architecture and the city. For Hilberseimer it was not just planning studies. These are "Studies of Architectural Variation, by maintaining the density"[98] and also architectural studies in the context of planning principles.

Master Thesis at IIT: Contextualization   The most complex and most sophisticated studies related to the Settlement-Unit concept emerged as master thesis at IIT under Hilberseimer's supervision. A detailed analysis and comparison of the theories is beyond the scope of this work, however.

The works are reorganizations of cities or landscapes of a specific region. The theses supervised by Hilberseimer all follow a similar structure. In a first step the analysis of geographical, social, economic and historical characteristics leads to the determination of relevant planning factors. In a second step planning principles are presented as diagrams. In the third step, the principles developed were inserted into the existing cities to intervene, to gradually highlight a possible reorganization of the city and its region. The works vary greatly in their appearance and depending on the needs of the region, different units and strategies are developed. In interaction to the topography, in the application highly differentiated studies result, which have no resemblance to the shape of the schemes of the settlement unit.

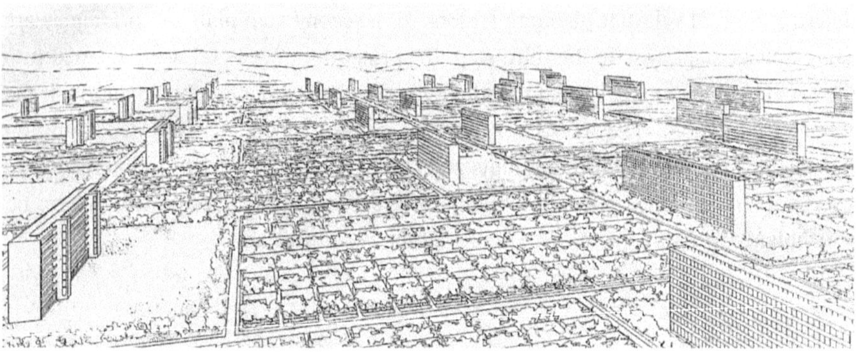

156   The Mereological City: a reading of the works of Ludwig Hilberseimer

fig. 1

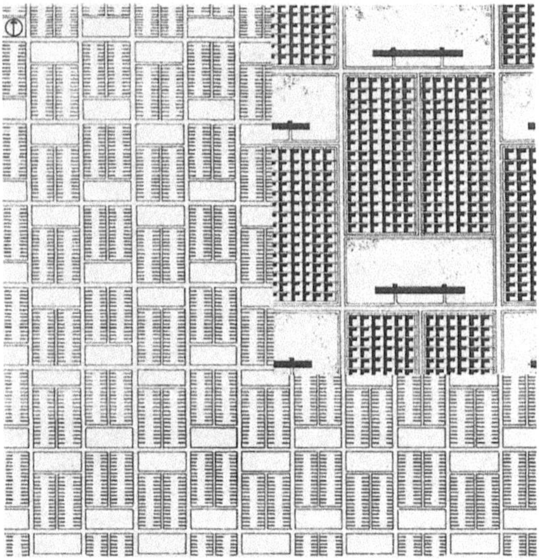

fig. 3

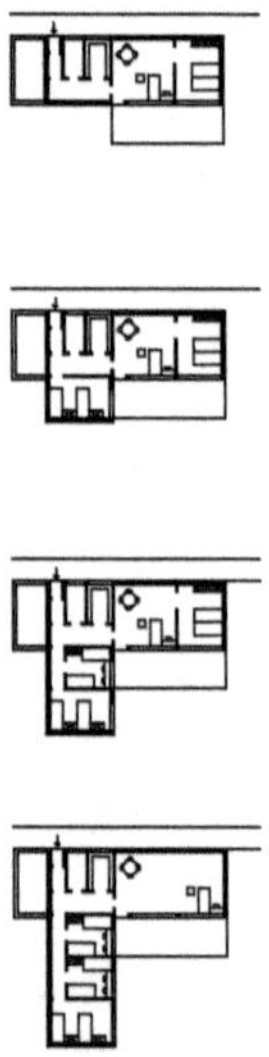

fig. 5, 6

fig. 7

Figure 4.13: Mixed-Building 1, free standing L-Shape houses and porch houses, 1931; top: perspective, middle left: siteplan, middle right: L-Shape house in different sizes, bottom: porch house

The unfolding of a planning idea 157

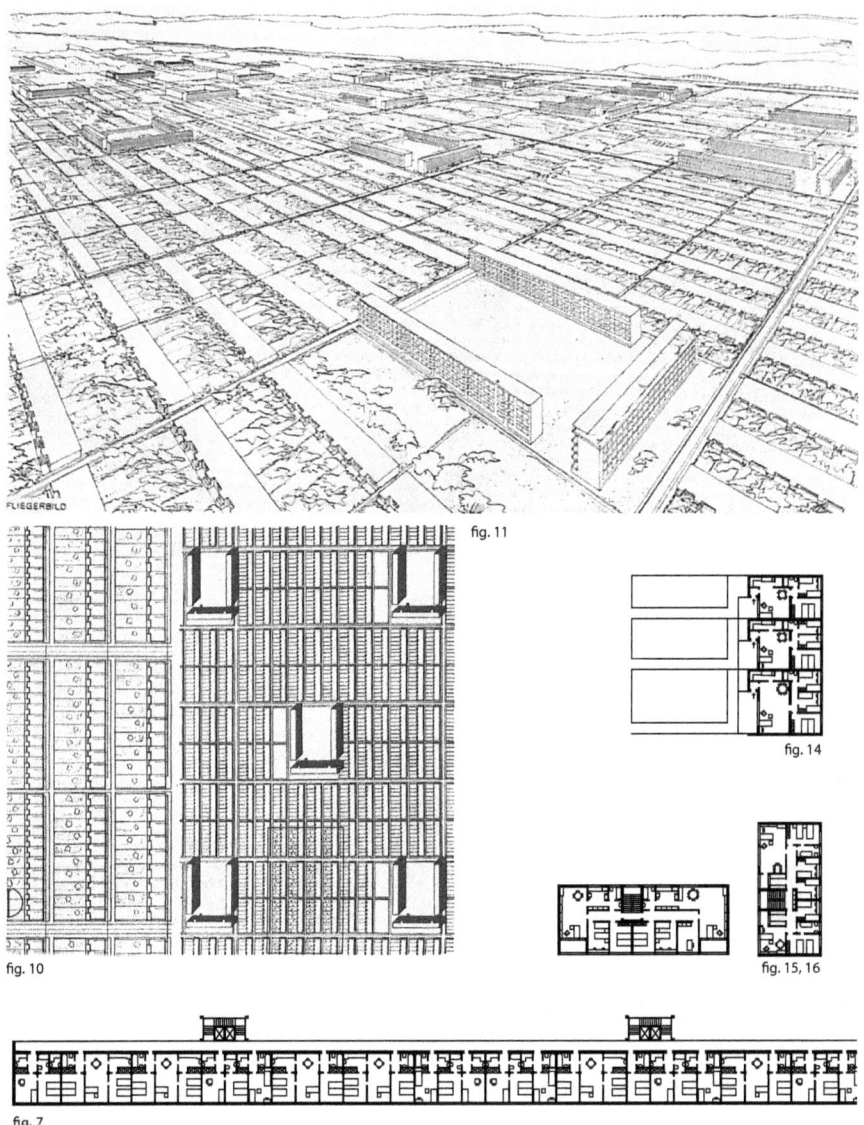

Figure 4.14: Mixed-Building 2, row houses, appartment houses and porch houses, 1931, top: perspective, middle left: siteplan, middle top right: row house, middle bottom right: appartment house; bottom: porch house

158   The Mereological City: a reading of the works of Ludwig Hilberseimer

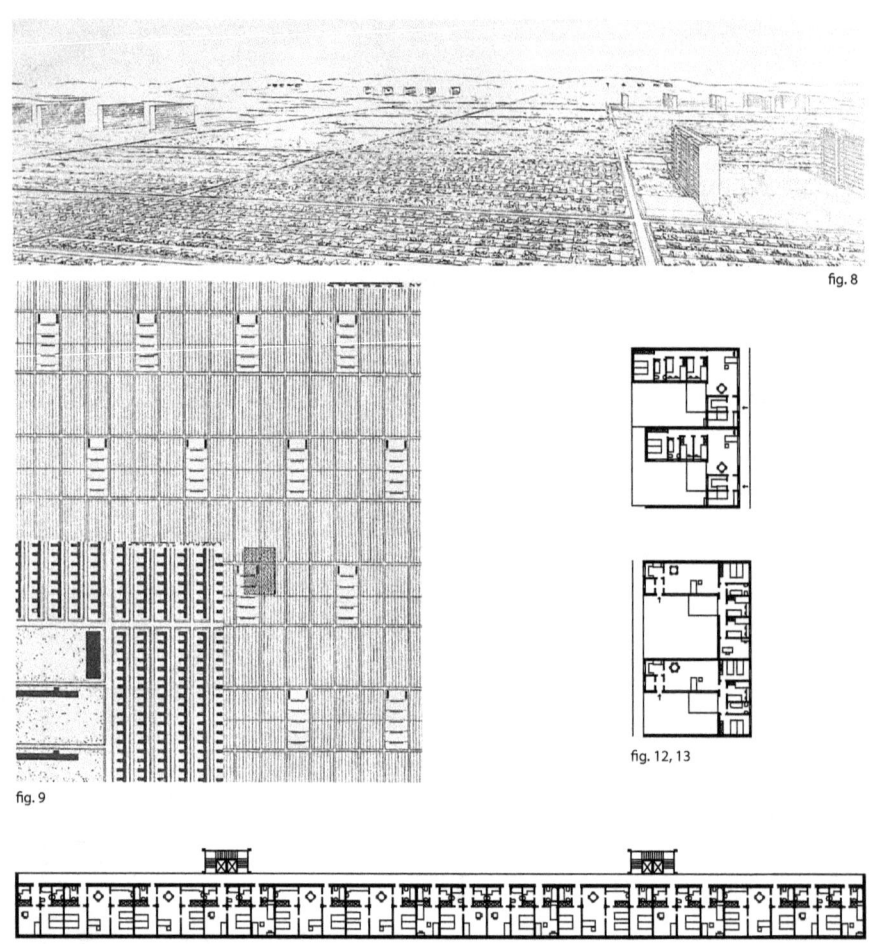

Figure 4.15: Mixed-Building 3, free standing L-Shape houses and porch houses, 1931, top: perspective, middle left: siteplan, middle right: L-Shape house in different sizes, bottom: porch house

The unfolding of a planning idea 159

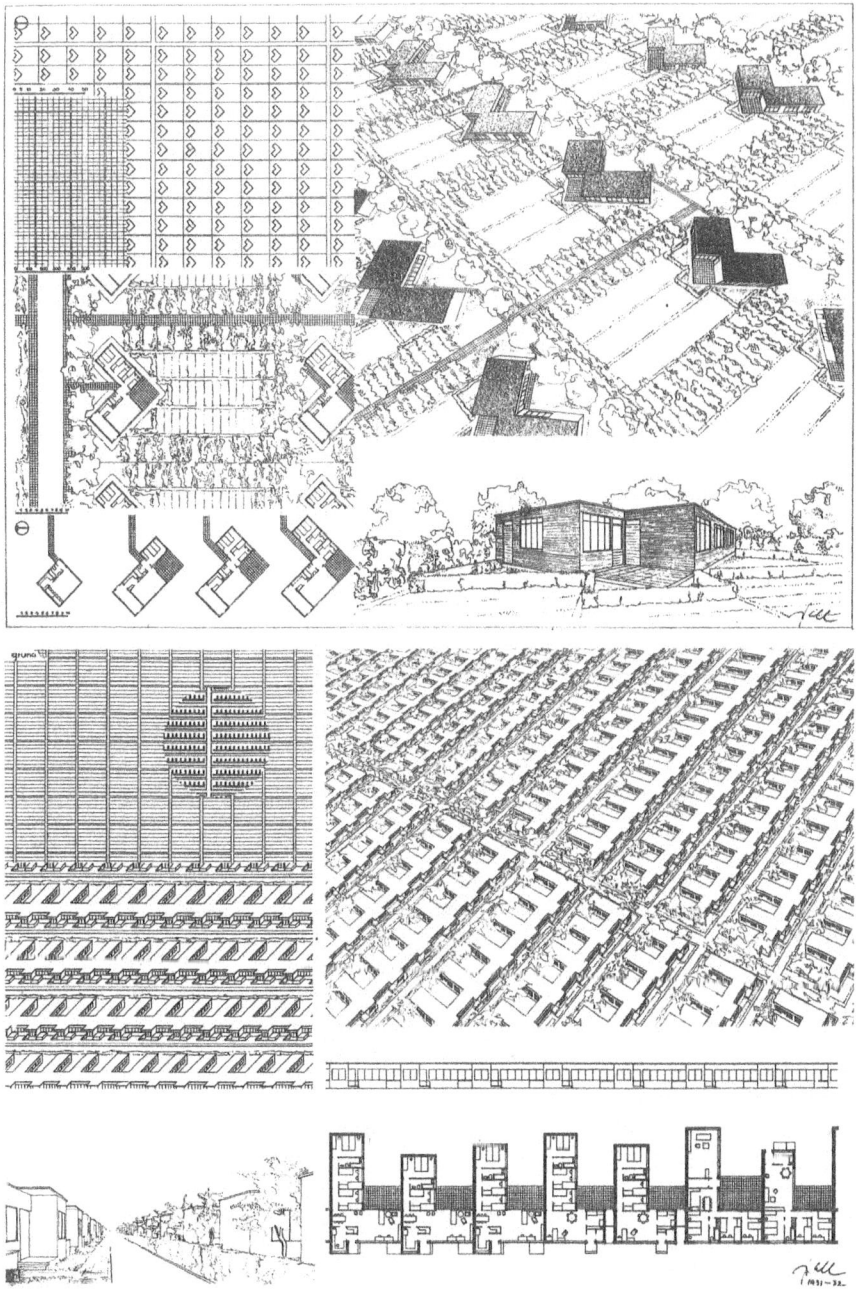

Figure 4.16: Pius Pahl: study on L-shaped housing settlements, 1931-1932, top: flat-buildings-settlement with L-formed, free-standing one family houses; bottom: chain building with expandable L-shaped row houses

160 The Mereological City: a reading of the works of Ludwig Hilberseimer

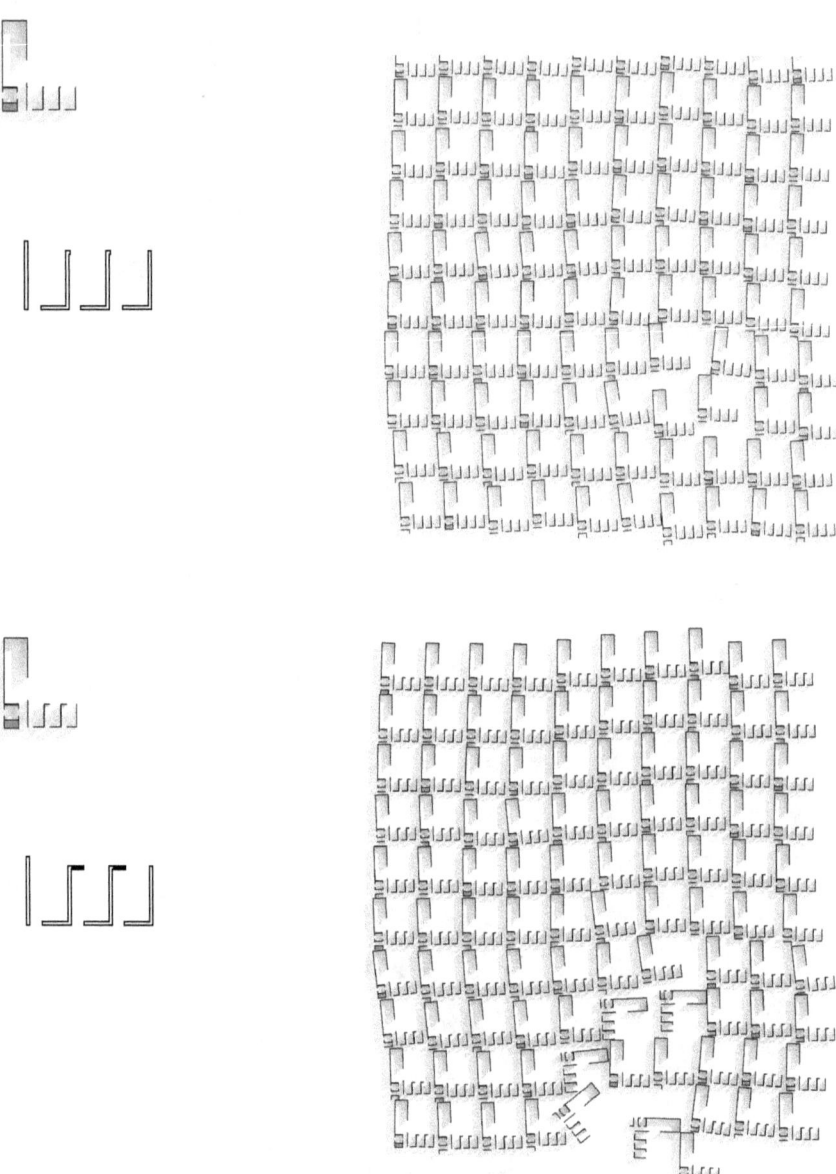

Figure 4.17: L-Shape house as settlement; differences in the composition of rooms lead to reorientation of the house and specific figurations of the settlement through the altered parthood relation of Room-Insolation. The black hatched area indicates the part, which provokes the character of the settlement layout

The unfolding of a planning idea 161

Figure 4.18: L-Shape house as settlement; differences in the composition of rooms lead to reorientation of the house and specific figurations of the settlement through the altered parthood relation of Room-Insolation. The black hatched area indicates the part, which provokes the character of the settlement layout

162 The Mereological City: a reading of the works of Ludwig Hilberseimer

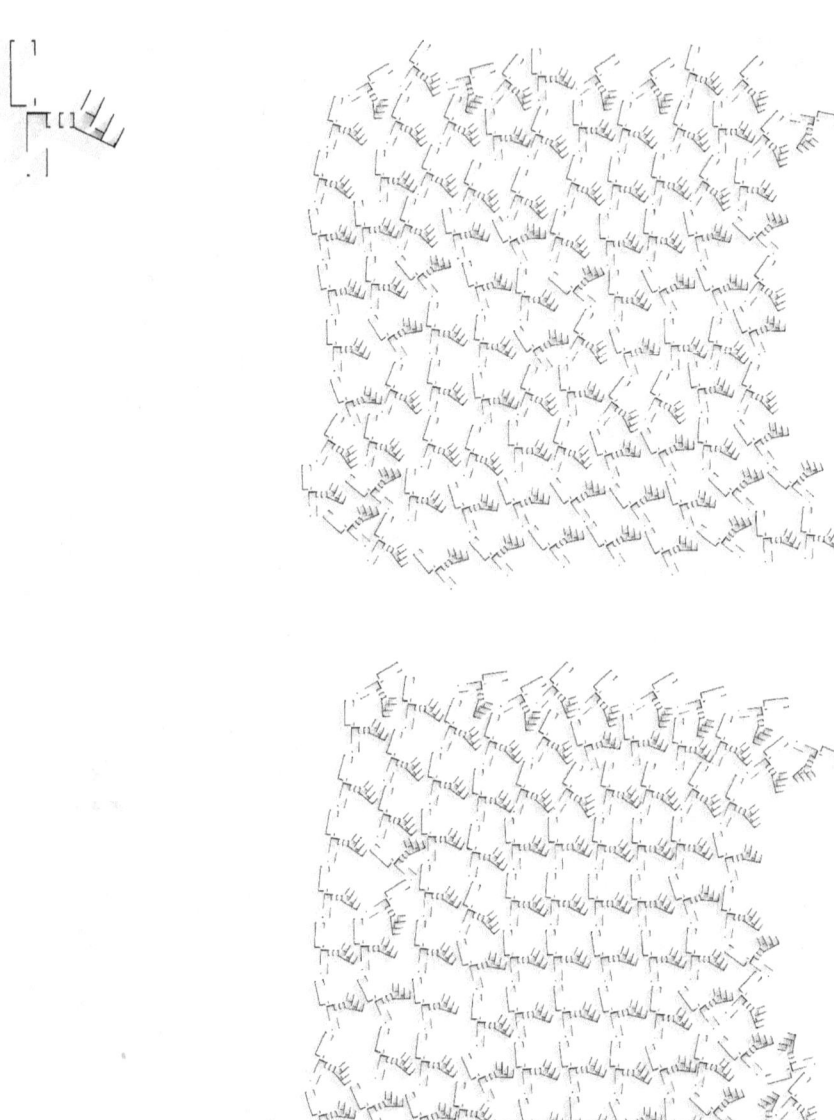

Figure 4.19: L-Shape house as settlement, study housetype C; a mereological schema provokes self-similar settlement layouts

The unfolding of a planning idea 163

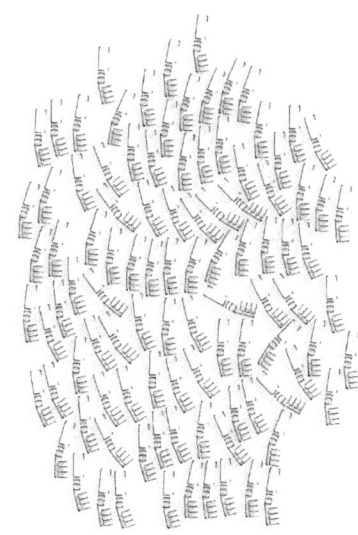

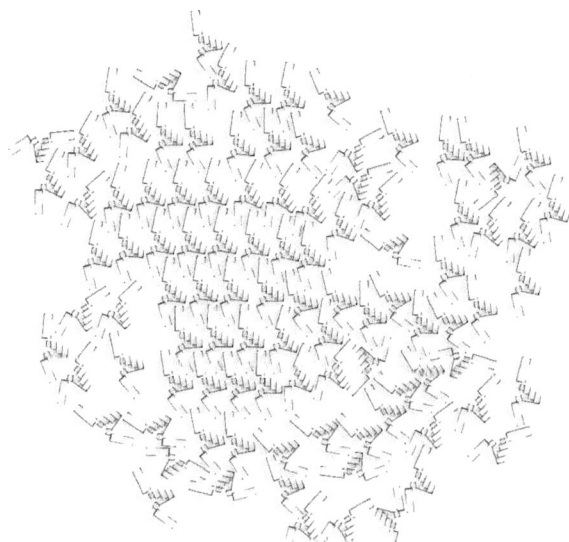

Figure 4.20: L-Shape house as settlement, top housetyp F, bottom housetyp H; each mereological schema incorporates a specific settlement layout

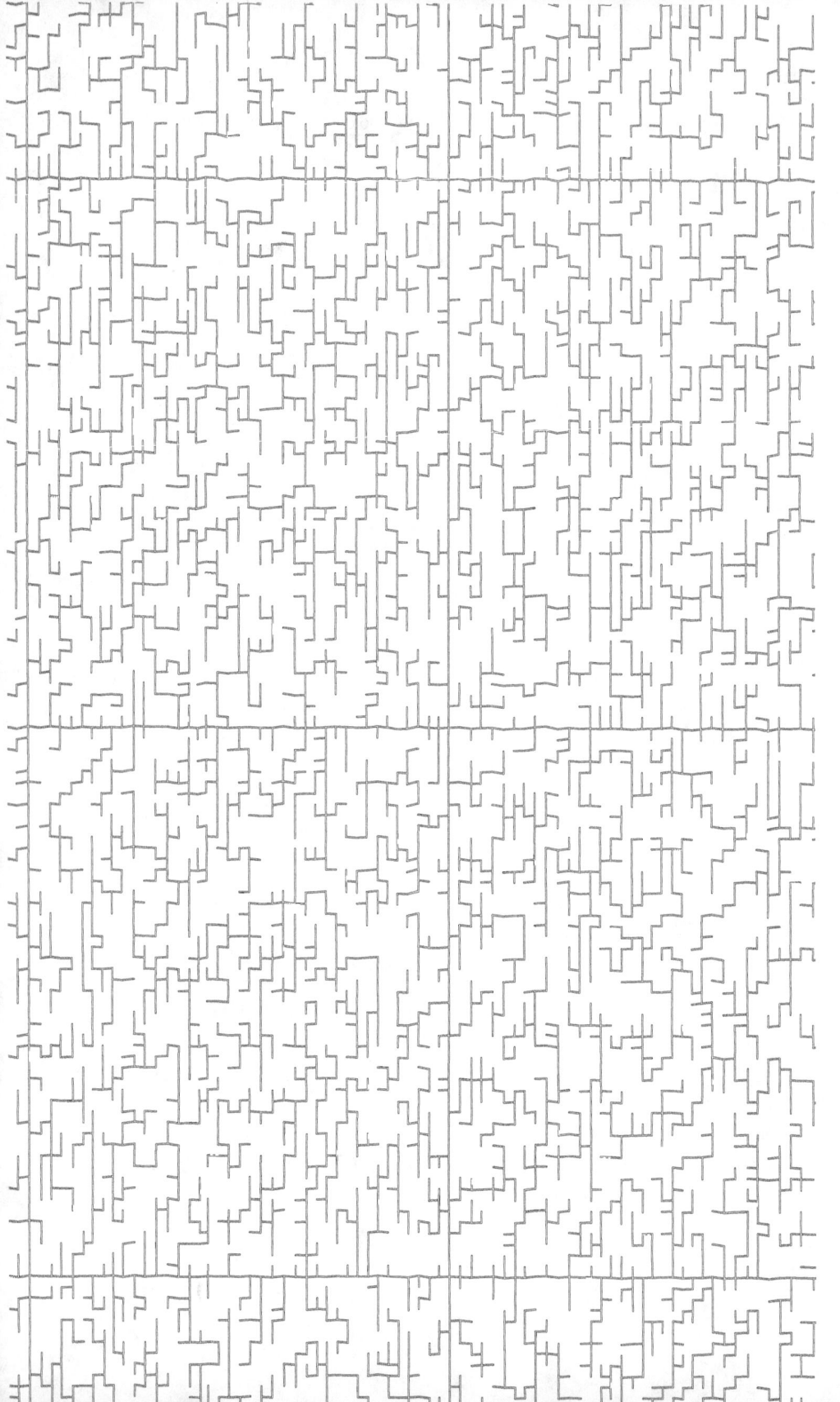

5 The punctualisation as architectural method

> Structure is the nature of architecture. A structure can be defined as relation of parts, and finally as an idea of parts. Structure is the embodiment of a conception. The form of architecture is a consequence of the structure. Form is fact made manifest.
> LUDWIG HILBERSEIMER. ARCHITECTURE: STRUCTURE AND FORM

5.1 THE CONCEPT OF FORM IN THE WORK OF HILBERSEIMER

Ludwig Hilberseimer developed architectural schemata as sensualisation of the term of the settlement for the planning of a house as part of the settlement. Part of the goals of this study was to clarify the concept of form in the work Hilberseimer's to record an appropriate representation of the formal relationship between the house and settlement. Let us now summarize what can be identified in the concept of form in the work Hilberseimer's:

Hilberseimer's formal operations associate the shape with contextual references. For Hilberseimer the form is not the outward appearance of a thing. Form is not the limitation of materiality. Form is not the opposite of matter as its contour or silhouette. As we have seen through the study of Nietzsche's concept of form, Hilberseimer uses the term analog to Nietzsche: Form as the equivalent of a region and a content. Form is not a hull, in the sense of an enclosure, but the zone of frenzy, of the contents. The edge is merely a cessation of the content but no limit. In contrary to the concept of form as contour, form do not limit the content and is the Matter, the frenzy itself.

With the analysis of the draft Chicago Tribune Towers it was apparent that the facade seals the building in terms of function, therefore naturally enclosures. But as part of the building its shape is the rhythm of columns and floor plates, so part of the zone of the building. The shape of the facade is the expression of a mereological relation between columns and plates and thus part of that area. The facade is not a textile carrier of a cultural narratives, their criticism or the similar, but the shape of the form of the house. The nakedness of the facade is the expression of the joining of architectural parts to each other. The social reference only happens indirectly through the economic and technical aspects of the parts.

Form results in the unity of spirituality and material[1]. For Hilberseimer form is the inscription of an idea into a material medium. By analyzing the inscription of the sun in an architectural design, we were able to see how the idea of Room-Insolation is transferred to the proportion between mass and free space. The political vision of a better constitution of society is transmitted as a therapeutic effect of the individual to the room in an idea of the joining of rooms and ultimately the reorganization of the cities. The postulated claim means a transformation of partial aspects between the elements of the various collectives. In this way the reference is uncoupled from reproduction. The design of the reference takes place reciprocally through the expression of the shape of the settlement as an expression of the form of the settlement, without a direct bridge between the collectives as a symbol. Through the inscription a shift takes place, which at first sight and depending on the view, allows to collapse one of the two opposites into the other. On the one hand, cultural aspects, represented by the individual seem to be expressible by nature. On the other hand, by definition incomprehensible nature becomes a design element, conceived as one element for the representatives of culture. If both are absorbed in constant change, what is the argument for the preservation even of one of the representatives? Here, a succeessful approach is the composition of real part without categorization into one of the two representatives.

In the link of idea and matter, Hilberseimer implements Nietzsche's concept of the Sensual-Corporeal. Both relate to each other in the designed work of art in a ratio of tension. The idea becomes the will, or more precisely to Alois Riegl's concept of Kunstwollen. The will opposes the corporeal, as representation, interpretation and abstraction of the corporeal.

The defined area of the form, the Sensual-Corporeal, is distinguished from the Other by the cessation of the Self. Thus form creates duration and continuity. The accidental characteristics of an object and thus the appearance are opposed to form. The thing is the expression of an inherent will. This representation of form is rooted in Aristotle's term $ευτελης$. Based on this concept from the autonomous object and its subjective viewing Kant builds and draws the conclusion, that form is a gift of the Spirit in addition to the perceived object. A recognition can only be done out from the corporeal. The recognition of a corporeal is therefore an interpretation, a perspective on others, to participate in the Other. Later, Konrad Fiedler and Adolf von

Hildebrand differentiated between the form of existence and the form of effect. As Heidegger showed in his interpretation of Nietzsche's aesthetics, a work of art arises from a back-coupled interaction of frenzy, beauty, creation and cognition and form. The form shifts from something that is circling to something that is spatial. Then to recognize something means resistance to something else corporeal. The interpretation of the Other from its own corporeal outwards is an interpretation and takes place with a sense of order: designing.

For the design this means, that the architectural elements are described as compositions by a specific participating-on-one-another, therefore mereologically. The architectural element is designed by the interpretation of the form of effect of the neighborhood. The recognition of the corporeal is reflected by the will of the other and by a requirement for the form of existence of the corporeal. The form is evaluated by beauty, in the classical sense of Alberti's concinnitas, just as a participating-on-the-other, as content of the parts for each other. Thus form aesthetically is the opposite of the sublime, appearance, contour and always explicitly tangible as a linkage whole.

The relevant part relationships in Hilberseimer's planning are minimum standards for the neighborhood relations. The figure is limited and specified by the sum of the mereological relations. As we have seen in the analysis of the urban schemata of the Vertical-City, it is only the reduction of limitation which allows diversity. Architecturally, the partial relationship translates to a distance, a proportion, a rhythm, a between, a free space of the settlement.

Because an idea is always absolute, form also is a unique totality. "Works of art are boundaries of the factual"[2]. Their limit makes them tangible, describable. A form is used to separate different ideas of the factual. The form becomes a statement. The form is complete in time and space and only assessable based on its own relation between ideas and material. The form of the distinction is thus not the distinction between One and Other, but the multiplicity of singularities of individual self-contained elements. The autonomy only becomes visible to the means of diplomacy. Only in the multitude the individual reaches an expression of autonomous form. Architecture as the diplomacy of autonomous elements means an architecture as a strategy to mereological composition by disposition of architectural elements. What remains is the design of the city by the determination of its elements by co-localization and their disposition. Form is always an order, an arrangement of parts.

Thus, the interaction between the organization of a single house and its disposition in the settlement is Hilberseimer's most important exercise in teaching. Since the era of the Bauhaus seminar, the designs were continuous variations of the same task: to design the building and its multiplicity in the settlement. The presentation took place in three drawings: the layout of the house to represent the individual form as the organization of rooms; a site plan schema as the multiplication of the individual house and third, a bird-view-perspective for the architectural evaluation of the surface of the settlement. This ratio was historically locatable in the formal analysis of the art historian Alois Riegl. It is the relationship between the form to surface, of the One as a figure and the Many as figuration.

At that point, Hilberseimer switches to the linear as representation technique. The figure is indeed characterized by its contour, by a boundary and therefore differs from an Other, buit at the same time remains transparent as a composition from parts. The figure is figuration and is only described by the complexity of the settlement as a shimmering rhythm consisting of landscape, houses, windows, roofs and gardens. The figure is produced in the space between the lines as a limitation of the parts. Meaning arises only in the figuration of directions and changes of direction, intervals and their sequences of parts as forms in the field of view of the surface of the settlement as ground. The architectural element on the one hand is created by a number of parthood-relationships and their overlap in an element and on the other hand, by the effect of its own multitude in an arrangement.

5.2 Punctualisation as method

Someone who is familiar with actor-network theory (ANT) will recognize a pattern throughout the previous study: The encapsulation of a network of relations to an actor. ANT originated as a critique of dialectical reasoning and technically can be seen as as a material-semiotic method in the field of philosophy of science. As a constructivist approach, ANT avoids existential statements as true or false and draws characters together, which are materially or semiotically involved in the production of the actor. As a discipline actor-network theory therefore deals with sociology and with strategies about how different elements relate to each other and are drawn together into a coherent whole. In sociology, ANT is therefore primarily a descriptive method to investigate so-called agencies as a sum of their parts. However, this does not happen in a structuralistic manner. As a contrast to structure ANT introduces the concept of the Agency. While structure refers to forces that affect an object, Agency is understood as the ability of an agent to act independently. Force, motion and limit are owned by the actors. A logical consequence of this is that a whole, an actor is always composed at the same time through a withdrawn network. A whole is always a composition of parts.

The punctualisation as architectural method 169

Figure 5.1: Alois Riegl: perforated bronzes; left: museum Klausenburg; bottom middle: collection Trau, Wien; bottom right: museum Linz

The way how a network is contracted to an actor and how a network is used as an actor is defined by ANT as punctualisation. As John Law[3] pointed out, punctualisation is a product being of a heterogeneous network. When a network acts as a single block, the network disappears from perception and is replaced by the action itself. The components of the action are absorbed from the figuration as a point: punctualized. The production and cause of the effect so becomes invisible. It is no longer relevant. By the habitual use of a network the pattern becomes a routine. The pattern is considered certain and repeatable and thus becomes a resource for more complex types of action. As punctualisation one describes the moment of absorption when objects participate in the constitution of a new entity[4].

Whitehead's point as the smallest element of an epistemological geometry The method of punctualisation borrowed its name from the geometric axiom "punct"[5]. According to a classical definition such as the Euclidean geometry, a point is defined as an axiom. The axiom usually describes the point as irreducible element without its own parts to determine an absolute position in space. It follows that each complex geometrical element like for example line or surface, builds on points. Each geometric element requiring the point as the absolute position in this way also becomes an absolute element. These geometries are thus simply unrelated to perceptible reality, they remain decoupled determinations. The elements do not form abstractions; but worlds of their own and are self-contained and independent from the presented. Alfred North Whitehead described the problem with the following words:

"The (Euclidean) geometry comes with the intention of studying specific forms of physical things. But in their initial definitions of the "point" and the "line" geometry seems to postulate directly certain fundamental physical things with very special properties. Even Plato seems to have had some clue about this confusion when he refused to acknowledge points as a separate class of things."[6]

Alfred North Whitehead attempted to solve this problem with a theory of space, in which all abstractions are based on concrete objects of our perception. In it position determinations cannot be made absolute, but only relative. As a relative position, the point itself becomes a complex entity consisting of the relations between the objects which construct the representational space[7]. It is a method to gain mathematical objects by abstraction of formal properties and concrete things through neglecting their specific qualities. The point so becomes the function of relations between empirically observed objects. The empirically non-perceptible point is abstracted from the concrete and perceptible. In return, the applicability on to our perceptual space should be ensured[8]. The point becomes an approximated minimum of the equivalence between the empirically perceived parts: the point as the smallest-possible-Common[9].

As approximations to a smallest-possible common, points are relative to the resolution of their mereological structure. Depending on the level of granulation[10] of the approximate smallest, the point must not necessarily be a point on another level of granulation. In a finer resolution points can turn out to be specific, structured entities.

This epistemologically founded term of the point accesses the punctualisation and thus indicates the approximate unit *and* the simultaneous multiplicity. It is precisely this moment of bifurcation that we are able recognize in Hilberseimer's ratio of house to settlement, form to surface. The moment between entity and network, the One and the Many. Without any question Hilberseimer could not have known the concepts of ANT's. However, the concept of punctualisation describes the demands raised in an old philosophical question. The roots can be traced back to Aristotle's definition of Hexis[11]. Hexis can be translated as being an active disposition as constitution. Similar to punctualisation Aristotle discussed Hexis as practical action, a behavior in time. In the context of practice Aristotle describes Hexis as an arrangement of parts (similar to the term Agency) in which the arrangement itself is a being and it has its own qualities[12]. Similar to Alberti's definition of concinnitas, Hexis only describes the constitutive character without external dialectical evaluation. In the Nicomachean Ethics Aristotle brings Hexis in direct reference to poiesis. The term poiesis alone describes a result-oriented action, the creation of a work with regard to the finished piece. The evaluation of the production is carried out not with looking at the action itself, but by the success and the use of a workpiece. A change of action takes place only indirectly by the finished work and the perception of the work piece. In the Nicomachean Ethics Aristotle explains that poiesis is created by $\tau\epsilon\chi\nu\eta$, the virtue of the disposition of the action ($\mu\epsilon\tau\alpha$ $\lambda o\gamma o\upsilon$ $\epsilon\xi\iota\varsigma$ $\pi o\iota\epsilon\tau\iota\kappa\epsilon$). Aristotle argues that $\tau\epsilon\chi\nu\eta$ cannot be anything else than the production itself. Opposed to Practice, where the act itself is knowledge and value (eg politics) and opposed to Theoria, which creates knowledge from the description of an action (eg metaphysics) Techne as the act of poiesis is only indirectly accessible. Knowledge is created through the evaluation of a poietic object. The production remains hidden. This also means that Techne has its origin in itself and consists only of knowledge of the disposition of the action. Purpose, use and material are requirements and qualities of the architectural element but not of the production. For the production purpose, use and material are transformed to quantitative statements to disposition, due to the evaluation of an architectural element[13].

So Hexis forms poiesis, which evaluates Hexis. It follows that an effective alteration of an architectural work can only be done by a self-reflection of its inner Techne as Hexis. For architecture it follows, that on the one hand an architectural element can not be evaluated during the making of the design, but only on the reflection of the positioned element. This indicates the disciplinary difference between Practice, so an evaluation during or by the emergence, and Poiesis, as formed Hexis. But there is one more difference to be noted between Poiesis and Theoria. The evaluation, innovation, the design itself, is not carried out by a Theoria, a consideration. The reflection of an architectural element takes place in the composition of its parts. Poiesis as Hexis as punctualisation means concatenating and opening, a de-punctuating of the ordinary. Architectural interventions are re-configurations of the existing architectural element. Poiesis designs by combining parts into a whole. A mereological understanding of the concept of form so becomes the basis for architecture.

Heidegger's beginning to an ecological metaphysics For the contemporary discourse the emphasis of punctualisation roots in the work of Martin Heidegger: In his introduction to the Bremen lectures, Heidegger in 1949 Heidegger begins with postmodernism's critique of technology[14]. Heidegger observed, that technology represents things as equipment, tools[15], as reliable serviceability of the environment for humanity. Heidegger reminds us that the representation of the environment as nature is an abstraction of real things. The role of technology as a tool of culture is to provide things ready-at-hand. Technique provides a conception of the real thing by assigning a role to the thing, with which you can rely on the thing as tool[16]. At this point it is Heidegger, who urges us to recognize things beside the tool-being, not as the hidden, but as the excluded:

"The tool grants in its reliability of this world an own necessity and proximity. While a world opens up, obtain all their things while and rush their far and near, their wide and narrowness. In worlding is those spaciousness gathered, from which the preserving grace of the gods is given away or fails."[17]

It is perhaps the origin of what we call ecological politics today. Far from the romanticized Wilderness and the Other or more efficient ornamentation of our houses with further technical artifacts Heidegger shows a course of action, which is absorbed later by Bruno Latour as a politics of nature:

"Political ecology does not speak about nature and has never sought to do so. It has to do with associations of beings that take complicated forms – rules, apparatuses, consumers, institutions, mores, cows, pigs, broods- and that is completely superfluous to include in an inhuman and ahistorical nature. Ecology dissolves nature's contours and redistributes its agents."[18]

The punctualisation is method as invitation. For the consideration, for the use, for the physics, to the space. The punctualisation opens the possibility of a conscious bifurcation between the disposition of the tool and the colocation of the thing in itself[19]. Here too, we are based on Heidegger and the subsequent interpretation Graham Harman's the tool-being. The presence of the tool and what is ready at hand of the thing "in worlding" as a competition between One and the Many, between the whole and its parts[20].

5.2.1 The punctualisation at Hilberseimer

Mies as a reference It is difficult to imagine an architectural object that is clearly a thing but simultaneously contains a plurality of entities. What more does the competition of One and Many hold for an architect than being simply a philosophical game of words? There is an architectural theory approach in the work of Mies van der Rohe's. As Michael Hays' analysis of the highrise Friedrichstrasse shows[21], the architectural object of the glass prism multiplies itself in the subjective perception of the flâneur. Or, as Richard Padovan's analysis of the Barcelona Pavilion[22] reconstructs it, unites the plurality of elements of the pavilion to a *Machines a mediter* in the subjective perception of the visitor. In the review of Mies' designs we already find the desired bifurcation between part and whole. It is only a small step to Ludwig Hilberseimer's settlement. While at Mies' highrise or pavilion, the bifurcation still occurs in dialogue with the viewer, the user of Hilberseimer can no longer maintain this dialogue in the distant view of the large scale. Hilberseimer must establish a detour. In the distance and multiplicity of the settlement, subject and object cannot be directly influenced. As Alois Riegl already pointed out, the down-sizing of the vision from near vision to far vision leads from a direct concern of the object, the haptic, to an indirect, spiritual relation: the optical[23]. Things receive their own autonomy. They begin to mean and to represent something. It is assumed that the observer reflects their vision as part of a cultural enrollment. Using a different cultural view, the object in view will appear strange, inaccessible as Riegl's Late Roman Art Industry.

In *Late Roman Art Industry* Riegl describes, how the late Roman art can be defined as altered art will to antiquity. The basic means of expression of the Kunstwollen is the relationship between form and surface. The intent of the Kunstwollen, Riegl divided into historical sequence in near vision, normal vision and distance vision. In a near vision a whole is detached from the ground and articulated by symmetry, accents, proportion. With its articulation, the whole thing resists the chaotic, withdrawn ground. The ground is suppressed, only the accent of the figure is crucial. With the normal view and the onset of individualization of the forms, the means of rhythm arises, ie the unity of the parts into a whole. The reason becomes figurative. The whole thing is differentiated by means of grouping and sequence of the similar (rhythm) and in this way stands out from the background.

The late Roman art era increases to distance vision until finally the single form detaches from the universal visual plane. The single form is isolated from the ground and only connected to other individual forms[24]. Thus the interval that is a part of the rhythm is emancipated and itself becomes a form-creating figure. As an intermediate space and the only coherent element of consideration, the definition of the interval becomes the ground. The figure became ground. For the single form and rhythm the following consequences unfold: The single form, detached from any context, can be represented only in loose appearance. For Riegl the single form arises in the abstraction of geometry. Furthermore, the rhythm will express itself in a different way: Instead of articulation and accentuation, so as contra-compositional contrast, the interval is now aspiring a uniform sequence.

More than 80 years later, Deleuze and Guattari appointed Riegl's intuition to a model of aesthetics of nomadic art[25]. The shift of figure-ground to figure-figuration, Deleuze and Guattari describe as the difference between a neurotic and psychopathic view.[26]. For Deleuze and Guattari a neurotic differentiates between the one and the other. In the neurotic model of thought, an object is defined by a contrast to an Other, so similar to Riegl's Egyptian Kunstwollen, where the figure is opposed to a background. For the neurotic one object can only be transmitted by another object, ie as a symbolic reference. But in contrast to the neurotic, the psychopath differentiates between the thing as One and the thing as Many. For the psychopath one thing always simultaneously is also an assembly of Many. A thing is defined in its figurative composition of other objects.

The removal of the ground My argument is, that house and settlement in the work Hilberseimer are linked analogous to Alois Riegl's relation between form and surface. The ground of a settlement is not the soil but its constituents, its houses themselves.

This would put Hilberseimer's project into radical contrast to the planning of the city based on a territory and its subdivision into plots: short city planning based on land speculation. This means that in Hilberseimer's work it must be possible to give ground a different meaning, as architectural and especially economic strategy. An approach can be found in Hilberseimer's requirement of population density in the form of the settlement. Together with the selected housing types, density determines approximately the size of the Settlement-Unit. To choice of density as a design element is unusual[27]. Usually it is only the density, which is shaped by various planning requirements. In the specific case of the Settlement-Unit one could assume, that the requirement of the Room-Insolation specifies a distance relation, which under maximization of the plot would lead to a building cubature and ultimately to a value of the density. But if the value of the density itself is part of the description of the figure, it can be assumed that one of the ordinary urban elements of design - cubature, housing typology, insolation-distance or plot – is obsolete. If cubature and housing typology are as well part of the specification, there are two scenarios:

(A) the insolation distance between the buildings is to ensure a minimum distance and only relevant to guarantee a minimum room-insolation. For larger plots the choice of building location and type would be unbound. The planning would allow thus a variable design. But with limited combinatorics of building types, by large plots a required density could no longer be achieved. Therefore, the plot size, too affects the parameters of the Room-Insolation and the maximum possible density. In this scenario, population density cannot be a requirement for the settlement.

(B) The definition of the ground as land parcel does not exist or is irrelevant for the planning. Requirements to the density, insolation distance and the combinatorics of housing types design a settlement. At low density and choice of housing types insolation distance is also no longer an issue. The determinates allow a variable design.

Already in his early theoretical texts[28] Hilberseimer speaks against land speculation and therefore against a planning role of the plot as the ground for architecture. The architectural interventions Hilberseimer's try to overcome the plot as ground. In his early designs Hilberseimer calls for the merger of small-scale plots to provide housing collectives[29]. Property is not defined by individual floor plots per house, but first as a consolidated common property[30]. The large city is no longer extended individually from house to house, but by means of satellites[31]. Large City Architecture here refers to the consolidation of plots, its impact on the size of the resulting "Großform" and the independence of architectural elements from land-speculation.

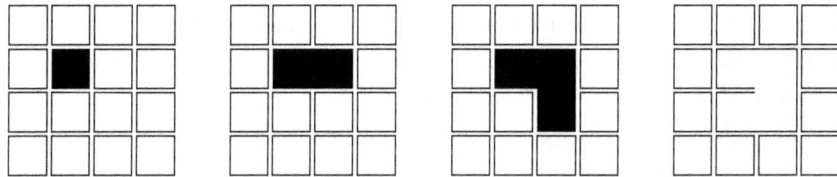

Figure 5.2: Schema: influence of road segments on the assignability of plots; from left to right: the removal of road segments leads to not closed and therefore ambigious land contours

The clearest strategy for the dissolvement of plots can be found in the late plan studies at IIT, studies on the reorganization of the city. Here, Hilberseimer and his thesis students used one strategy repeatedly: The subtraction of street segments. Based on the existing and mostly closely meshed network of streets, they are extracted in steady, temporal sequence[32]. The interruption of the street space creates the famous Cul-de-Sacs, the dead ends and the tree-like layout of the settlement unit. In terms of spacial planning, this intervention has far-reaching consequences for the American city. In a rasterized city the plots of land are clearly defined by its boundary, the boundary lines of the streets. The rasterized subdivision of the city thus produces convex plot figures. By subtracting an edge and street segment plots are at first consolidated. Mostly oblonged or L-shaped plot contours arise. But if one extracts more street segments dead end streets emerge. Therefore the plot contour becomes non-convex and thus not clearly attributable anymore. The previously clear defined convex demarcation transforms into a continuous, free space through the elimination of streets. With the blurring of plots the ground loses its necessary unique affiliation for speculation and thus its meaning. The subtraction of the street disempowers the economic speculation on the plot as ground of the city. What is left to speculation are the architectural elements themselves. Thus, one of the first demands Hilberseimer achieved: from the speculation of the plot to a speculation of the commonplace object, which will bring the quality and specific articulation of the object to the foreground.

Similar to a three-set, first the element to be designed is extracted by analyzing and describing its parts. In the second step, the city is read as a plurality of the extracted element and its transforming parts. In the third step, a time-operative intervention of the part leads to the reorganization of the city and thus to the revaluation of the element to be designed.

From the beginning on, Hilberseimer understood city planning as a political tool[33]. As a planning tool, city planning sets the framework for economy and not vice versa. A political demand so becomes a spatial planning requirement for the reorganization of the industrial city[34]. The urbanistic conclusion of the reorganization is a political-economic promotion of object instead of land speculation[35]. The apartment becomes an economic object itself. In order for the apartment to be an object, it must be able to break away from the plot. If the soil is no longer the ground of the city, architecture must be economically grounded in other ways. Hilberseimer's approach is the transformation of architectural elements into economical products: to utilities, which are determined by their intended use[36]. The apartment and its qualitative properties themselves are to be regarded as an economic product. The title Vertical-City should be just that: the vertical organization of the city, rather than a horizontal speculation over the plot. The ground of the building is no longer the land parcel, but the structure of the cells, of the rooms, the houses in the city[37]. The later Settlement-Unit is the formulation of previous planning requirements. Demands for the architectural organization describe the settlement according to its mass and as an economic product. The economic value of the house is created by its disposition in a settlement. Speculation loses its immovable mobility of reference. While in the Cartesian localization of the plot speculation is transferable and interchangeable here, through the concatenation of the neighborhoods, speculation is intransparent. The value of the architectural object is speculative, unique and non-transferable by its specification as overdetermination through composition.

The ground as Synoikism Like in any of his other strategies, Hilberseimer abstracts his economic strategy from a historical conception. The idea that the value of a house is gained by its disposition in the settlement, Hilberseimer takes from the Aristotelian description of the Greek polis, or more precisely from the concept of Syn-

The punctualisation as architectural method 177

Existing

1. Phase

2. Phase

3. Phase

Figure 5.3: Hilberseimer, Plan of Chicago, Southside District, Chicago, 1951

oikism. In *The New City* Hilberseimer proposes a concept of property, which defines property not by individual floor plots per house, but first as consolidated communal property. Each owner bearing on the joint ownership shares the value of their house. Each owner would bear on the joint ownership shares in the value of his house[38].

In *Politika*[39] Aristotle describes the house as a corporation of building, family, slaves, goods. The village is an extension of the house. The state is a community of several houses. A community Aristotle defines as those consisting for the "good life", beyond self-sufficiency[40]. For this Aristotle chooses the word: Synoikism. The cause of a whole as a surplus value for its parts. A surplus is created when multiple elements form a larger entity. Hilberseimer takes over this concept of Synoikism[41]. For Hilberseimer, the city's history is a story of the advantage of living in increasingly larger communities. From the hut as weather protection for a family to village gatherings for trading, to the walled cities of the Greeks and medieval times in need for protection against war: the larger settlement always leads to better conditions for its inhabitants. But according to Aristotle and Hilberseimer, it is the city which first enables culture. Only above a certain size and diversity of the co-existence of its parts, cultural exchange is enabled. But the city is, according to Aristotle, limited in size: it should be small enough for every citizen to hear a speaker at the Agora [42]. The city should create a ground for each of its citizens. Each effect should be effective for each part of a whole. The qualities of the whole are self-reflective. Therefore, the greatest form of Synoikism is the autonomous, self-sufficient settlement, while any demand of a part can be met from the effects of the whole. According to Aristotle, the size of the territory, the region of a city, is determined by the needs of its residents [43]. The development of the New Regional Pattern is taken by Hilberseimer directly from Aristotle's *Politeia*:

"Every State," said Aristotle, "is a community of some kind, and every community is established with the view to some good; for mankind always acts in order to obtain that which it thinks good. But, if all communities aim at some good, the state or political community, which is the highest of all, and which embraces all the rest, aims at good in a greater degree than any other, and at the highest good."[44]

Against this background Hilberseimer limits the size of the Settlement-Unit. Later, in *The Nature of Cities*[45], Hilberseimer explains the reasons for limiting in detail. On the one hand, a settlement unit should be large enough to enable the essentials of a community. This means that the settlement should be large enough to carry all the necessary cultural, hygienic and shared facilities and to enable a variety of living and working conditions for each individual. At the same time a settlement unit should be small enough in order for each resident to actively influence communal activities.

Here too, we find parallels to Plato's *Politeia* und Aristotle's *Politeia*, which Hilberseimer mentioned explicitly:

"Aristotle, however, recognized other considerations influencing the size of a city. It should be small enough, he thought, so that every citizen could hear the speaker on the Agora; large enough lo provide as many hoplites as any neighboring city with which it might come into conflict. It had to be prepared against aggression."[46]

The Agora is the "Open Space" of the Settlement Unit. In each scale of the settlement planning, principles are formulated which limit the design and its objects to enable open space. Open Space is the new symbol of the American Agora: the agora as unoccupied space to individual development. The only buildings in Open Space are schools[47]. While all other administrative and commercial buildings are located in the distance between Green Highway and living area, the schools are in the open park landscape, so the Open Space, located between residential areas. They also serve as a community center, library and exhibition halls[48]. As the Open Space is a transformation of the Greek Agora, the school replaces another type of Greek city: the Prytaneion. While the Agora was the meeting place of all citizens, their representatives met in Prytaneion for the practice of daily politics. In Prytaneion the holy fire of Hestia, goddess of the domestic hearth, was burning. The catering in the Prytaneion was allowed only to the most outstanding honorary citizens of a city. Max Weber pointed out, that the Prytaneion as a house with cultic meals represented the act of synoikism[49]. The catering as table community Weber sees as a consequence of the brotherhood of individual city families. As the hearth of the individual house, the Prytaneion is the hearth of the city. Hilberseimer replaces the Prytaneion as a place of common physical strengthening with the school as a place of common spiritual education and community gathering place. The ancient Greek city serves as a quantitative model for the Settlement Unit. However, Hilberseimer mixed the model of Greek democracy with the model of the physical ancient city. While during ancient times it was possible to design a city as part of democracy, since residents and city constituted the same political entity, this possibility no longer exists in modern times. The transfer of synoikism as an idea of ground in Hilberseimer leads to a politics of elements. Hilberseimer dissolves the city from its real inhabitants, just by the functional and schematic inscription into architectural elements. The city so becomes a hermeneutic entity. The space of the elements negotiated by politics, for its inhabitants becomes open space, decoupled from politics.

180 The Mereological City: a reading of the works of Ludwig Hilberseimer

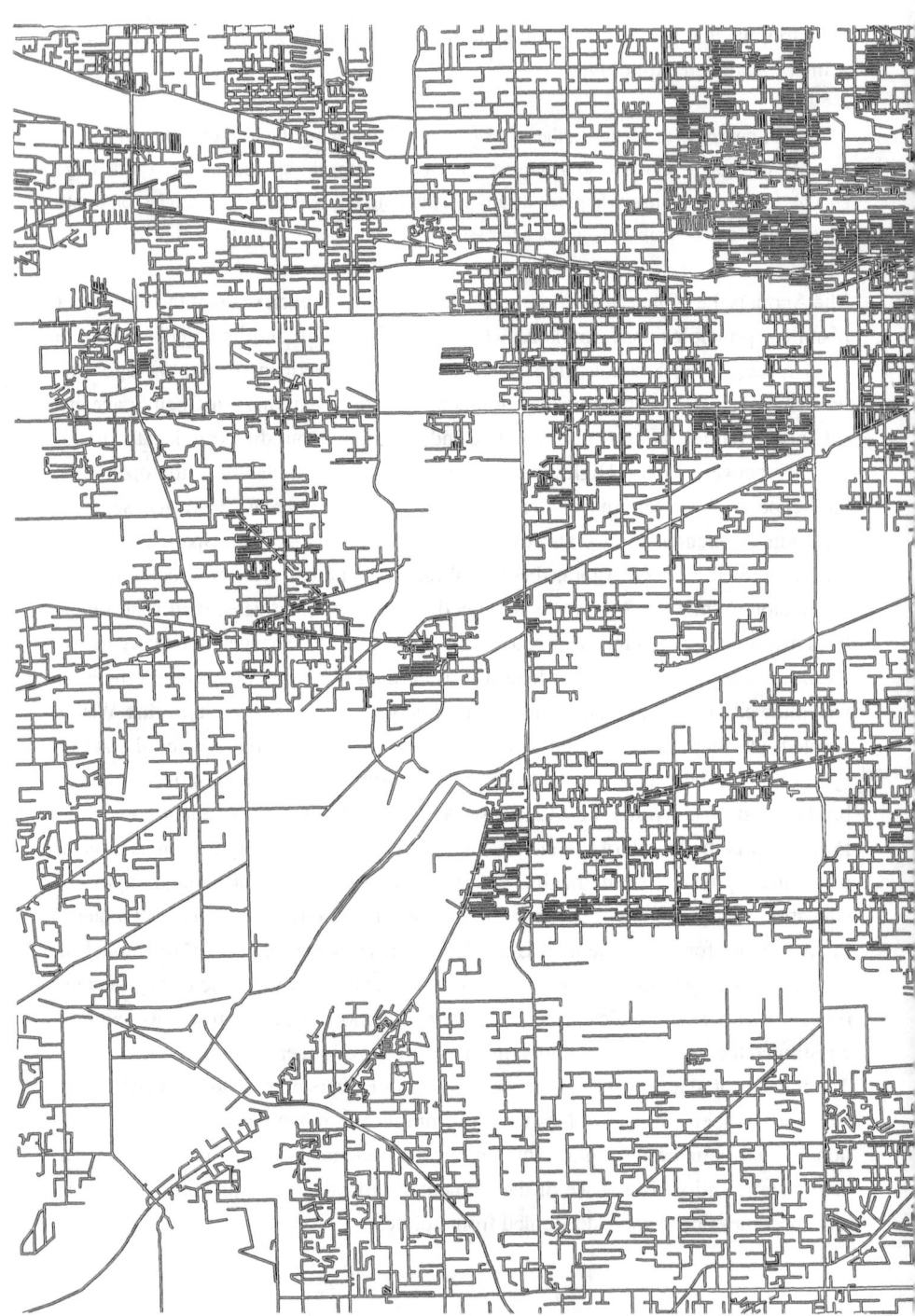

Figure 5.4: Plan of Chicago, according to the schema of removing street segments

The punctualisation as architectural method 181

5.3 ROOM, HOUSE, TOWN, REGION:
A MEREOLOGICAL ANALYSIS

Finally, I would like to analyze the mereological relation between house and settlement graphically. Hilberseimer, in his manuscript *Physical Planning, a textbook*[50] described four plateaus on which the elements are negotiated with respect to each other: Room-House-Town-Region. Each plateau is regarded as a figure, ie, as a whole, which is linked via parthood-relations to other plateaus. *The Whole is a part for the part as whole.* As we were able to demonstrate with the concept of form in Hilberseimer's work, the transformation is done in two steps: First, an object for another object is reduced to a utility as economic relation. In the second step, the relationship to architectural elements is transformed by the entanglement of a plurality of the part. As a result, the economic value in proportion to the parts simultaneously negotiates the strategy of the plateau.

Room, house, settlement and region can be described mereologically, so by the kind of their parthood-relations, in two ways: Through their mereological *Bottom*, so by a part which each part of the composition has in common, or as mereological *Bound*, so the part which is part of the composition. The figure of the whole as bottom is a mereological overlap of parts. The overlap as distance, wall, door, proportion, is considered its own part in the relationship between two other parts. For instance, the house is described by the disposition of the kitchen near the entrance. The schema of the house is expressed in the physical *Overlap* between the kitchen and the entrance: so the house is a part of the house. The bound the figure of the whole is described as a part of something else with a requirement for a part of the whole. As mereological bottom, the whole forms an *Underlap* with the part. Thus, the figure of the settlement is expressed as the maximum walking distance from one house to another settlement area: the settlement becomes measurable by the geometric path length depending on the position of the house. In both cases, the whole is a part for the part as a whole. Within the meaning of punctualisation, the one is described as one in relation to others or as a composition of many. The fabric of the parthood-relations defines the city as materiality, similar to the fabric of the mereological line from the introduction of this investigation. In the following, the mereological relations of room, house, settlement and region are presented. The type of relations are distinguished between mereological *Bottom* and *Bound*. Each architectural element here is described on the one hand as composition of parts, so as *Underlap*, or on the other hand as part of a composition, ie, as *Overlap*[51]

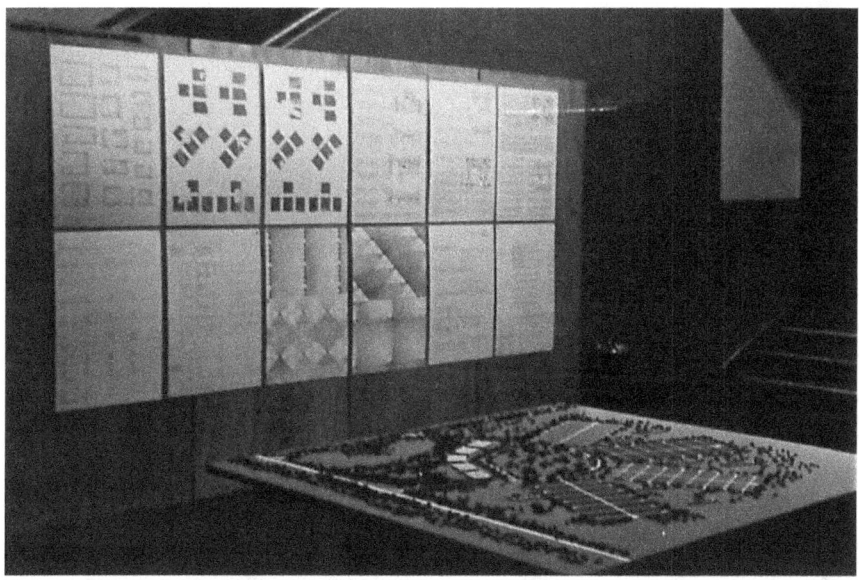

Figure 5.5: exhibition »Open House«at IIT, ca. 1950; coherent planning of a settlement from the design of a room to the influence of the region

Room   At first sight it is not really obvious why city planning can be described by relations of individual rooms and even relations of individual room elements. Hilberseimer explains the relations of a room and his part-being within the settlement in *Physical Planning, a textbook*[52] summarized as follows: The proportion of the room has an influence on motion sequences, as well as the position of furniture towards each other. Location and size of doors and windows not only affect exposure and accessibility, but also utility and sense of the room arrangement and the furniture. The wall openings bind the room to a spatial structure: the house. The location and size of the openings depends on the one hand on the arrangement of the furniture, on the other hand on the orientation of the house itself and the location of the room inside the spatial structure. If a room should have more than a certain amount of sun insolation duration, conditions this its orientation, the size of the openings (depending on the reveal depth). However, rooms are also weighed by their distinction of exposure duration, like the living room and side room. In addition, the orientation of the rooms will also have an influence on figure and orientation of the house. The distance between the houses also determines the sun insolation of a room. Thus, indirectly, the duration of exposure has an influence on the settlement pattern, as the proportion of the houses towards each other. By linking the settlement to the physical elements of a room such as wall, ceiling, opening, surface, etc., the settlement becomes explicite.

Probably, the best known relation of a room is the Room-Insolation. The light prism is the overlap of the settlement and the room. The settlement is as part transformed to a part of the room volume. The light prism depends essentially on two parts: the opening between room and settlement and the orientation of the room. The type of the opening is designed in detail by its proportion, size, location of the opening and its revealed depth. The opening is framed (Bound) between the boundaries of the room and is influenced by the neighborhood, the visibility from other houses. The orientation of the room depends on the organization of the house and the density of the settlement. On the one hand, for the light prism the figure serves for evaluation of room and settlement, on the other hand the light prism is framed by part relations between room-settlement and house-settlement.

The Room-Insolation is alternately described on different plateaus as a bottom (plateau room) or bound (Plateau room element, settlement). The abstract term of Room-Insolation can thus be replaced by explicit architectural elements in the intersection of plateaus. The mereologically complementary relations transform the dynamic element of the sun in the static element of the window opening or room orientation.By the relation of Room-Insolation it can be demonstrated well , that a parthood relation is an individual object. The overlap is not the room itself, which is never fully described by mereological relations. As a linkage-whole, every relation creates its own shape, here on the hand as differentiated edge line of the settlement or as marked part of the room volume.

Further parthood-relations of the room are: In the private rooms as well as in the master bedroom, the position of furniture depends both on the position of the door and the length of the walls perpendicular to the outer wall. If the room does not have enough space to set up the furniture, one of the inner walls is folded into a niche. If a private room has far more area than is required for positioning the furniture, another room with less space is created. The position of the desk in a private room is located on the outer wall and the revealed height and remaining floor space decide whether the table is oriented tangentially or perpendicular to the outer wall. The value in use of a kitchen is determined by the quality of the work area. Depending on the proportion of the kitchen, the position of the doors can extend the work area. The sequence of furniture decides on their use.

The previous part relations are descriptions of rooms using their geometric subordinate elements, such as wall openings, furniture, ie internal parthood-relations. The following part-relations are descriptions of the room as the overlap from room to room, house to room and settlement to room.

The living room can on the one hand be divided by the disposition of walls and openings and on the other hand by the superposition with other rooms, as crossing, as an insertion or tangential position. The corridor can be determined as the shortest connection of bathroom and private rooms. The location of the terrace is determined as the intersection of the living room and garden.

The garden as a room spans another parthood relation: Gardens are intended at a certain size, to be used as vegetable gardens. Due to the possibility of self-sufficiency, for Hilberseimer the dependence is reduced to an employment relationship. Larger gardens mean more leisure time for the people, working hours in a company can be reduced. The ability to self-sufficiency means more stability in difficult economic times[53]. Indirectly, larger gardens mean for the settlement, that the proportional relations between residential and industrial sectors are weakened. This applies both to the size ratio between the two, which number of residents is coupled with the number of employees to parameters such as the walking distance between the two areas, which has influence on the contour of the settlement.

House A house can be described by parthood relations of architectural elements in relation to rooms. So the house is the fixed neighborhood and thus wall element between the kitchen and living room, between the entrance and kitchen or between private rooms and a garden. The house can also be described as parthood relation of separation. So the house is the maximum distance between the entrance and private rooms. The entrance is in fixed relation between the personal and living rooms and so divides the house into two areas. The house can also be described by the ratio of properties of rooms to each other. In this case, the areas of private and living room are proportional to each other.

The figure of the building is dependent on the orientation of the rooms. The parthood relation of sufficient sunlight for rooms results in a high density of settlement to the folding of the house around a private space, the garden: an L-house is produced. The house stands between street space and private space and divides the settlement in publicly-developed and undeveloped areas. The conditions of neighborhood of the house determine the allocation of the facade of the house in enclosed areas, small or large wall openings. The exterior walls adjacent to neighboring houses are closed, the outer walls to the street have small openings, while the garden is framed to the outer wall with large openings. The division of the facade is not, as in a classic case, in relation to the elevation of the house, but in the intersection of outdoor and indoor use.

Settlement A central parthood relation of a house in the settlement is the minimum room insolation and its influence on the density of the settlement. The maximum settlement density depends on the sun radiance angle and thus resulting insolation of the house and on the other hand depends on the cubature and thus the self-shadowing of a house. The settlement density is therefore determined by the parts' sun radiance angle and buildings' cubature; generalized: the settlement is described as Bound and included as part of the region and the house. In the case of the Vertical-City, this was the only parthood relation between the elements: sun-density-building. From the study of Room-Insolation[54] Hilberseimer develops additional parthood relations between sun-density-building. These relations are complementary defined as bottom of the settlement. As an overlap of regional latitude the minimum proportion varies between the buildings' cubature and maximum settlement density. Furthermore, parts of the building are described as a bottom of the settlement density. The design of the roof as well as the storey height affect the minimum distance between buildings and thus the maximum settlement density. Only in the two-sided mereological description as a bottom *and* bound the insolation finds a design expression.

With reference to the relation between the house and settlement density as inscription of a minimum distance as part of the house, it becomes clear why the essential exercise in Hilberseimer's seminars is to design a house and its settlement. The settlement becomes the part of the house, a speculation of its own relation to a possible neighborhood. The drawing of the settlement is no longer a master plan, no frame, but the projection of an inner multiplicity. The settlement is the description of a possible neighbor relationship, designed by a minimum possible mutual interference.

A similarly constructed relation between house and settlement is the demand for privacy. This requirement is considered as parthood relation inscribed in the isolation and intransigence of the house in relation to neighboring houses. The lowest possible insight into a building leads to different articulations of the buildings' figure depending on the size of the free space. The higher the settlement density, the more fixed and uniform the building figure becomes as a result of entering an overlap with other buildings from several sides. With lower density, so if there is no overlap with neighboring buildings, the shape of the building is also not limited by the partial relation of insight. The house figures can vary greatly in the settlements of lower density.

The materiality of the settlement fabric in this way for example does not correspond to a continuous network, while linked nodes are connected to each other at any time. In the contrary: Without a superposition of partial relations, house figures do not affect each other. This is evident in the peripheral areas of a settlement with low density, Figure 5.15: In the inner part of the settlement, the parthood relations between the houses do not affect each other due to low densities. The house-figures there correspond the prototypical house types. In the peripheral areas it comes to modification and variation of house types, due to the entanglement with the new part relationships. Analogous to the Hippodamus plan of Millet, the settlement fabric is matter of an organic design, which only becomes visible under friction. Similarly to the difference between a heap and a collection of loose stones, a specific figure results only through friction and resistance of objects when touching. But in contrast to a pile of stones as a collection of rigid objects, the house and the settlement affect each other through a plurality of disparate, complementary or contradictory parthood relations. The heap becomes an entanglement. The circularity of the mereological relations requires a softness of the elements.

Streets are passive elements in the settlement. Congruent to Hilberseimer's demand for a city planning that is independent of land speculation, the street in the Settlement-Unit is not a design element but is designed. The used basic type of a fish bone pattern is always the same and is based on economic considerations of a ribbon city. But instead of being laid out on a territory to predetermine the allocation of houses, the street layout is incorporated into the settlement and is dependent on the desired orientation of the houses, a position from house to garage or the relief of the territory.

Nature is for Hilberseimer a figurative element and utility. For Hilberseimer as modernist, Nature is a designed product for the benefit of man[55]. Therefore, Hilberseimer distinguishes between *Wilderness* as untouched and *Nature* as cultivated landscape. On the architectural level, nature serves as figurative element to camouflage free-standing single-family-houses[56]. The settlement interweaves with the landscape, is visualized as rhythm, only accentuated by the solitaries of the apartment houses. Nature as designed element is the symbol of the settlement as a community. No single building embodies the vision of the settlement community, but the designed region into which the settlement is integrated. The subtlety of the landscape refuses symbolic signification of a single object. If the landscape is designed as a utility value for the single individual, expresses by inference the landscape the value of each individual. As David Spaeth noticed, with this Hilberseimer was able to transform the dominance of the humanistic approach into a balanced interaction between man and nature[57][58].

Man and nature are not opposed as in Alois Riegl's notion of Kunstwollen, but both are parts of a larger whole: the region[59]. Nature, man, house, settlement, etc. are part of an ecology which it is designed to[60]. With the lack of contrast between culture and nature, an outside disappears and the city dissolves into the landscape. While in*Proposal to City Building* the interior still was an anticipation of the big interiors of shopping malls, here the landscape, the park, also becomes a commercial zone.

Region The best known parthood-relation of the region is the relation of the wind shadow, the slipstream as distribution of residential and industrial areas in the region. Residential areas must not be in the wind shadow of the exhaust-causing industry. The wind shadow forms an overlap between the areas of a settlement.

In the Master's thesis work at IIT, additional parthood relations between the region and settlement, supervised by Hilberseimer, can be found. Their structure is similar: A design element of the settlement is set depending on regional aspects. For example, historical settlement patterns can lead to a different street layout. From a cultural analysis of the region, also prototypical settlement units may arise. The regional studies become more complex over time and try to build more and more parthood relations. Characteristics of the territory such as soil composition, climate, terrain profile are included to determine street layout, settlement distribution and density. More references are made also to economic, social, cultural, ie dynamic factors. The analyzes are becoming more extensive, but the settlement patterns remain similar. Thus, parameters become arguments and are used to justify without really exerting design influence.

Parthood relations are only relevant in design if they are mereologically defined as Bottom *and* Bound defined; as Under- *and* Overlap. For example, in the study *Mito and its Region Replanned*[61], the analysis of the historical settlement patterns becomes design-relevant through the explicit parthood relation of the distance of the house and the street. Through the intermediate step of a part, the settlement can thus be reterritorialized. However, different for graphs of employment conditions, soil qualities and similar: These relations mereologically are established only one-sided as Bound or Bottom. The dynamic element is not exchanged on any other plateau with an architectural element. The influence on the design of the settlement remains physically indeterminate.

When used in the regional scale[62] Hilberseimer's design scheme reaches its limits: It is not possible to define a mereological Bound for a region. The *New Regional Pattern* ultimately fails in this: It is the attempt of a definition of the region as a completed whole. For Hilberseimer a region initially is a geographical entity. The regional studies begin with the study of soil and climate. Congruent to the apartment as a utility, the geographical unit is classified according to its value in use. The analysis shows usable resources of a region, which act on the economic potential of production, industry and agriculture as a region[63]. As with the apartment, Hilberseimer introduces the determination of the region parameter, which would produce a surplus through its economic use. For the apartment the value of use was determined by the arrangement of the neighborhood, the settlement, so through the multiplicity of the determination of use. The usage value of an apartment was architecturally evaluated in proportional relationships. Unlike this happens in the determination of use for a region: The region as largest unit may not be reproduced and evaluated in a proportional relationship. The free space, the proportion between the elements, is missing. It lacks the element which Hilberseimer's mereological schemes distinguished.

Due to the lack of the free space, the region and all its elements down to the cell and the room are part of one specifically-featured city; Part of a holistic perspective: The regional pattern becomes the "Republic Hilberseimer". For the following reason: The definition of the region is no longer made by use of the poietic object, but only on the practice of its parts, so non-architecturally, but politically, economically, sociologically. A better definition of region of can only be made by the addition of properties. The composition of static, physical elements is supplemented by dynamic elements: infrastructure, social organization, politics, technology, markets[64]. While the relationship between the house and settlement was a relation between architecture and urban design, the relationship between settlement and region is one between urban design and the practical sciences. Architectural methods are spoken into the void. In the progress of the studies, the list of relevant relations will get longer. Compared to the compositions on the scale of the room of the house or settlement, there is this one crucial difference: soft, dynamic parameters are directly part of a form through the detour of inscription into a static object. Equating politics and architecture without the transformation of politics into elements of architecture will ultimately lead to the failure of the system of Hilberseimer.

190　The Mereological City: a reading of the works of Ludwig Hilberseimer

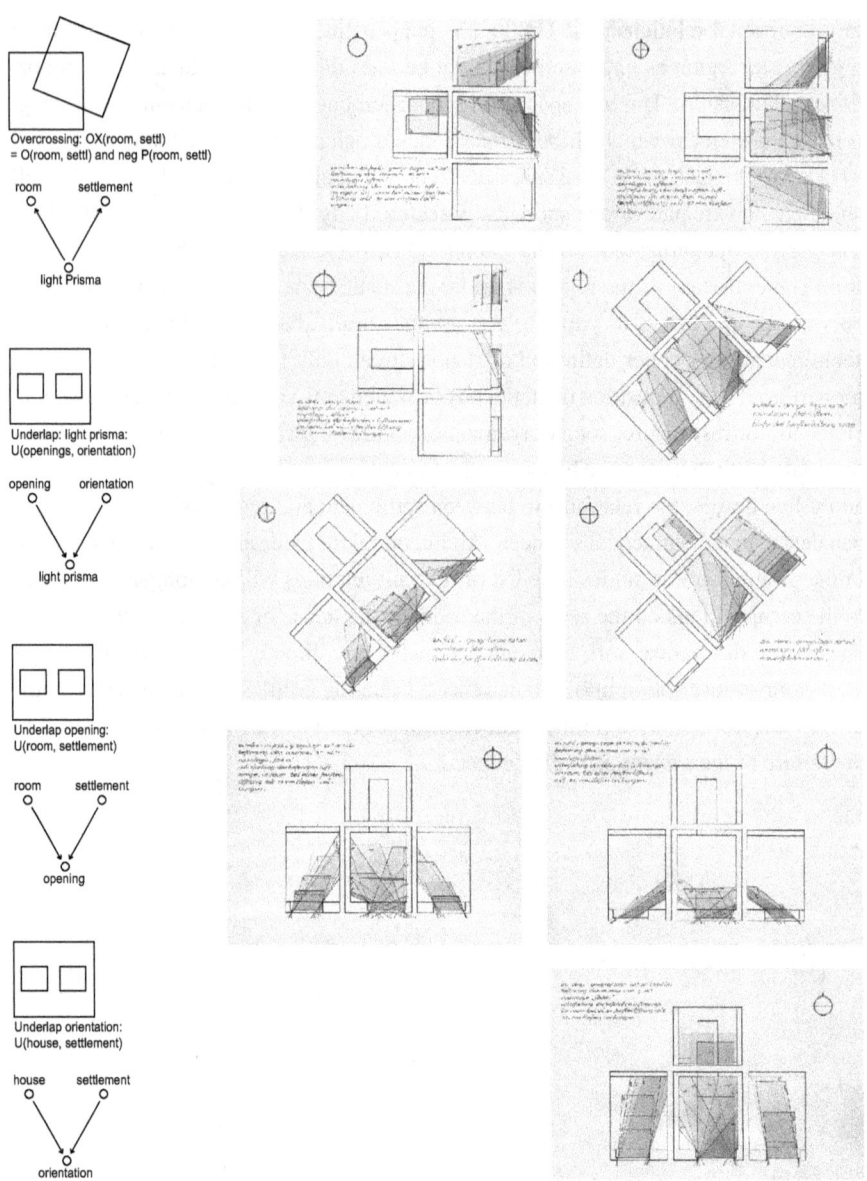

Figure 5.6: mereological analysis Room-Insolation

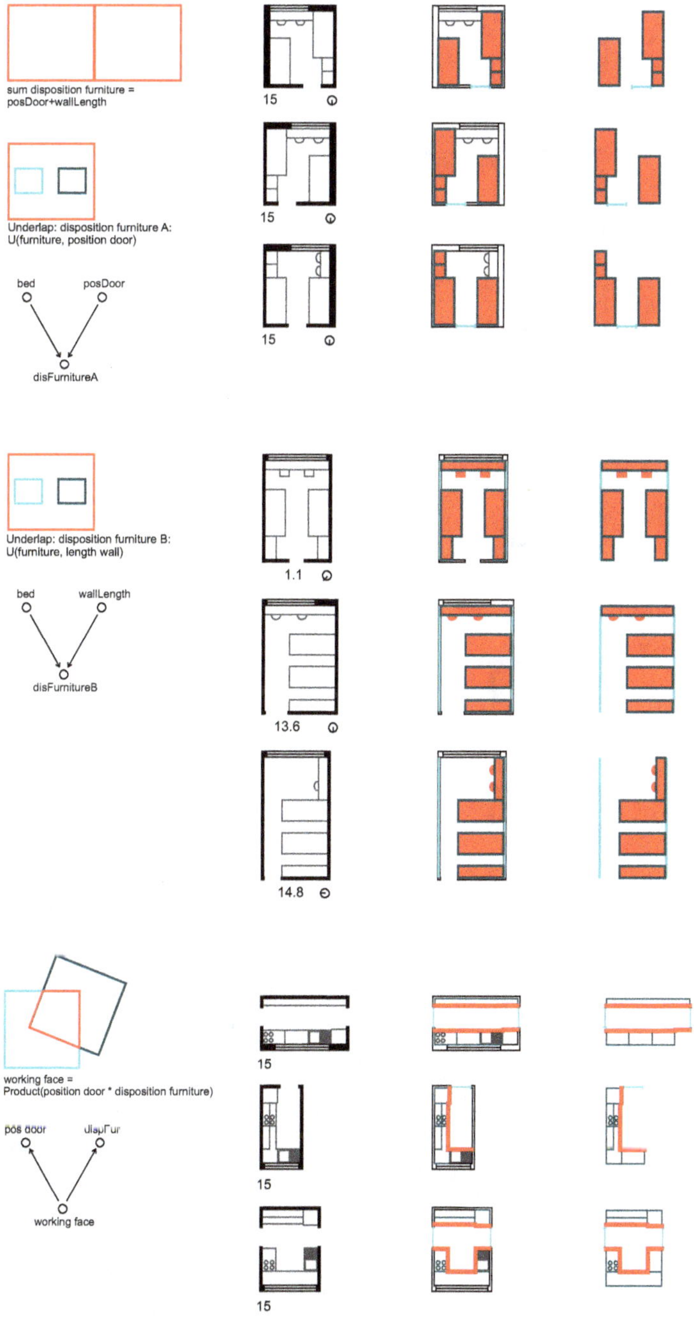

Figure 5.7: mereological analysis of private room as the sum of the disposition of furniture

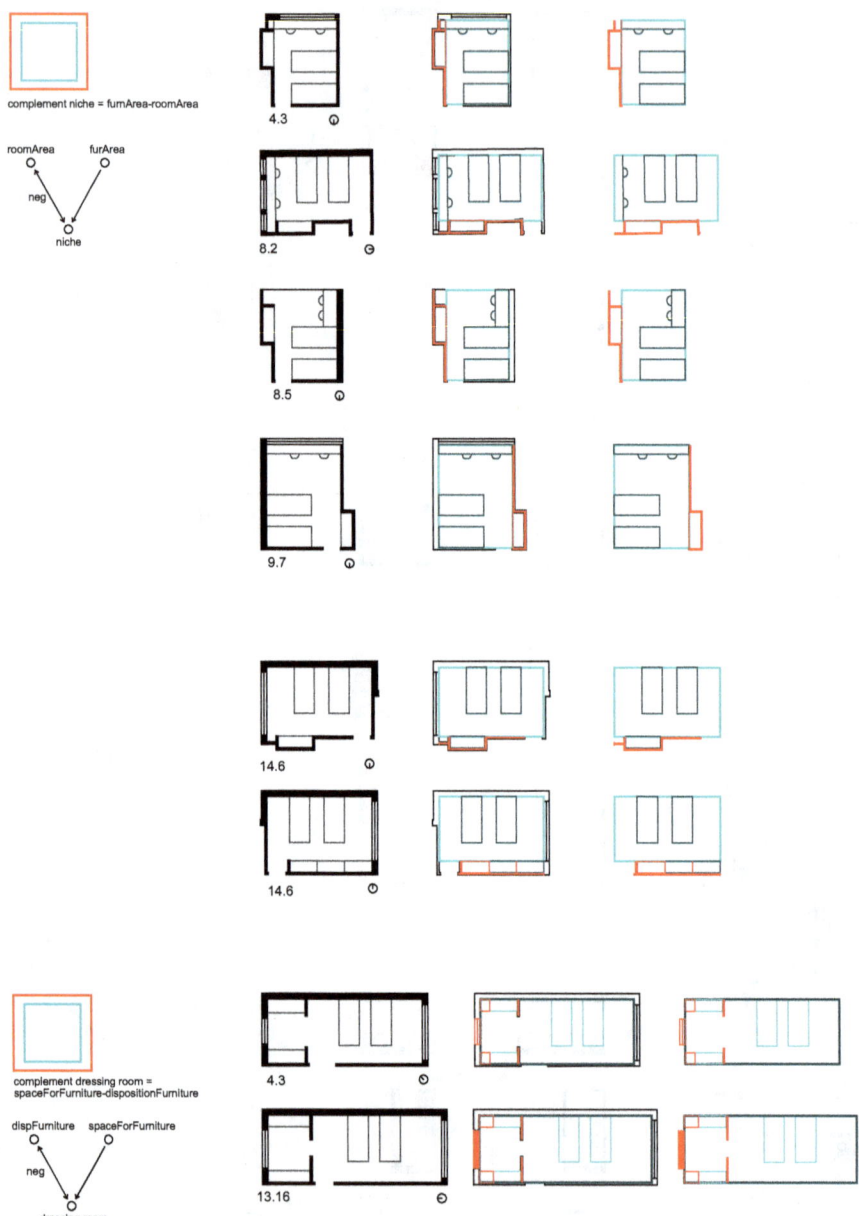

Figure 5.8: top: complementary overlap of room to floor space leads to the formation of a wall niche; bottom: complementary overlap of floor space to room area leads to an additional room

The punctualisation as architectural method 193

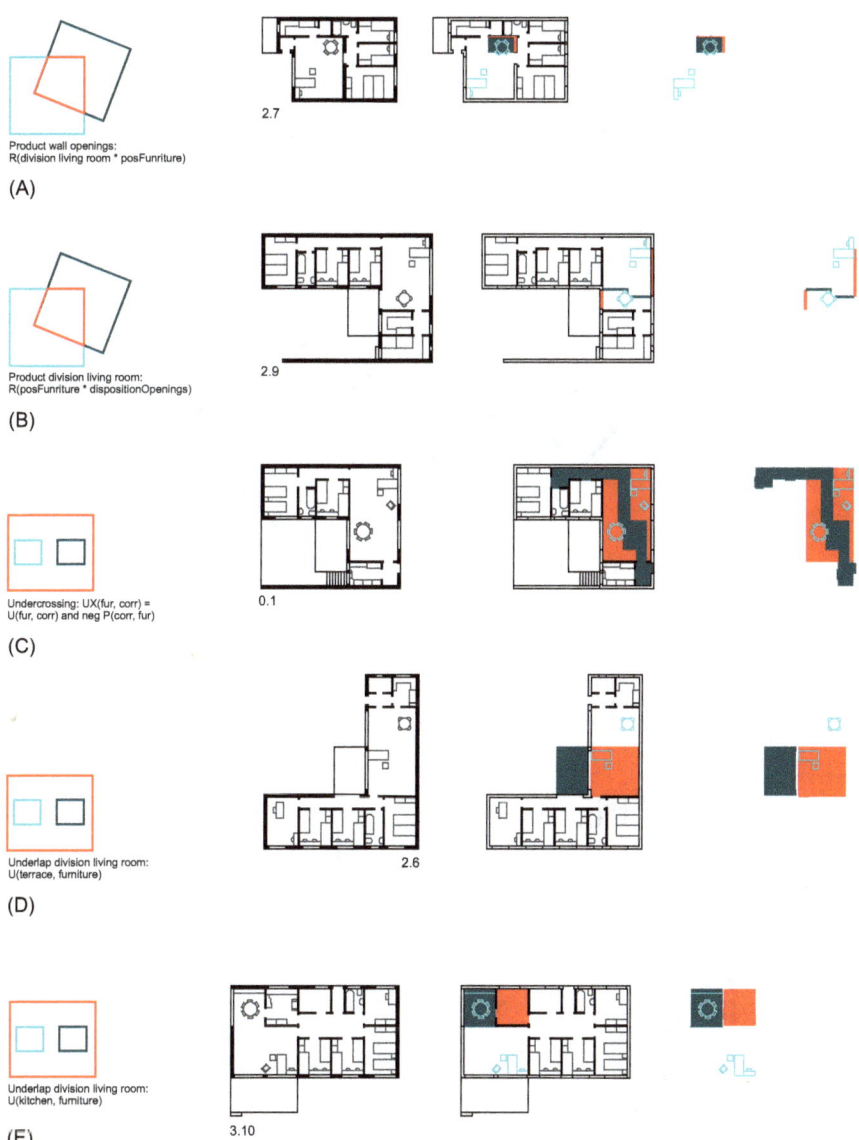

Figure 5.9: mereological analysis living room; (A): wall positions zoning the living room; (B): wall openings zoning the living room; (C): partition of the living room with the superposition of a corridor; (D) division of the living room with adjoining terrace; (E): partition of living space with an additional inserted room

Figure 5.10: mereological analysis room to house to settlement; (A): corridor as the shortest path between private room and bathroom; (B): terrace as part of the living room and garden; (C): size of the garden indirectly influence the demographic composition of the settlement up to an influence on the proportional dependencies between residential and industrial sectors

The punctualisation as architectural method 195

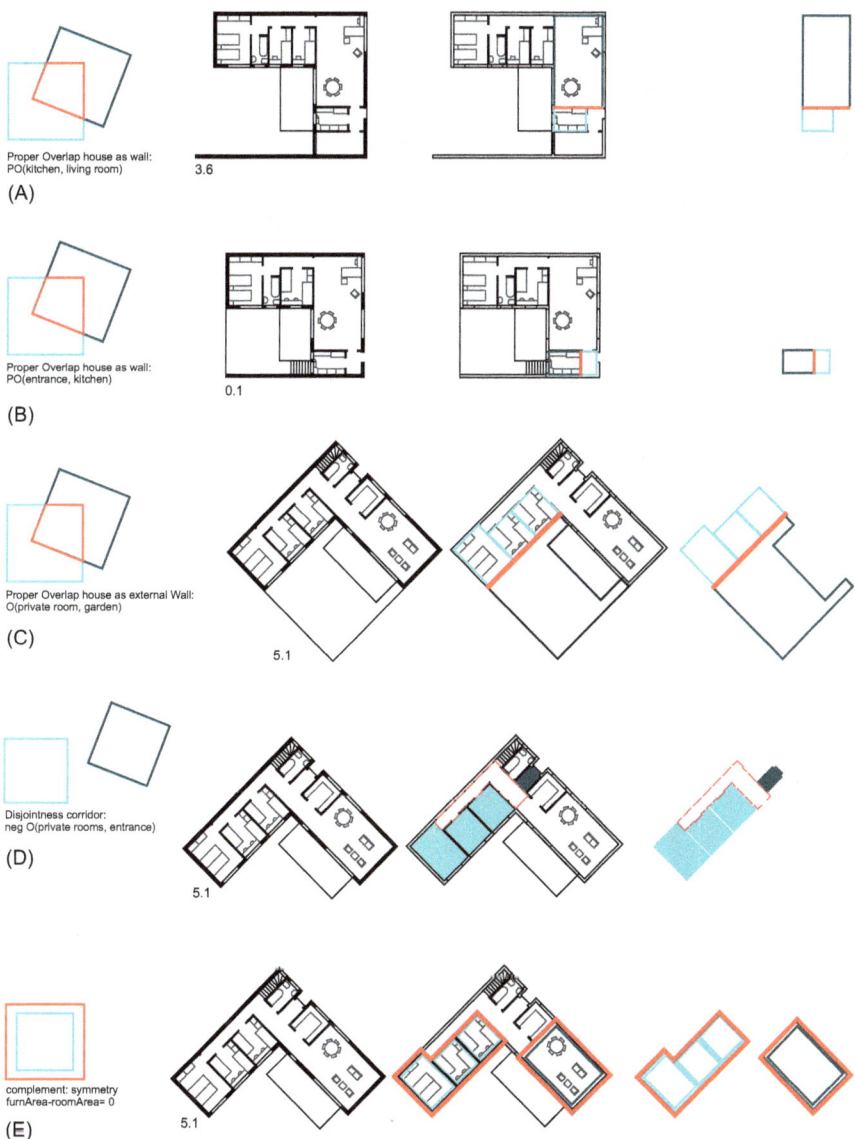

Figure 5.11: mereological analysis house as parthood relation of rooms; (A): House as a wall between the kitchen and living room; (B): House as a wall between entrance and kitchen; (C): House as a wall between private rooms and garden; (D): House as a separation between entrance and private spaces; (E): House as a symmetrical relation between living and private rooms

196   The Mereological City: a reading of the works of Ludwig Hilberseimer

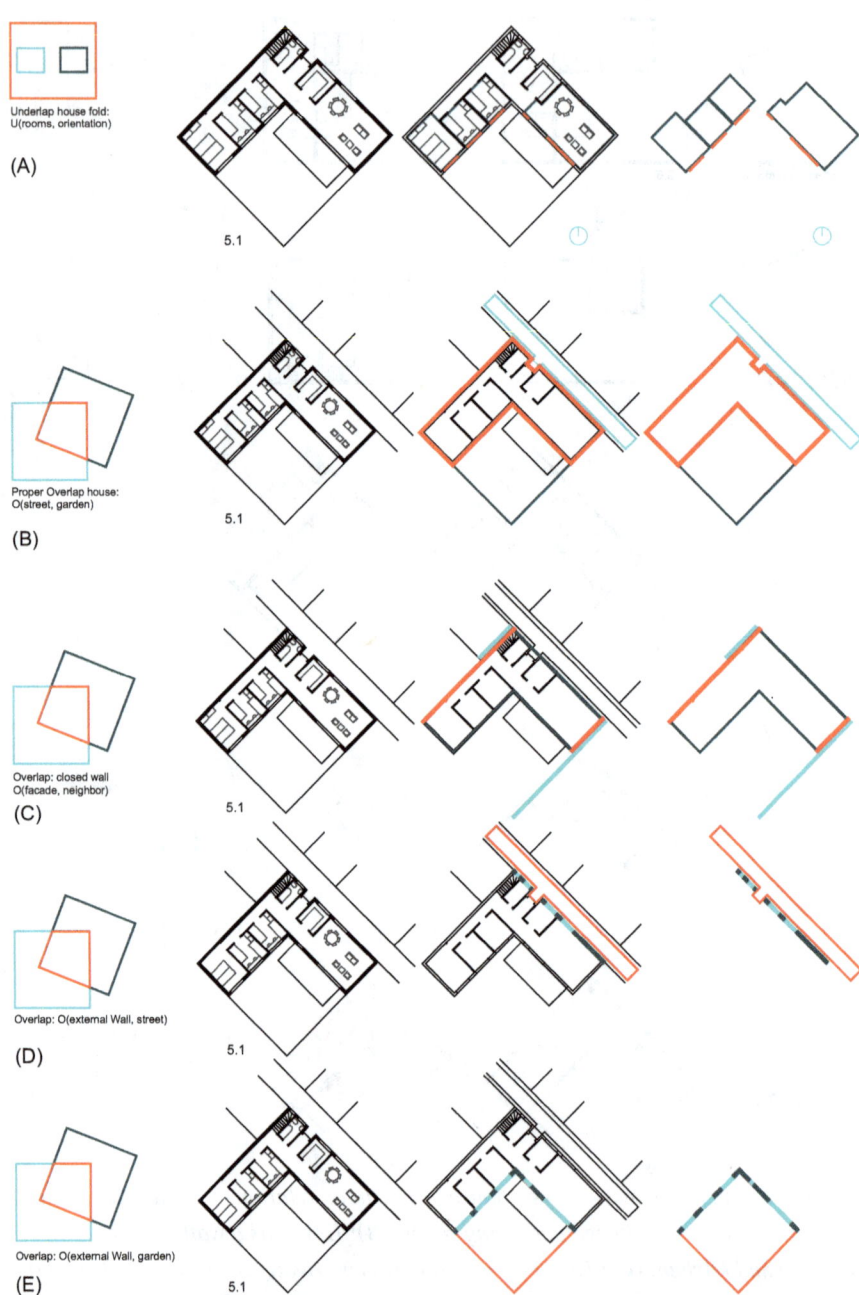

Figure 5.12: mereological analysis house to settlement; (A): the figure of the house in dependence to the orientation of the rooms; (B): the house as the separation of street and garden; (C, D, E) parthood-relations of the facade

The punctualisation as architectural method 197

Figure 5.13: mereological analysis of the house figure depending on settlement density

198   The Mereological City: a reading of the works of Ludwig Hilberseimer

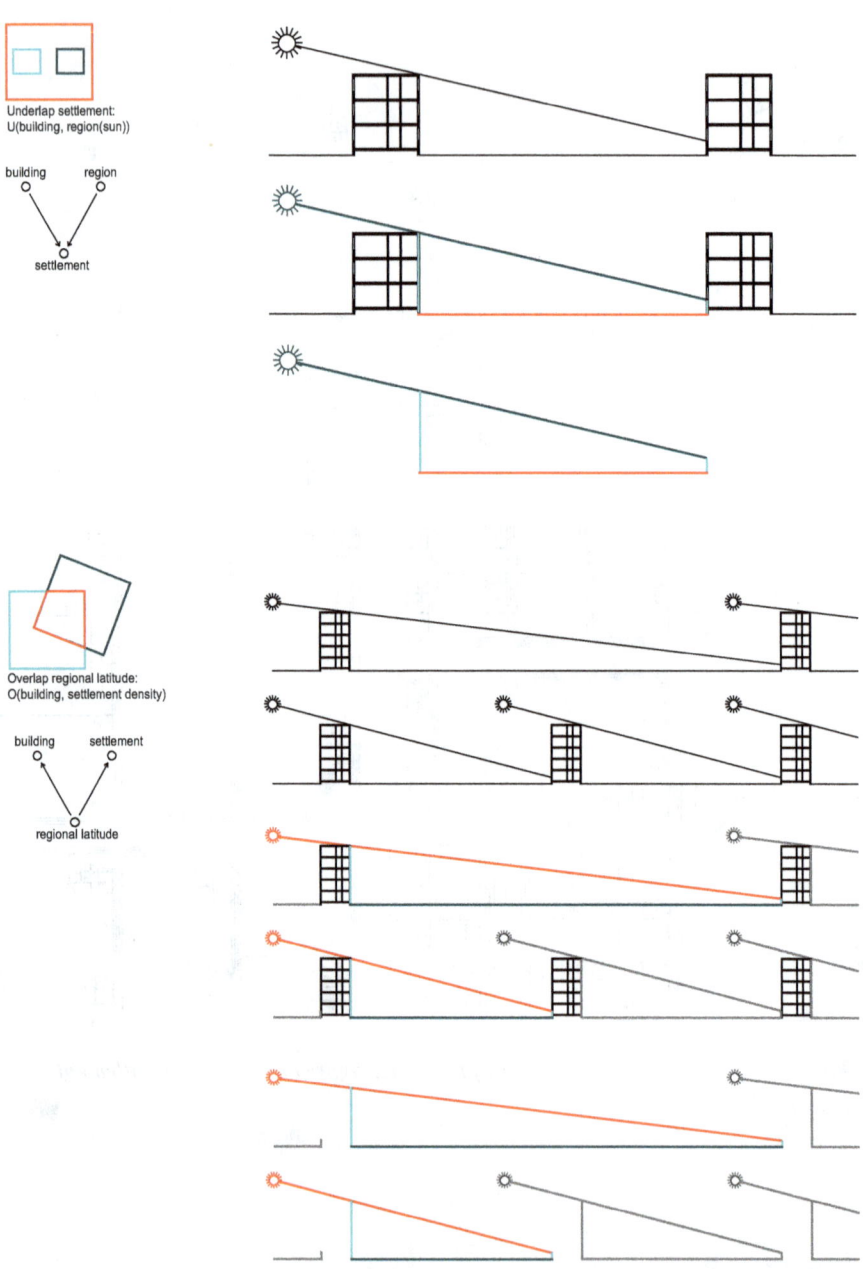

Figure 5.14: mereological analysis of settlement density; top: the settlement density is dependent on the sun angle and the cubature of the buildings; bottom: the ratio of the density and the building cubature depends on the regional latitude

The punctualisation as architectural method 199

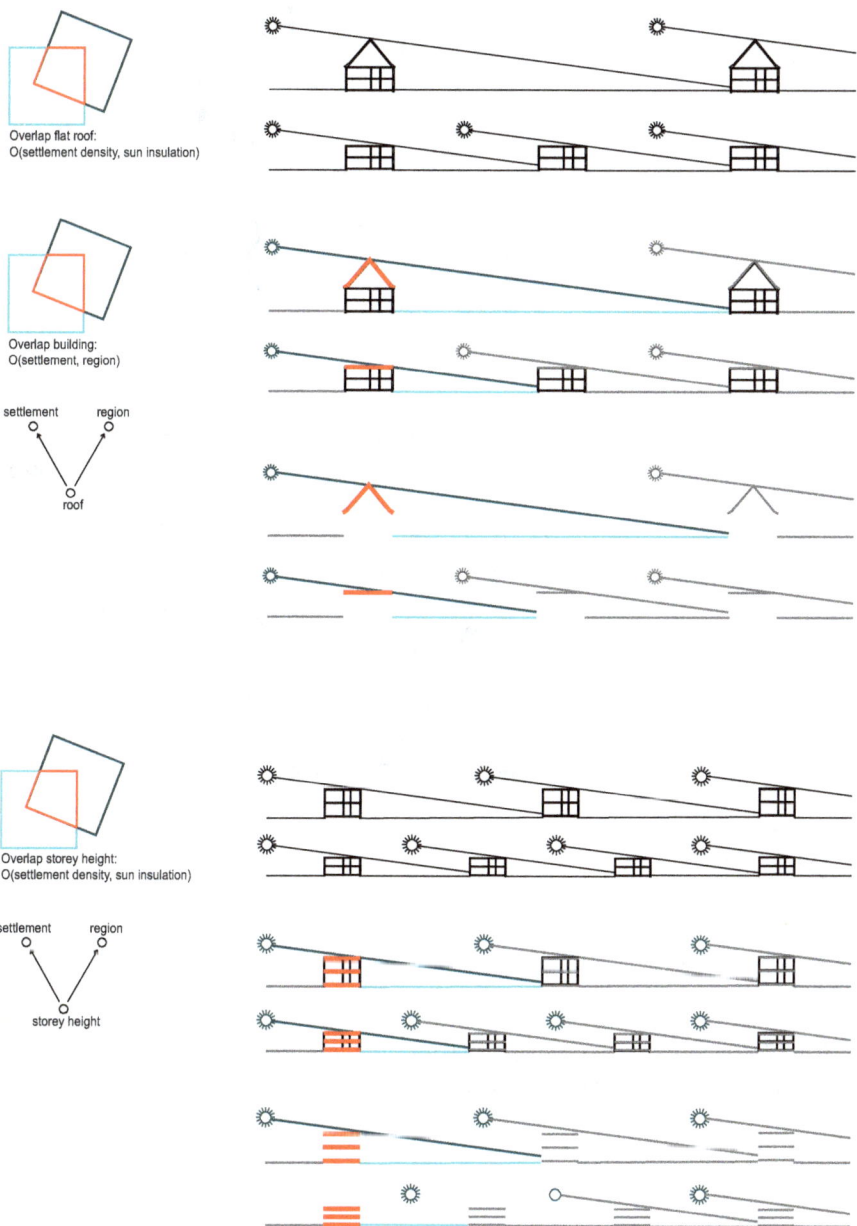

Figure 5.15: mereological analysis of minimum density – room-insolation

200   The Mereological City: a reading of the works of Ludwig Hilberseimer

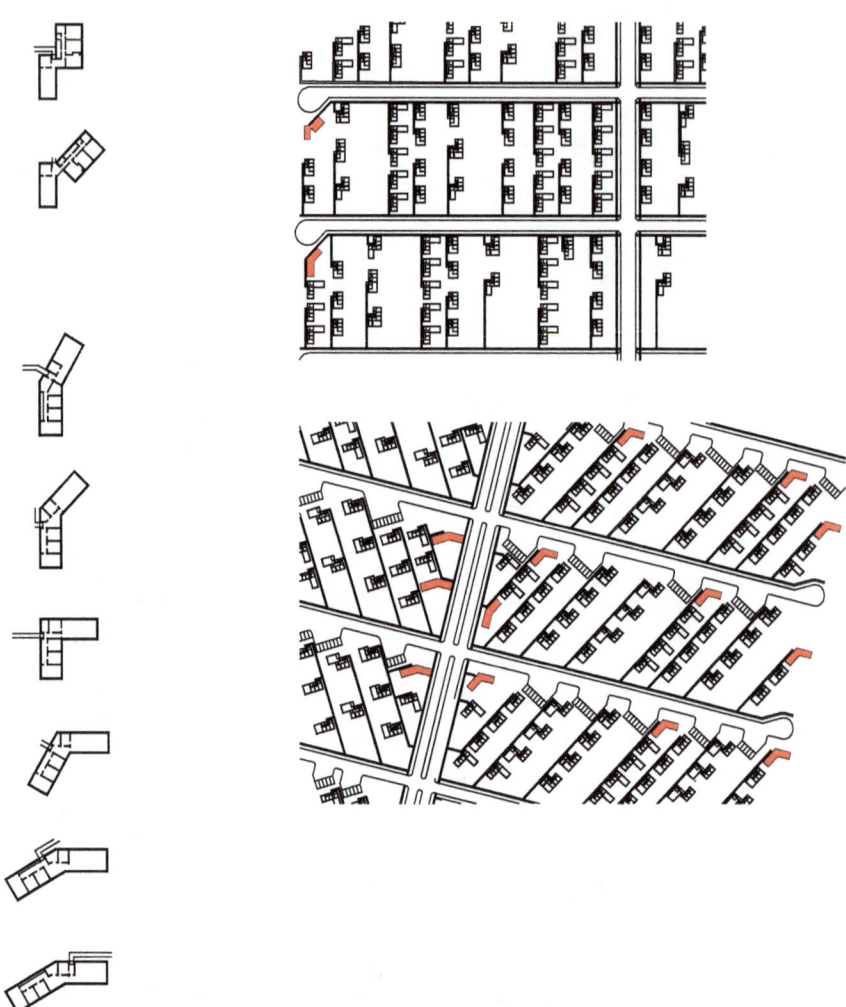

Figure 5.16: Variation in the peripheral area of the settlement as a result of new overlaps with other parthood relations

The punctualisation as architectural method 201

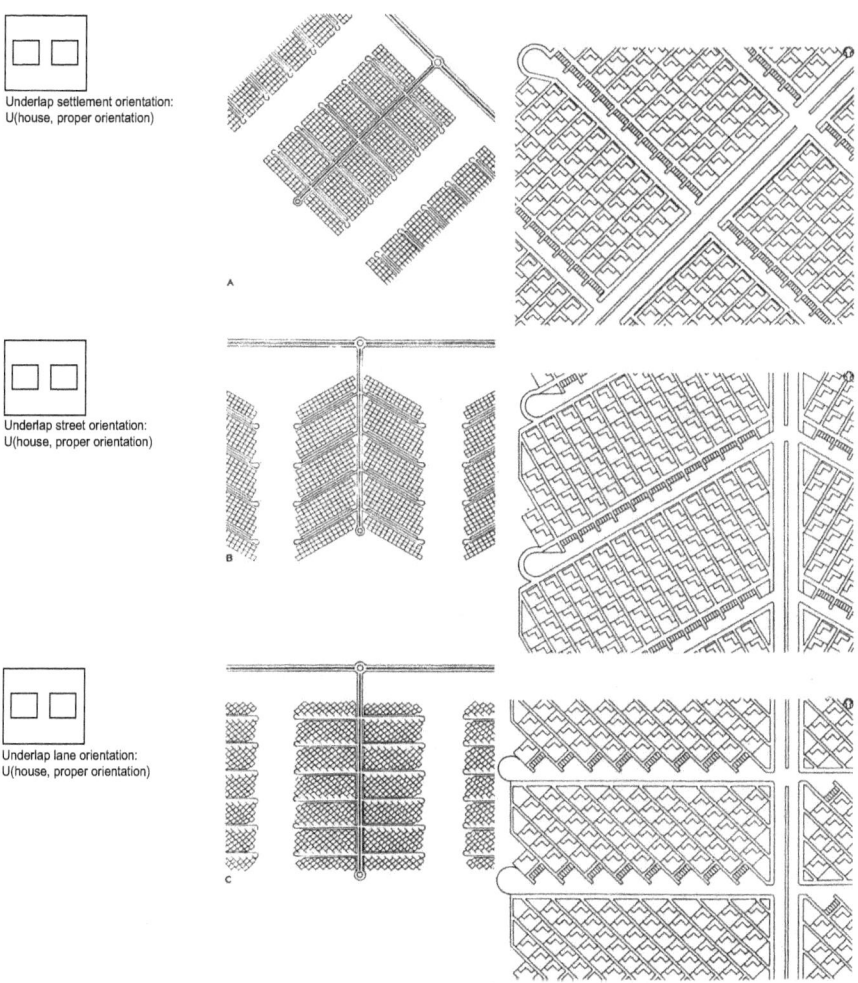

Figure 5.17: mereological analysis orientation house – settlement

202 The Mereological City: a reading of the works of Ludwig Hilberseimer

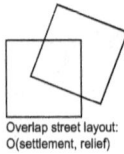

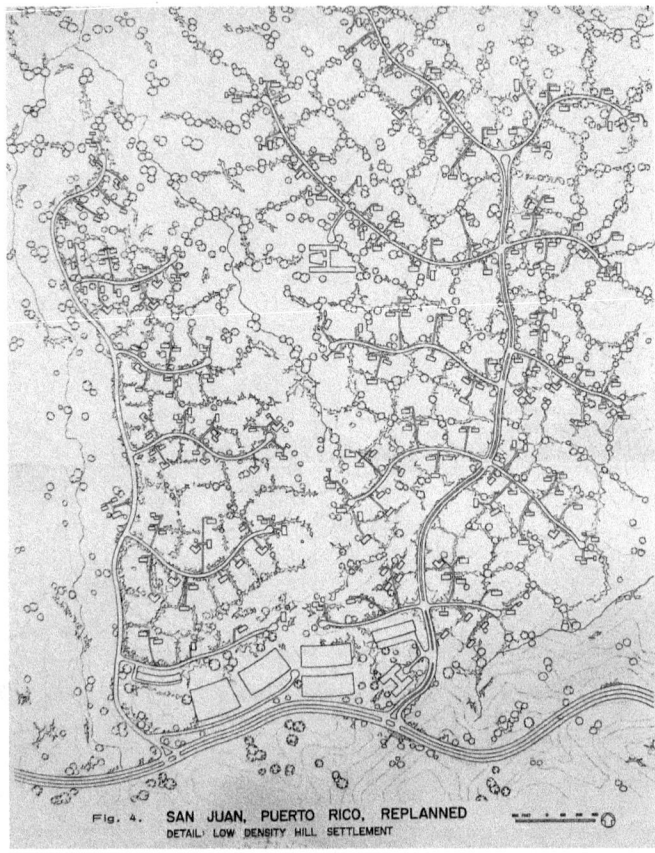

Figure 5.18: mereological analysis street layout following the relief; original drawing: John Ast, San Juan Replanned, 1964

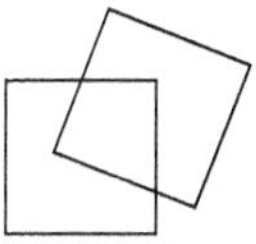

The punctualisation as architectural method 203

Overlap nature:
O(low rise house, carmouflage settlement)

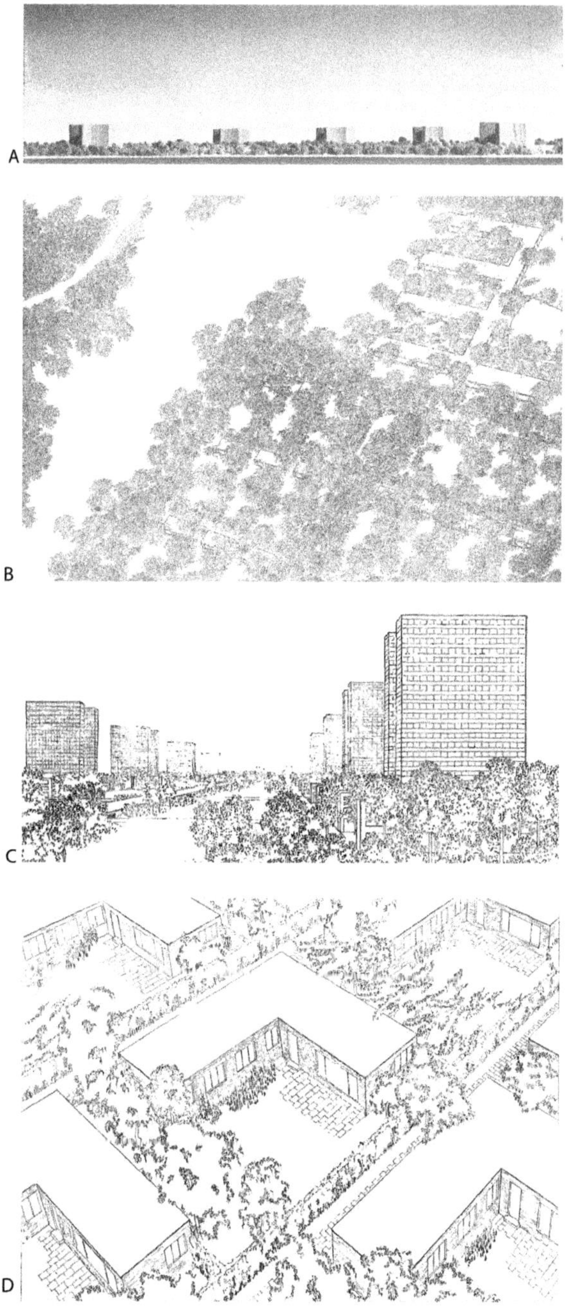

Figure 5.19: mereological analysis Nature – Settlement-Unit; top: Apartment houses for orientation; bottom: Nature as an element to camouflage single houses

204   The Mereological City: a reading of the works of Ludwig Hilberseimer

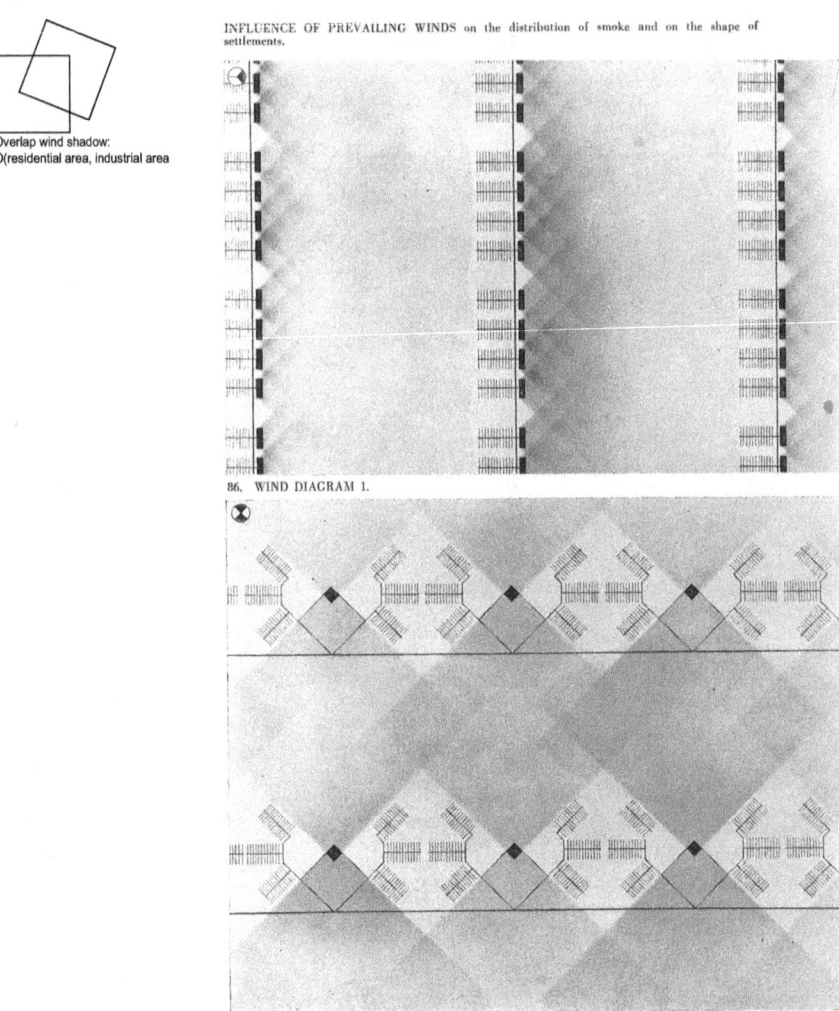

Overlap wind shadow:
O(residential area, industrial area

Figure 5.20: mereological analysis residential area – industrial area; original drawing: Hilberseimer, Influence of prevailing winds

The punctualisation as architectural method   205

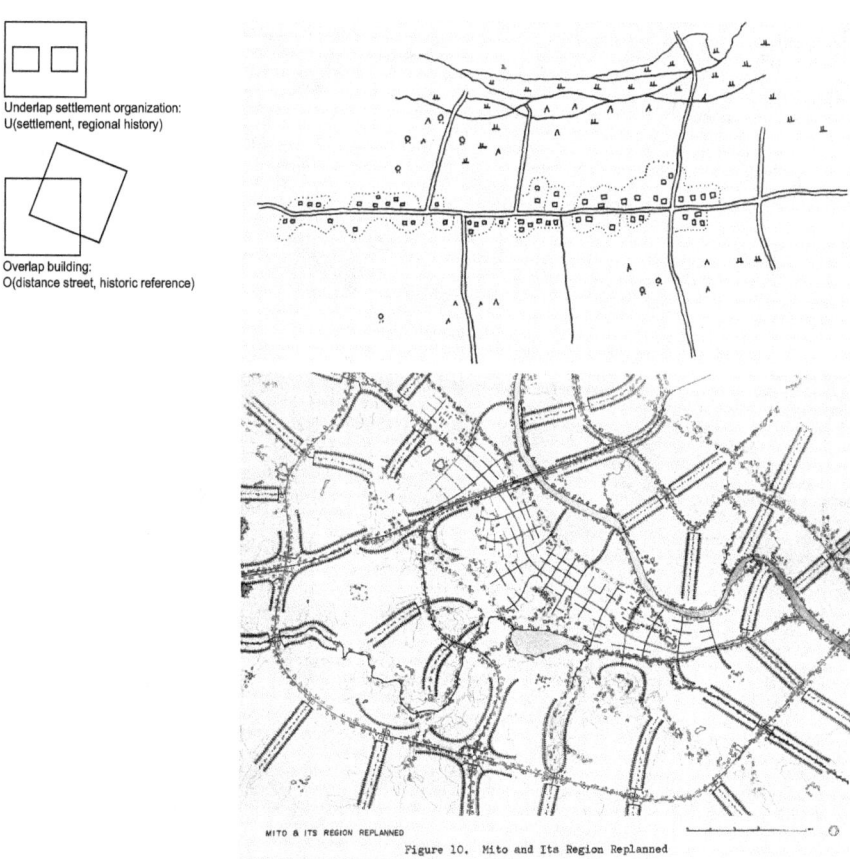

Figure 5.21: mereological analysis of the disposition of buildings – region; the abstraction of historic settlements as the distance of the house to the street specifies the new settlement layout

206   The Mereological City: a reading of the works of Ludwig Hilberseimer

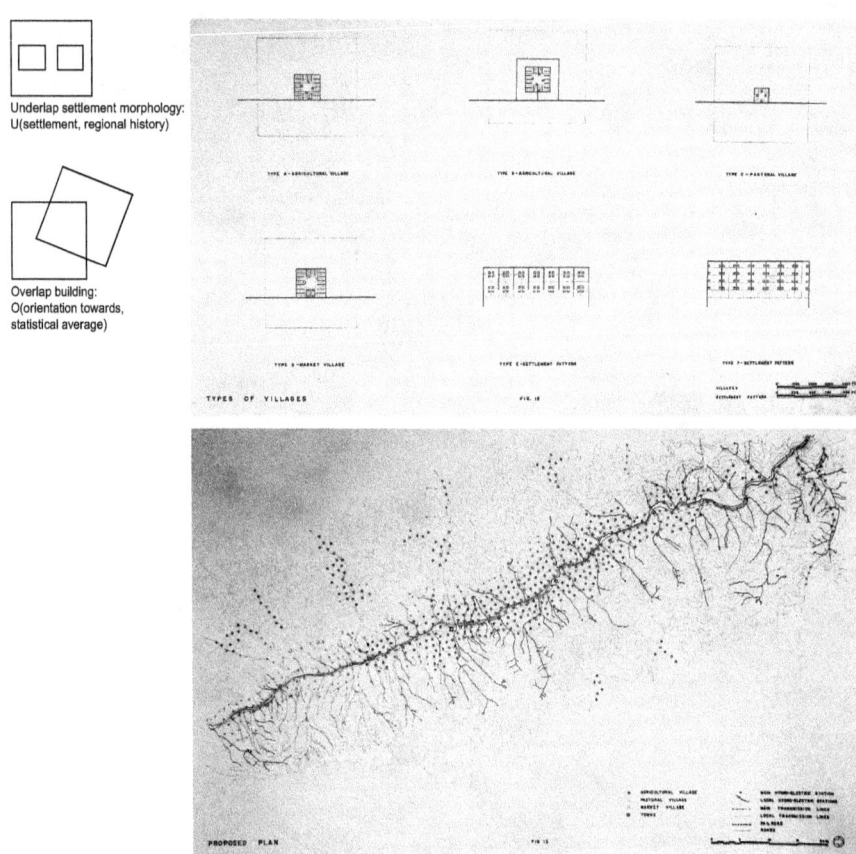

Figure 5.22: mereological analysis of the disposition of buildings – region; the classification of villages in region-specific typologies leads to region specific settlement layout

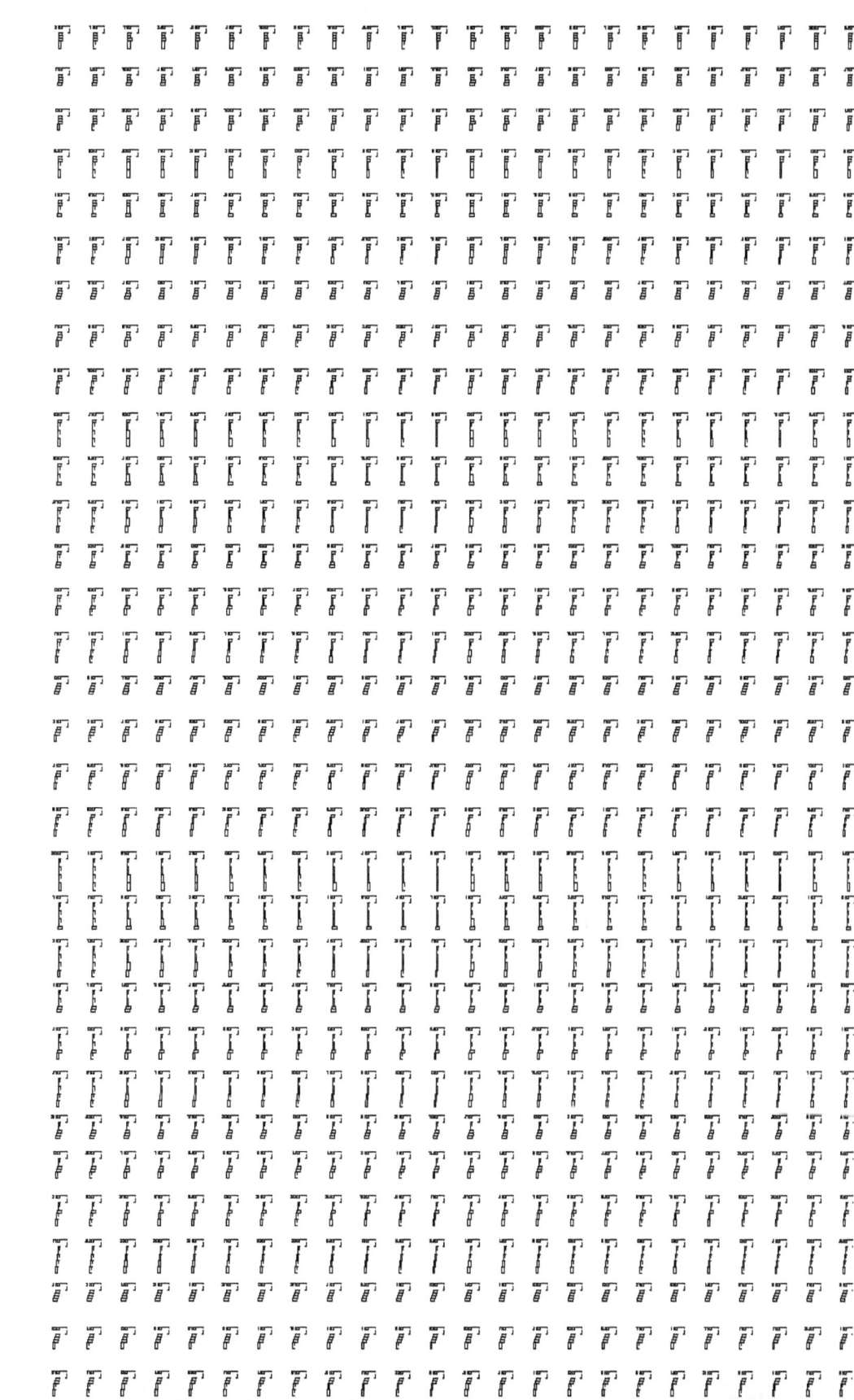

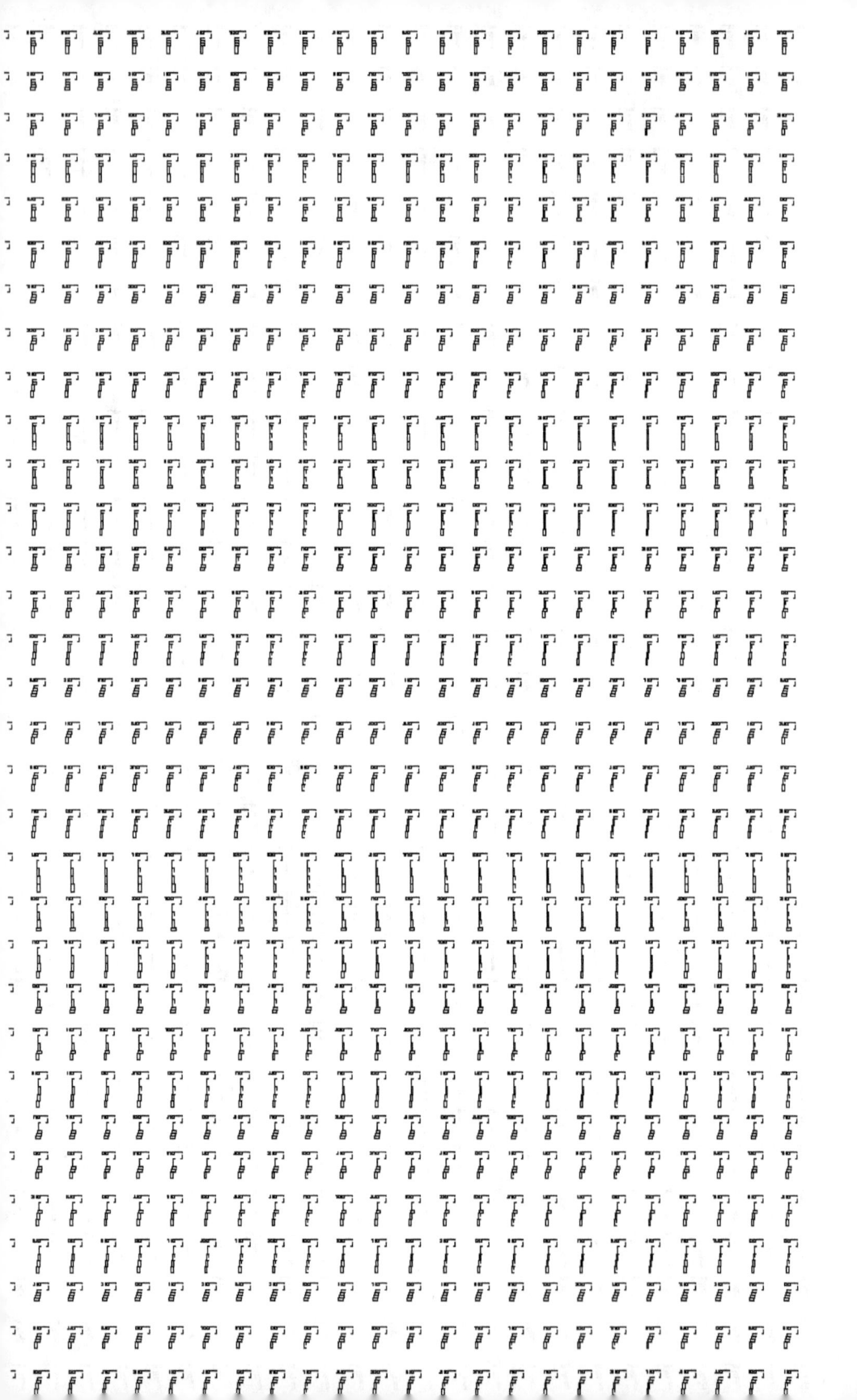

6 Conclusion: The Art of City-Planning

Let us remember Alois Riegl's concept of Kunstwollen: The artistic intention is rooted in intuition and abstraction, in opposition to the of its era. In the same spirit, approximately half a century later, Hilberseimer emphasized:

"The dependency of city planning on a scientific basis does not limit its artistic expression. On the contrary, it is the beginning of new possibilities, for the problem of city planning as a whole consists in the creative mastery of all conditions and means. [. . .] But a wholly rational discussion of the problems of city planning must always remain incomplete. The art of city planning: is not susceptible of analysis by reason alone. Artistic ability, which cannot be taught, is beyond technical means. Not in the measurable, but rather in the immeasurable, lies the essence of art. Only by mastering the technical means can the city planner realize his aims with artistic freedom. [. . .] Artistic freedom in city planning is not possible without this link with reality. All that is created by man is bound to time and space and can be executed only in time and space. Spiritual creativeness alone can turn the transitory into the permanent, the temporal into the eternal."[1]

Architecture should evolve from the materiality of its time, acknowledge its economy, integrate its technical achievements, address its social issues. But architecture is to do one thing: Designing.The majority of all models and schemata Hilberseimer's describe, how architecture can integrate external parameters however, at first it is city architecture, the design of the city. The large city should be experienced spatial. City architecture and architecture evolve from an artistic will. The architectural sensibility forms the space[2]. It is precisely the spiritual element, which first helps architecture to its specific expression. The essence of architecture is based on the materiality of a society and is taken back by society through designed objects. Therefore, it is never in contradiction, never a criticism, but goes beyond this.

Let us remember Nietzsche: The will to architecture means the eternal union of the Apollonian and Dionysian. Each step of the reproduction of a part obtains the inscription and thus a reference, a function. But in their composition, the frenzy as

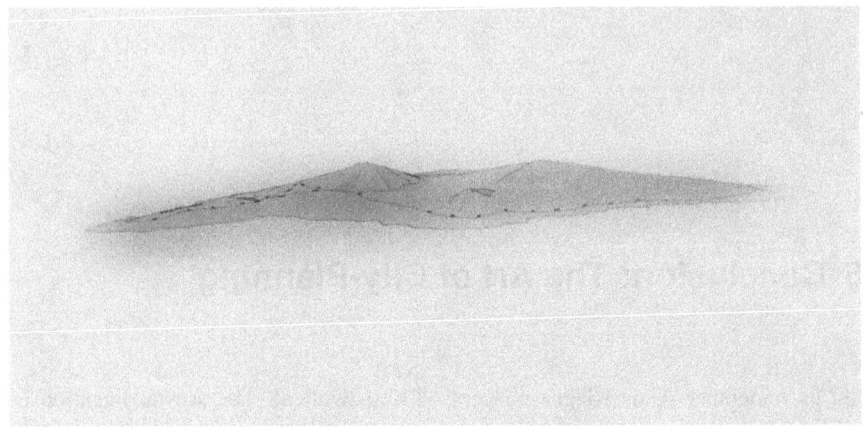

Figure 6.1: John Frega, Island of Jamaica, IIT Master Thesis, supervisor Ludwig Hilberseimer, 1957

rhythm, a sur plus evolves[3] without reproducing a reference. Through the prior inscription, the incorporation as form, architecture liberated itself from the role of being a hull for content by the step of the composition. At the basis of architecture, architecture in in the meaning of Aristotle poiesis[4] Disposition and Colocation overlap on the fabricated object[5]. Only the disposition of the thing produces knowledge about the quality of the colocation of the composition. This is reflected in the interaction of house and settlement: The disposition of the house in the settlement determines the design of the house. In this step, the disposition overlaps and is inseparable from the colocation: The settlement is part of the house, more precisely: The whole is part of the part as a whole: this is the punctualisation as architectural method.

The figure of the settlement never exists as a whole in itself like an economic plot. The ground is a figurative composition in itself. The figure of the settlement is always located in a state of transition between part and whole. Even more: the operations that are necessary to link the scale of the individual house and a settlement do not accept a hierarchy of scale. The whole of the settlement in Hilberseimer's settlements is only negotiable as part of the part, so the house as a whole. The class of the settlement can only be understood by the consistency of the houses. There is no settlement without its elements: the houses and their grounding negotiation of each other. Sense of scale so undergoes a revaluation and is at the disposition of One and the colocation of Many. The house is not only part of a field of the settlement. The house is not only placed and determined by a frame or a plot. A house is also described by its own field, projected by the multiplicity of itself in a settlement. The projection of the house as a settlement transforms mereological dependencies into proportional fabrics. In the settlement studies of Hilberseimer they are economic demands to the house as a utility, which are visible in the projected neighborhood of the figure of the house. The neighborhood is aesthetically tangible through the meaningfulness of the parts to each other: their mereological relationship. Thus, the proportion of a possible neighborhood becomes punctualized in the house. Each potential neighborhood, every relation of the parts to each other, becomes physically tangible as the contour of the smallest influence. Ultimately, the house is as an architectural "punct" of the settlement, is an epistemological superposition of several mereological schemata. It is a specific entity depending on the fabric of the settlement by the internal representation of a settlement. The contour as the difference from one to the other becomes an area of many. In the density of the figuration of contours the form becomes again surface. In this way the punctualisation describes a continuous closing- and opening circulation of the architectural element.

Hilberseimer recognizes that a mereological reading of architecture, as a composition of elements, means a new creative potential[6]. And so begins urban design with the smallest element, the room[7]. The objectives of the Urban Design, City Planning, City Architecture[8] is therefore similar to that of the architecture: "The ordering and shaping of space with the buildings which constitute a city."[9]

The difference is in the scale and in the meaning: It is the relation of the buildings to each other, the open spaces of the city, the topography as a landscape. It can be described as the opposite of the architecture: the Void, the intermediate space, as a form of the thing[10]. The artistic expression of the artist are explicitly: perspective. contrast[11]: "clarity of structure. proportion. Proportional relation of mass and harmony of appearance."[12] The proportion is the relation of the parts to the whole and the whole to its parts. In city architecture, the whole thing is the urban area, the parts are the buildings and open spaces. Two matters are worth to be emphasized here: First, there is a mutual relation between part and whole. Secondly, mass and space are specifically designed elements. By means of contrast and perspective dimensions and proportions can thus visually be amplified and transformed.[13]. In *The New City* Hilberseimer devotes an entire chapter *The Art of City Planning* to the artistic principles of urban design and extracts several proportional principles of historical examples. Cathedrals are an example of the contrast between small-large and high-low. The relative proportion of the Frauenkirche in Dresden is compared to the absolute proportion of the Gothic cathedral, the contrast between the massive structure and small-scale buildings. The silhouette of a city like for example Prague, is explained through the grouping of buildings. Contrast by large, detached buildings, such as the church buildings in the cityscape of Stralsund; perspective shortenings as in the Piazza San Marco in Venice. These are artistic decisions that the schemata of the city first turn into the architecture of the city.

The punctualisation as a balancing act between One and Many in the design practice is the tension between material and Kunstwollen. The strength of Hilberseimer's schemata lies in the idea of a practice as materiality of time, its technology, economy and culture in a composition. Urban composition is non-specific, a mereological description, as a schema a picture schema in becoming.

The punctualisation is also a transfer of human characteristics to the room. Thus, the assessment of the figure of the external view of a subject moves to the form of the house to designed. The shift is ultimately a transfer of Kant's synthetic model. The relationship between subject and object here becomes a relationship between object and object. The architectural scale of the moderns always designs with the humanistic distribution of roles: The form of existence of an object is reflected in its form of effect as part of a subject. Hilberseimer's urban operation as the displacement of the form of effect in the architectural figure finally allows a revaluation of modernity, a revaluation of the contrast between nature and culture. Through the multiplication the form of effect in the vicinity of the settlement fabric, the humanistic contrast becomes a compositional parthood relation.

The notion of materiality does not correspond to the real situation or things, but as an abstraction is opposed to them. The idea of a parthood-fabric, a composition, is the first step of decomposition of the real and thus expresses a tension when related to the Kunstwollen. In a second step, there are interventions within the presented materiality that again negotiate the parthood fabric. These are Hilberseimer's schemata, the minimum distance, the light prisms of the rooms, the non-intersecting street segments, which serve as compositional subtraction or addition of parthood relations, speculative projections of the city. The compositional intervention in the city's scheme is always designed by a specific architectural element. The idea of a settlement, the Many, is ultimately the house. Such architecture can be described as a matter of composition.

Finally, to reorganize the industrial, infinite city, Hilberseimer promotes object instead of land speculation. If the soil is no longer the ground of the city, architecture must be economically grounded in other ways. Hilberseimer's approach is the transformation of architectural elements into economical products: to utilities, which are determined by their intended use. Each time, economic value is created by its disposition as an element of the city. Here economic value is understood as an "interest in interests". As historian Albert Hirschmann showed[14], capitalism in its beginning was promoted by thinkers including Montesquieu, Sir James Steuart as the transformation of passion to an interest. Similar to Hilberseimer's object-speculation, these early thoughts based on the notion that the interest of capital, as opposed to the landlords, with its fixed property will be able to thwart the efforts (of the state) and to make its intentions to lay hands on private wealth destroyed[15]. Individuality is obtained by interest.

Analogous in the beginning of the city, the Greek polis, the public sphere, the political was sharply distinguished from the house (gr: oikos), the economic. Politics was the word and reason[16]. Whereas, the economic, the oikos, was the sphere of the family and was understood as composite of house, family and goods. The economic was thought to follow an inaccessable interest, desire. In the ancient line of city-architecture speculation is isolated a part of the house. In this way the *Mereological City* creates a mobile immovability of reference. Finally, when the whole becomes a part for the part as whole, Hilberseimer's conception of the city is far from being a simple body-metaphor. When the ground (gr.: logos) of the city is defined by its parts (gr.: meros): its architecture, it reminds us that in turn the city is always part of the architecture as its desire as well.

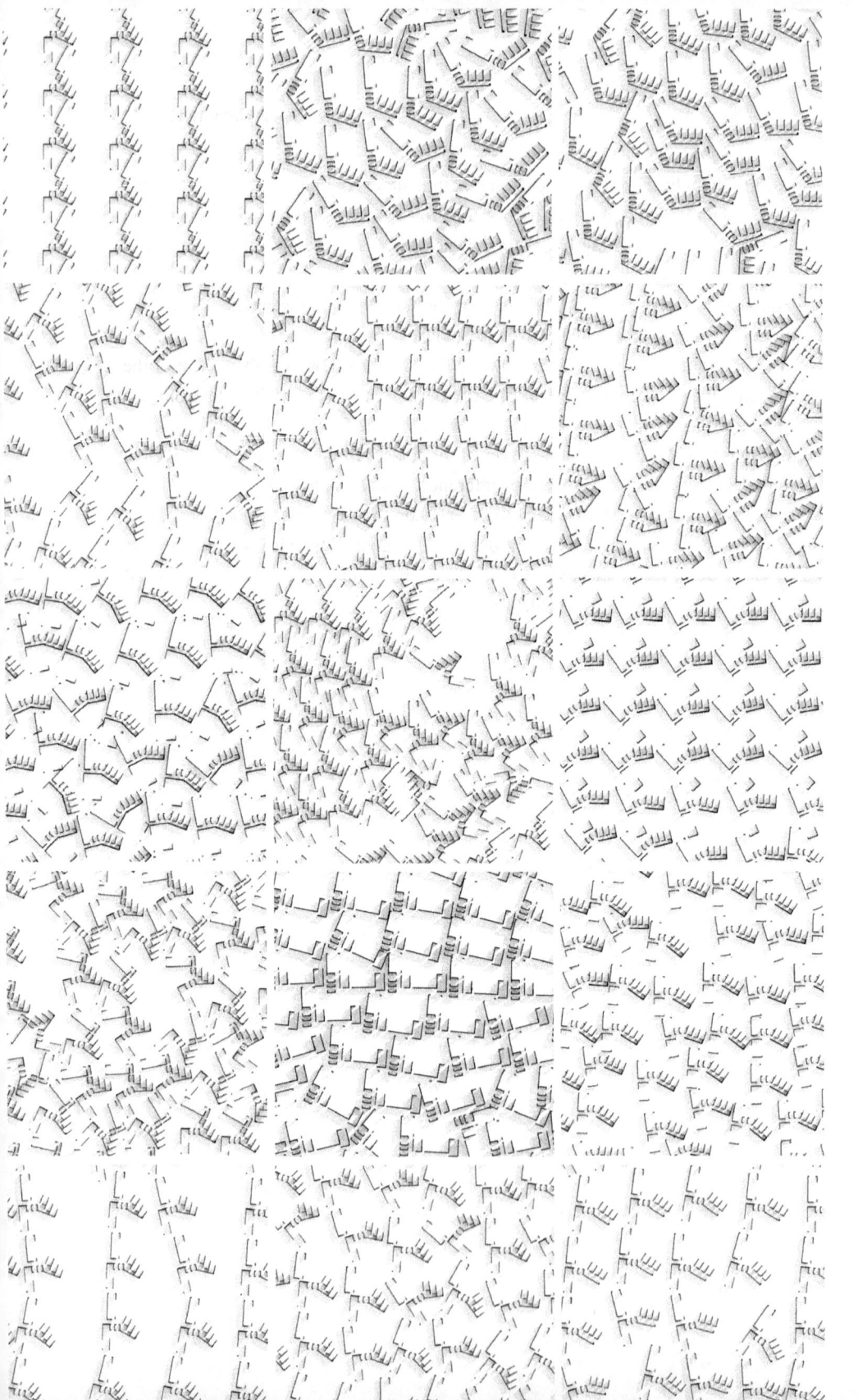

Notes

Prologue:
Architecture as a Discipline of Composition

1   "Even though the word *composition* is a bit too long and windy, what is nice is that it underlines that things have to be put together (Latin *componere*) while retaining their heterogeneity. Also, it is connected with composure; it has clear roots in art, painting, music, theater, dance, and thus is associated with choreography and scenography; it is not too far from *compromise* and *compromising*, retaining a certain diplomatic and prudential flavor. [...] From universalism it takes up the task of building a common world; from relativism, the certainty that this common world has to be built from utterly heterogeneous parts that will never make a whole, but at best a fragile, revisable, and diverse composite material." in: Latour 2010, 3-4.

2   One of the core arguments of ecological thought is exactly this: accepting a largest whole. The most obvious example is Gaia in the work of James Lovelock.

3   The recognition of the irrelevance of any criticism leads to the requirement of a formal research: "The point here is that the failure for change to occur despite compelling critiques of the dominant social order cannot simply be attributed to ideological mystifications. Social and political thought needs to expand its domain of inquiry, diminish its obsessive focus on content, and increase attention to regimes of attraction and problems of resonance between objects. [...] content alone is not enough and that political theorists need to enhance their capacity of resonance with respect to nonhuman actors and regimes of attraction." Bryant 2011, 227.

4   Stadtarchipelago Entwurf, Berlin, 1977.

5   Alexander 1966.

6   Branzi 2006, 66-68.

7   Aureli 2008, 112.

8   Rossi and Eisenman 1988 in Aureli 2014, Aureli's text provides an overall overview of the role model Hilberseimer in the 2nd half of the 20th century.

9   Pope 1996.

10 Koolhaas 1998b, 198-203.
11 Tafuri 1985, c1976.
12 Hays 1992.
13 Aureli 2012.
14 Schumacher 2012b, 59.
15 Lévi-Strauss 1973, 154.
16 Robin Mackay and Armen Avanessian, editors. 2014. *#accelerate#*. [Falmouth, United Kingdom] and Berlin: Urbanomic Media Ltd. / in association with Merve, 23: "the only radical political response to capitalism is not to protest, disrupt, or critique, but to accelerate and exacerbate its uprooting, alienating, decoding, abstractive tendencies."
17 Ecological politics unfolds here from the critical examination of Marx's economic collectives: "there is a tenuous relation between the Communist and the Compositionist Manifesto. (…) the two manifestos have something in common, namely the *search for the Common*. The thirst for the Common World is what there is of communism in compositionism, with this small but crucial difference that it has to be slowly composed instead of being taken for granted and *imposed* on all. Everything happens as if the human race were on the move again, expelled from one utopia, that of economics, and in search of another, that of ecology. Two different interpretations of one precious little root, *eikos*, the first being a dystopia and the second a promise that as yet no one knows how to fulfill. How can a livable and breathable "home" be built for those errant masses?" in: Latour 2010, 17-18.
18 Latour and Porter 2004.
19 Descola 2011.
20 446-447.
21 Harman demonstrates that the natural sciences as well as the humanities, in its focus on materiality or relationship, does not do justice to reality and calls for a third science that lies between two world-views Harman 2012.
22 Bryant 2011, 243-289.
23 "A thing is nothing more than the difference between that which is in this thing and that in which this thing is." Garcia 2014, 13.
24 "If a network Acts as a single block, then it disappears, to be replaced by the action itself and the seemingly simple author of that action. At the same time, the way in which the effect is generated is also effaced: for the time being it is neither visible, nor relevant." Law 1992, page 384.
25 Classical categorization; first made by Aristotle in his categorization of Sciences in theoria, poiesis and praxis. In this context, Aristotle assigns the architecture explicitly to poiesis: Aristoteles 2006, 1103 b 31-35.
26 Aureli 2012.

Introduction:
Topic, State of Knowledge, Method

1   "Hilbs was a very private person, how much so we really didn't discover until late in his life. He had little to be engulfed socially in large groups, and when he was asked to address some professional organization he usually managed to get out of it by persuading one of his colleagues to present his paper on his behalf." Graham Foundation 21.03.1987, 41-42.
2   Mengin 1986a.
3   Kilian 2002, 7-11.
4   Ostendorf 1918.
5   Baumeister 1876.
6   Alois Riegl already described the proponents of the thesis as "Semperianer", but this is not directed against Semper, but a generalization of his theses. Mallgrave and Semper 2001.
7   Pommer 1988; Michelis 1986.
8   Hilberseimer 1908-1911.
9   Kohlmeyer 1986.
10 Hilberseimer 1963b, 122.
11 Hilberseimer 1925d.
12 Hilberseimer 1927b.
13 Kieren 1998.
14 Spaeth 1981.
15 Kilian 2002, 7-11.
16 Danforth 1988.
17 Blum 2000, 18.
18 Apparently there should be a analogue settlement layout in Spain.
19 Saliga 1993, 57.
20 Ryerson and Burnham Archives Finding Aids, The Art Institute of Chicago.
21 "Some photographic illustrations of student work took Hilberseimer himself to America. Probably for educational purposes." Christian Wolsdorff 1986, 45 They are now part of the collection of the Busch-Reisinger Museum, belonging to the Harvard Art Museum, Cambridge.
22 There is still missing an extensive research among former students and their descendants.
23 Häring 1926.
24 "However the uniformity of the block resulted in an excessive uniformity. All natural things were excluded: No trees, no grass surface broke the monotony. [...] It was not the intention of the study to solve the architectural problem of the city; it was merely an attempt to find a technical solution to the traffic problem. This goal was achieved, but at what cost! As seen as a whole, the concept of this high-rise city was already wrong as thought. The result was more of a Necropolis as a Metropolis, a sterile landscape of asphalt and cement, inhuman in every respect." (Hilberseimer 1963b, 22).

25 William J. R. Curtis 1996.
26 Alexander 1966.
27 Hilberseimer 1963a, 16.
28 Pope 1996.
29 For a detailed definition of elliptical space see Jameson no date.
30 Pope 1996, 72.
31 139.
32 262-279.
33 Koolhaas 1998a.
34 New insights show, that Koolhaas had a crucial role in the development of the archipelago concept during the "Urban Garden" summerschool in 1978, organized by Ungers; in: Ungers et al. 2013.
35 Tafuri 1985, c1976.
36 Incidentally Tafuri himself points out that his interpretation on Hilberseimer goes far beyond his own intention: "Thus the large city is, properly speaking, a unity. Reading *beyond the author's intentions* we may interpret his assertions to mean that, in its structure, the entire modern city becomes an enormous social machine." 104.
37 In Scheffler there is also a description of the location unbound industrial worker who works for foreign markets than for its neighborhood. Scheffler sees the house as something rather random for industrial workers. So home and symbols can not achieve impact anymore. The generic is valid and the typical is places in the foreground. Scheffler 1913.
38 Chapter *State and City* in Geddes and Branford 1917, Geddes compares City and Citicans. The city is an organic object for Geddes, that is subjected to evolution, it grows and shrinks. Hilberseimer explicitly builds his regional pattern on Geddes theses, Hilberseimer 1949c, 88-110; in Hilberseimer courses Geddes book was a required reading at the IIT.
39 Or Schmarsow's approach of architecture as hull: Schmarsow 1893.
40 Note that the German "Raum" means equally room or space. In German language doesn't exist a difference between both.
41 Hake 2008.
42 Hilberseimer 1927b.
43 Aureli 2011.
44 Aureli clearly refers to O.M. Ungers Stadtarchipelago project from 1977, for a detailed presentation of the draft, see: Ungers et al. 2013.
45 This concept origins in the work of Oswald Mathias Ungers, who introduced Nikolaus von Kuehn's term: *coincidentia oppositorum* into urban design: confrontations, accidents and complements as a theme for architecture Cepl 2007, 415.
46 Definition from Eisenman in: Eisenman 2010.
47 Aureli 2011, 2-7.
48 13-16.

Notes

49 "Thus the form of the city emerges from the repetition of a single typology, and reflects the logic of the most conventional geometry possible – that of the grid" 14.

50 "As each unit would contain all the essentials of a community, its population should be large enough to meet the social and personal requirements of the individual, large enough to offer varies in work and in life, large enough to support necessary communal, cultural , and hygienic institutions. But it should also be small enough to preserve an organic community lire, so that democracy might prevail and each individual participate in community activities." Hilberseimer 1955, 193.

51 "The city, as a vast ocean of houses, will disappear, and residential zones will be embedded into the landscape and become a part of it." Hilberseimer 12/ 1940, page 12.

52 Hilberseimer 1964.

53 104.

54 Aureli 2012.

55 Page 16.

56 Hays 1992, 270.

57 Kilian 2002, 36.

58 Anderson 2014.

59 26.

60 62.

61 Tafuri 1985, c1976, 106.

62 Kant 1919, A140.

63 Heidegger 1991, 96.

64 96.

65 98.

66 98.

67 The term of logical form Hoyningen-Huene 1998, 23-27.

68 Probably the most comprehensive and most accomplished classification into the philosophical and historical context provided Wladyslaw Tatarkiewicz with his essay on the history of the form: (Tatarkiewicz 1980, 220-243). The overview presented here is based in large part on Tatarkiewiczs consideration.

69 Focillon 1989.

70 Tatarkiewicz 1980, 232.

71 Probably best defined by Tristan Garcia: "Nothing is the absence of something, the empty place left by something. Nothing is what remains when one has removed something. In other words, nothing is the negative form of something without this something." Garcia 2014, 46.

72 Wölfflin 1915.

73 Rowe and Koetter 1997.

74 Aureli 2008.

75 Venturi, Scott Brown, and Izenour 1977.

76 Schumacher 2012a.
77 Alberti 1456, 203.
78 Alberti and Theuer 1452, 293.
79 Müller-Sievers 1997.
80 Shaviro 2014, 134-137.
81 Hildebrand 1918, 16-18. Contemporarly Graham Harman differentiates similar between Real Object and Sensual Object in his definition of an object: Harman 2011, 114.
82 Riegl 1893.
83 Hilberseimer 1988, 94.
84 Alberti 1541.
85 Already former reviews pointed to a parallel between Hilberseimer and Alberti. Markus Kilian portrayed the settlement unit as horizontal proportional study according to the rules of Alberti. But a precise study, presentation of the thesis is still lacking Kilian 2002, 134-135.
86 Alberti and Edward Owen 1755, 23.
87 Hilberseimer 1944, 74-75.
88 "Architecture is largely dependent on the solution of two factors: the single cell of the room and the entire city organism. The room as a part of the combined houses into a street-block will determine in its appearance and becomes a factor of shaping the urban layout, the actual goals of the architecture. Conversely, the design the city plan will gain significant influence on the formation of rooms and houses." Hilberseimer 1925d, 4.
89 Alberti 1541, 12; in englisch: "the city is like some large house, and the house is in turn like some small city," Alberti and Edward Owen 1755, 23.
90 For a contemporary analysis of the concept of beauty in Alberti see Carpo 2011. Carpo argues that Alberti's definition allows for a precise articulation and translation of thought into a building. By the proportional relationship architecture is copyable, regardless of location. The idea and thus the authorship of the architect is strengthened, the building is the Replique of the plan. Carpo however also shows that the general rule of a proportion is not dissimilar to what we today call algorithm. To describe this kind of architecture includes the potential for infinite variance. In more recent texts Carpo argues that the solution set is unpredictable due to the number of combinations. The task of the architect shifts, from a determinative determination of properties to feeling and finding of possibilities.
91 Alberti and Theuer 1452, 492.
92 Hilberseimer translates the German word Städtebau, as City Architecture, and not as urban design see: Hilberseimer 1963a.
93 Alberti 1541, 288; in Italian: "Tre cose danno vaghezza a la fabrica, il *numero*, la *figura*, e la *collocatione*. [...] come ricerca la convenienza" Alberti 1456, 202; in English: "That the Beauty of all Edifices arises principally from three Things, namely, the *Number*, *Figure* and *Collocation* of the several Members." Alberti and Edward Owen 1755, 651.
94 Hilberseimer 1956, 36 as well in: Hilberseimer 1949a, 108.

95 Its goal is to achieve an optimal order adequate to the city's physical order. City architecture has but limited means for the realization of such aims. Hilberseimer 1955, 161.
96 Hilberseimer 1963a, 1-2.
97 Hilberseimer 1944, XV.
98 St. Augustin, De Ordine, 386, llib.II.,c. XIV. col. 1014, t. I., in English: "From here, the ratio step further to the forces of the eyes, and as she looked to earth and sky, she felt that she only liked the beauty, and beauty the forms in the forms the dimensions and in the dimensions the numbers." Augustinus 386 / 1940, 75.
99 Riegl 1901, 213.
100 De Ordine lib. IJ., c. xvru, t. J., col. 1017, in: Augustinus 386 / 1940, 75.
101 Riegl 1901, 212.
102 The order of a city means the order of all its parts; the order of a house means the order of all its parts, everything in the house. Yet, to understand order, we could well begin with a chair, or even with the simplest household utensil, a fork or a plate. Before we can say it has its proper place, it must first be proper itself. Does it serve its use in the best possible way? Does it belong to itself? Has it a true identity? Is it not perhaps the ambiguous aping of something else? Is it clear what it is? was it created out of the life of our time, out of our spirit, needs, methods – like this chair? Hilberseimer 1949a, 10.
103 Augustinus 386 / 1940, 75.
104 "To the knowledge of things no one should struggle without the ability to talk logically and without insight into the theory of numbers." 79.
105 An introductory overview of the formal logic of mereology provides Peter Simons in Simons 2000 ; for the first time mereology was mentioned as such by Stanislaw Lesniewski 1929 see:Stanislaw Lesniewski 1929.
106 The here presented, historical framework has been adopted in large parts by: Casati and Varzi 1999, 29-30. Casati's and Varzi's framework was extended to include the exact philosophical sources and own conclusions.
107 Aristoteles 1837, V 25 1023b 10.
108 Aristoteles et al. 1978, V 25 1023b 25.
109 Husserl 1901, 224-230.
110 Ridder 2002, 393.
111 Husserl 1901, 286.
112 Ehrenfels 1890.
113 See among others Konrad Fiedler and Adolf Hildebrand's notion of form
114 Rescher and Oppenheim 1955.
115 All definitions in: pages 91-93; w = whole; D = decomposition; Q = attribute; Pt = parts; G = set of attributes; T = theory.
116 Page 100.
117 Simons 2000, 356-360.

118 Latour 2014, 253.
119 A detailed bibliography of mereology supplies Barry Smith: Smith 1982.
120 Ridder 2002, 58.
121 63-64.
122 Casati and Varzi 1999, 30.
123 Varzi 2014.
124 The formal descriptions of mereological conditions were never unified, most authors provide their own connotations. The here given overview follows the connotatio n of: Casati and Varzi 1999.
125 Compare Bryant: "To understand why this mereology is such a strange mereology, we must recall that all objects are independent or autonomous from one another. Objects can enter into exo-relations with one another, but they are not constituted by their relations." Bryant 2011, 214.
126 compare Bryant: »While I do not go as far as Latour in claiming that *every* relation between objects generates a third object, the important point is that the object that emerges out of other objects does not erase the objects out of which it is composed, but rather generates a third autonomous object related to these other autonomous objects.«217
127 Compare with: Schumacher 2012b, 10-96.
128 The term component includes already the subordination under a whole. The design of a component is determined by decomposition, because the whole is an inherent part of the term component. The contrast of the component is the element.
129 Lynn 1999.
130 For an overview how space and time were transformed through industrialization see: Schivelbusch 1986.
131 Mitchell Schwarzer showed extensively, how the "Rhetoric of the Line" had a strong role in German architectural theory of the second half of the 19. century: M. Schwarzer 1995.
132 Henry van de Velde explained in this way his works: van Velde 1955; as head of the "Großherzoglich Sächsischen Kunstgewerbeschule Weimar" and one of the founder of the "Deutscher Werkbund" his commitment made him as one of the precursors of German Modernism and especially the Bauhaus.
133 Schmarsow 1893.
134 M. W. Schwarzer 1991, pages 52-56.
135 Lynn 1998, 44-45.
136 "the loss of internal boundaries allows both the influence of external events within the organism and the expansion of the interior outward" 44-45.
137 45.
138 Spuybroek 2011.
139 Theodor Lipps 1906.
140 Otto and Rasch 2001, 69.

141 Schaur and Otto 1992.
142 Spuybroek and Rudolph 2004, 352-355.
143 Compare to the formal exercises at the Bauhaus, like: Kadinsky 1926. Today's interfaces of design-software with extra shelfes of points, curves and surfaces are based on such formal understandings.
144 Bryant 2011, 19.
145 See Whiteheads method of extensive abstraction and the resulting definition of geometric elements in: Whitehead 1987, 513-557; detailed description, see Chapter 4
146 See Whitehead's description Euclidean elements as a smooth loci in: 544.

The Large City:
The will to elemental architecture

1   Recent authors translated Groszstadt with Metropolis. But the translation of Groszstadt as Metropolis is in my opinion misleading. Metropolis literally from the Greek origin means "Mother-City", referring today to a city as political center, as ie. capital. Whereas Hilberseimer Schemata refer to the quantity of the city, its size and architectural problem of an order of masses. Therefore I will translate the Groszstadt with Large City, to amplify the quantific aspect of the architectural problem and Hilberseimer himself translated Groszstadt-Architektur even just as: "City Architecture" in: Hilberseimer 1963a.
2   Endell 1908, 1984, 18.
3   O. Wagner 1911.
4   Hilberseimer 1914.
5   Scheffler 1913.
6   See Anderson's. introduction to the English translation of Large-City-Architecture, which, however, is an edited, no neutral translation by a different layout, differently named paragraphs and exuberant illustrations. Anderson 2014.
7   Quote of Riegl 1901, 5 in: Hilberseimer 1914.
8   On the influence of Alois Riegl's concept of Kunstwollen on Hilberseimer's architectural theory approach has already been mentioned several times, a more detailed analysis is still missing. Marco de Michelis sees the Kunstwollen as an argument of the large city as an expression of their productive, capitalist characteristics. "the will to conceive art as creation and not as reproduction. [. . .] try to attribute the specificity of the modern metropolis to the project of domination expressed by anonymous capital." in: Michelis 1986, 7-9. As an art historian Agnes Kohlmeyer recognizes that Hilberseimer used the concept of Kunstwollen as art historical continuation by Nietzsche's concept of the Dionysian: "Alois Riegl's concept of Kunstwollen is superimposed over Nietsche's Dionysian concept." in: Kohlmeyer 1986. Michael Hays is interested in the Kunstwollen as an expression of the relationship between architectural object and the user: "Hilberseimer understands Riegl's concept of Kunstwollen as a complex and medi-

ated relationship between subject and object" in: Hays 1992, 208-209. Mark Kilian understand the Kunstwollen in Hilberseimer as an argument for the development of a scientific planning methodology: "Kunstwollen as the question of the position of art in the age of Enlightenment" in: Kilian 2002, 36.

9   Tafuri 1985, c1976, 106.

10 Also Tessenow can serve as a model according to Richard Pommer. Pommer, in its analysis also points out that Hilberseimer early drafts have a comparable similarity with designs of Tessenow. Pommer 1988.

11 "The Wonders of the present are the wonders of technology. Their one-sided overestimation created as a basis automatism. [...] Instead of bringing freedom, enslaved automatism. Instead of man the machine became Lord over all. Man was degraded to an automaton. So was the vaunted development, progress has been turned on its head. Was to step back. The spirit succumbed to matter, rather than to shape their formation associated with it" Hilberseimer 1922c, 40.

12 Hilberseimer 1922b.

13 Hilberseimer 2.02.1919, page 30.

14 Hilberseimer equals the idea with the will, does not distinguish between both: the will of the body understands Hilberseimer as the materialization of the Kantian thing-in-itself.

15 Hilberseimer 26.01.1919, page 17.

16 On the last page of every magazine you will find a programmatic opinion of the magazine: "The only [...] knows no parties. He stands on a strictly individualistic ground and fight against each mass suggestion and mass psychosis. He is of the opinion that the rescue of the confused presence into a clearer future appeal to the ego, is to be found by going back to individuals like Stirner and Nietzsche only again, whose ideas he developed before all others, and will continue to expand"; So a work against the immaturity of the industrial worker, automation and mass-ornament.

17 Worringer 2004b, 231.

18 Worringer 2004a.

19 See Erich Panofski's essay on the KunstwollenPanofsky 1920.

20 Mallgrave and Semper 2001, 372-399.

21 Riegl 1889.

22 Riegl 1893.

23 Riegl 1901.

24 According to Malgrave the Rapture Riegl's from Semper had far-reaching consequences, Mallgrave speaks of a sacrificial ritual that Semper's theory finally was reviewed semperianian, art as pure materialistic, from now. Distorted, was the work of Semper by Riegl as a secondary source, as insignificant in the first half of the 20th century, until the start of the post-modernist discourse Semper was rediscovered.

25 5.

26 Hilberseimer 1956, 11.
27 Riegl 1893, 30.
28 Hilberseimer 1949c, 15.
29 Sedlmayr 1928, XIX.
30 XVIII.
31 Riegl 1966, 217.
32 22.
33 208-216.
34 Hilberseimer 1955, 133-160.
35 Mertins and Lambert 2014, 242.
36 Hilberseimer 1944, 19-22.
37 Hilberseimer 1955, 133.
38 Mertins and Lambert 2014, 246.
39 Hilberseimer 1944, 19.
40 Detailed information by: Sungho Choi, Michael Fara 2006.
41 Both comparisons takes Hilberseimer from Frobenius and Fox 1999. As anthropologist Frobenius dealt with the formalization of African tribes.
42 Riegl 1928, 60.
43 Riegl 1966, 21.
44 August Schmarsow, Heinrich Wölfflin, Konrad Fiedler und Robert Vischer.
45 Riegl 1928, 61.
46 Riegl 1901, 17-33.
47 Hilberseimer 1914, 5.
48 Hilberseimer 1922d.
49 Originally planned Hilberseimer the publication of an art-critical essay collection entitled "Creation and Development"; the published version of the text is significantly reduced compared to the manuscript version: Hilberseimer 1922c.
50 10.
51 The first time in: Hilberseimer 1944, 19-28.
52 Le Corbusier 1925, 1987.
53 In: Hilberseimer 1922c, 12 and: Hilberseimer 26.01.1919, page 17.
54 Hilberseimer 1922c, 17.
55 Hilberseimer is not alone. After Posener many of the modernist architect borrowed from the work of Nietzsche Posener 2013b.
56 Hilberseimer 2.02.1919, pages 30-31.
57 Hilberseimer 26.01.1919.
58 Hilberseimer 1923a.
59 Nietzsche 1922, 259-260.
60 Hilberseimer 1922a, page 531.

61 "the art, the will" in: Hilberseimer 1922c, 14.
62 Heidegger 1961.
63 Nietzsche and Wohlfart 1872, 2010.
64 Dorn 2006.
65 Heidegger 1961, 122.
66 Schäfer 2011.
67 Nietzsche and Wohlfart 1872, 2010, 29.
68 Schäfer 2011, page 178.
69 Bohrer 2007, 218.
70 Schäfer 2011, page 184.
71 Nietzsche and Wohlfart 1872, 2010, 105-106.
72 Schäfer 2011, page 189.
73 Nietzsche uses a German word switch: Vor-Schein, in English literally pre-shine, but in German the word means as well appearance.
74 Nietzsche and Wohlfart 1872, 2010, 61-62.
75 Hilberseimer 1922c, 8-9.
76 Schäfer 2011, page 197.
77 Heidegger 1961, 114-121.
78 Hilberseimer 1922c, 14.
79 14.
80 Heidegger 1961, 131.
81 133.
82 138.
83 138-139.
84 Nietzsche's paragraph 842: "Musik und der große Stil" in: Nietzsche 1922, 129-260.
85 Heidegger 1961, 140.
86 142.
87 Hilberseimer 1923a, page 136.
88 Page 140.
89 Page 140.
90 Hilberseimer 1925d, 26.
91 7, 22, 28.
92 "Primary is the abstraction. Secondary naturalization. Because naturalization is always corollary. Its cause is loss of contents. Disbelief seeks the realization of reality. Routine. Technology. Unbroken purity of will created the works of the exotic plastic. Deep religiosity is the cause of their creation. Her worship natural consequence" Hilberseimer 1921, 20.
93 Heidegger 1961, 168-169.
94 156.
95 Tafuri 1985, c1976, 106.

96 In German: übersinnlich, literally translated: above-sensual.
97 Heidegger 1961, 87.
98 Hilberseimer 1922c, 20.
99 20.
100 Heidegger 1961, 212-213.
101 208.
102 223.
103 265.
104 Hilberseimer 26.01.1919, page 16.
105 Hilberseimer 1927b.
106 Hilberseimer 1925d.
107 Hilberseimer 1914.
108 Hilberseimer 1922a.
109 Hilberseimer 1923a.
110 Hilberseimer 1922c.
111 Hilberseimer 1926.
112 On pages Hilberseimer 1927b, 17-20; published for the first time, but only by means of two diagrams: Hilberseimer 1925d.
113 Hilberseimer 1955.
114 Hilberseimer 1944.
115 Blum 1990, 119.
116 German: Sozialistische Monatshefte; entire edition available online at http://library.fes.de/sozmon/.
117 Hilberseimer 1919, page 273.
118 Hilberseimer 28.06.1920, page 523.
119 Hilberseimer 1923c.
120 Hilberseimer 1925c.
121 Hilberseimer, März 1926.
122 Mark Kilian points out that the critical operational method, which develops Hilberseimer, is influenced by the Dadaists in Berlin whose circles he frequented was Kilian 2002, 39-40. In their immediate artistic accomplishment of the social reality Hilberseimer recognizes a possibility which by inference in a position to influence society.
123 An irritating title as the exhibition itself consisted almost exclusively of photographic material. Detailed historical context in: Kieren 1998. The name "International" is to be seen against Hilberseimers political background. "The Internationale" was a synonym for a global labor movement. One intention is that Hilberseimer referred with the exhibition title not only to the geographical gathering of projects but their political will as well.
124 Initiated by the then chairman of the German Werkbund: Peter Bruckmann.
125 Curator: Mies van der Rohe.
126 Hilberseimer 1927b, 18.

127 Hilberseimer 1955, 276.
128 Mengin 1986b.
129 Proposal for City buildings von 1928-30 in: Hilberseimer 1930.
130 First published in G, 1922. English translation in: Jennings and Mertins 2011.
131 In: Hilberseimer 1920; Hilberseimer 1922a; Hilberseimer 1923b; Hilberseimer 1925a; Hilberseimer, März 1926.
132 Holl 1980.
133 Hilberseimer 1927b, 39-40.
134 Hays 1992.
135 Hilberseimer 1927b, 12.
136 99.
137 The following description is a summary of: 17-19.
138 See: Hilberseimer 1929e and Hilberseimer 1930.
139 The same requirement will result in horizontal arrangement – in the settlement unit – to its typical herringbone structure.
140 Fig. 22 in: Hilberseimer 1927b, 17.
141 Possible divisions of the layouts of the workshops, offices and the ground floor plan of the residential city with shops, community facilities and entrances to the houses do not exist.
142 See figure 3.24.
143 Kilian 2002, 71-77.
144 "Schema einer Wohnstadt", Fig. 25, p 25 in: Hilberseimer 1925d.
145 Analogous to the residential city were placed in the plan drawings of the city element solitaires at the ends of the east-west streets; unlike in the original plan schema by Hilberseimer
146 Depending on the block 32-37 rows at 14 storeys.
147 Hilberseimer 1927b, 99 originally in: Hilberseimer 1925d, 2.
148 Hilberseimer 1927b, 100.
149 The architecture of the 'Twenties was characterized by its objectivity, its directness, and its simplicity. Its trend was toward architectural autonomy. It aimed to free itself from all external influences, from all traditional bonds, to be self-determined, and to realize its goals by the true means of architecture. It tried to discover the elements of architecture and to use them in their purest form. Hilberseimer 1964, 104.
150 Mertins and Lambert 2014, 242.
151 Kaufmann 1933.
152 Hildebrand 1918, 16-17.
153 Müller-Sievers 1997.
154 Mertins and Lambert 2014, 241-242.
155 Jennings and Mertins 2011, 76.
156 Bergdoll 1994, 103-170.
157 Schinkel 1829.

158 Hilberseimer 1964, 116.
159 Hilberseimer 1922a, page 526.
160 Hilberseimer 1923a, page 138.
161 Hilberseimer 1927b, 17-19.
162 102.
163 Hilberseimer 1925d.
164 Hilberseimer used intentionally not the word facade from Latin facies: face; Cover and appearance.
165 Hilberseimer 1927b, 100.
166 100 and Hilberseimer 1922a, page 531.
167 Hays 1992, 263.
168 Wolfendale 2014, 15.

The unfolding of a planning idea

1 The exhibition was shown also a year later in Stuttgart. All photos are obtained from Stuttgart. Only in the photos is mentioned as author Hilberseimer. A portrait of him in front of a tower of stacked high-rise buildings is regarded as an indication of its authorship. Hilberseimer itself mentions the city design itself not in any of its publications. Pommer 1988, 39.
2 Vittorio Gregotti et al. 1986, 14.
3 Hilberseimer 1925d, 25.
4 Hilberseimer 1929e.
5 The in *Kunstblatt* published article contains only a mass study in axonometric view. In the mass study the canopy of the courtyards was not shown, but textually mentioned as a possibility. Was not until in the article in *Der Form* published contains all other representations of the study. Only in the mass study the blocks are connected on the pedestrian level. The connection to the underground, public transport network, by means of escalators and elevators is missing. Hilberseimer 1930.
6 Because only the abstraction allows to show the particular case, like the disparate elements that make up a city, can be brought into an evocative order to the city. Hilberseimer 1929e, page 93.
7 Hays 1992, 176-183.
8 183.
9 Hilberseimer 1929a.
10 238.
11 Hilberseimer 1931c, 130.
12 Hilberseimer 1964, 182.
13 Hilberseimer 1931c.
14 Hilberseimer 1929a, 239.

15 Hilberseimer 1929e.
16 Hilberseimer 1930.
17 Hilberseimer 1944, 103.
18 The Art Institute of Chicago 1988, 138-139.
19 Pommer 1988.
20 Hilberseimer 1927a.
21 Hilberseimer 1929b.
22 Alberti and Theuer 1452, 293.
23 Hays 1992, 136-143.
24 26.
25 Mertins and Lambert 2014, 196.
26 Hannes Meyer deliberately used the word Bau- building instead of architecture Droste 1989, 135.
27 Winkler 2003, 115.
28 115.
29 115.
30 115-116.
31 Posener 2013a.
32 Kremer 1984, 205.
33 210-213.
34 Hilberseimer 1929b, 4.
35 M. 1. Wagner 1932.
36 Hilberseimer 1929b.
37 Hilberseimer 1929c.
38 Sitte 2002.
39 Not only to communities and housing projects, but also to any other group of buildings can the same planning principles be applied, see: Hilberseimer 1963a, 24.
40 Compare: Hilberseimer 1944, 160.
41 The sequence is based on Hilberseimer own annotation of research used in: Hilberseimer 1929b, 1.
42 Hilberseimer 1923d.
43 Hilberseimer uses the term "city of princes" for the despotic city. The term of the "Fürstenstadt" was introduced by Max Weber about 1914 in his sociological studies on economy and society. See also: Weber and Nippel 1999, 11-13. It suggests that Hilberseimer statements are based on a wide-ranging investigation of that former literature to the city.
44 Hilberseimer 1925b.
45 Hilberseimer 1924.
46 See also: "The best apartment will be be the one that has become a perfect commodity and thus reduces the resistance of everyday life to a minimum." Hilberseimer 1927a, page 69.

47 Hilberseimer 1925e.
48 Hilberseimer 1925d.
49 Hilberseimer 1927b.
50 26.
51 Hilberseimer 1928.
52 With folding bed in the living room none at all Hilberseimer 1927b, 23.
53 Note: Parents are no longer seen as individuals.
54 Hilberseimer 1923a, page 136.
55 Hilberseimer 1931a, page 250.
56 Hilberseimer 1931b.
57 The difference in the qualitative or quantitative marking of a significant has substantial impact on the economics of an object; see Deleuze & Guattaris distinction between neurosis and psychosis in: Deleuze and Guattari 1992, 43-59.
58 See, the concept of the Linear by:Wölfflin 1915, 15-17.
59 Hilberseimer 1944, 74-75.
60 Hilberseimer 1932.
61 These are standard descriptions of programm languages, for a broad overview of the history of object-oriented-programming see: Sebesta, Mukherjee, and Bhattacharjee 2013.
62 For a general introduction: Eastman 2011.
63 Christian Wolsdorff 1986, 45.
64 Mertins and Lambert 2014, 196-197.
65 See Blaser's analysis of the courtyard house project of the American student Dearstyne Howard, developed in 1931 "a spatial solution with brick walls that surround the house and yard: the space is the primary, the position of the walls is determined by him. The inner and outer form a whole." Blaser 1977, 7.
66 Mertins and Lambert 2014, 223-225.
67 Saliga 1993, 57-58.
68 Hilberseimer 1935, Hilberseimer 2.1936.
69 Both articles become a section in: Hilberseimer 1944, 78-91.
70 Hilberseimer 1933.
71 Compare Table 1. Average time insolation in: Hilberseimer 1935, page 3; at another place: The beneficial effects of the ultra-violet rays may be obtained only when the sun can penetrate into the room at the season when they are at their maximum intensity the season between May and September and the hours of 8 am. to 4 pm. Hilberseimer 1944, 85.
72 Kilian 2002, 93.
73 Compare: "In a social organized society where production does not meet the needs of the people, the greed for profit of individual Privileged, turns also the city into a meaningful contemporary organism, transforms from a destructive to constructive entity." Hilberseimer 1927b, 2.

74 See Gilbert Simondons Analysis of the technical object: "The machine is embedded and kept, fixed human gesture, stereotypy and capacity became to resumption." Simondon 2012, 127.
75 Hilberseimer 1935, page 30.
76 An extensive argument for a concept of radiation builds up Lars Spuybroek, based on his research on Greek aesthetics in: Lars Spuybroek. 2014. Charis and radiance: The ontological dimensions of beauty. In *Giving and taking: Antidotes to a culture of greed,* edited by Joke Brouwer and Sjoerd van Tuinen, pages 119–149. Rotterdam: NAI.
77 Hilberseimer 1949a.
78 19-27.
79 Kilian 2002.
80 Pommer 1988.
81 Hilberseimer 12/ 1940.
82 Hilberseimer 1923d.
83 Hilberseimer lists more precursors in: Hilberseimer 1940: Ebenezer Howard, Ludwig Sierks, Frank Loyd Wright, N. A. Miljutin, Henry Ford; in the manuscript text Hilberseimer, n.d. places Hilberseimer his own work in a linear development to finally present the city as an organism. The list includes: Camillo Sitte, E.R. Lever, Ebenezer Howard, Richard Olmsted, Brix, Le Corbusier, Martin Mächler, Ludwig Sierks, Soria Y Mata, Mijutin and Hilberseimer.
84 Unwin 1929; Hilberseimer shows Unwins ribbon structure in: Hilberseimer 1944, 105.
85 For spatial planning analysis, see: Pope 1996.
86 "The group pattern determines the appropriate traffic system." Hilberseimer, n.d. 6; see also: Hilberseimer 1965.
87 "The question arises whether the traffic must be regarded as the main problem of city planning, or whether it would be possible to remove the mechanical, local traffic through the establishment of a reasonable relationship between the various elements that determine an urban settlement." Hilberseimer 1947.
88 Posener 2013a.
89 Industrial sector may also consist of commercial buildings, crafts and workshops.
90 The distribution of settlement units according to the wind direction appears in a study on the reorganization of Dessau for the first time. The study was developed in the 30s with the help of Bauhaus students, it is unclear whether the Bauhaus at that time still existed, or whether it was a commissioned work. The Dessau-study is also the first study Hilberseimers, which reorganized an existing city with schematic settlement units. For the first time published in: Hilberseimer 1944, 134-135.
91 For houses of the residential area without sufficient large gardens. The concept of self-sufficiency takes Hilberseimer from Peter Kropotkin: Kropotkin 1913.
92 Hilberseimer 1955, 216.

93 Settlement aggregates could be of varied shapes, such as triangles, squares, octagons, any geometric figures which added to each other fit together. Hilberseimer 1949c.
94 The name of the article is also the title of the second part of *The New City*.
95 Hilberseimer 1944, 76.
96 85-86.
97 Bauhaus Archiv 1986, 174-175.
98 Hilberseimer 1955, 212.

The punctualisation as architectural method

1 Hilberseimer 1964, 15-22.
2 Hilberseimer 1922c, 20.
3 Law 1992.
4 For a detailed overview of the nature of technological elements and the nature of their design, see: Simondon 2012.
5 "Whitehead distinguishes points in the instantaneous, time-bound space called by him puncts or event-particles, from the points of the timeless space of physics, for which he reserves the term points." Ridder 2002, 215.
6 Whitehead 1987, 544-545.
7 Ridder 2002, 197.
8 197-198.
9 "The relevant steps which leads Whitehead to his abstract geometric point term and which constitute his method of extensive abstraction can be summarized as follows: 1. Declaration of a relation of the non-tangential part between regions on the basis of the primitive connection relation. 2. Distinction of infinite, non-tangential nested sequences of regions that approximate an extensive minimum (abstract sets). 3. Defining of an equivalence relation on the set of all abstract sets (mutual overlap).4. Formation of equivalence classes (geometric elements) 5. Generating a strict order on the set of geometric elements (incidence relation) 6. Definition of a point as minimal element with respect to this order." in: 239.
10 304.
11 Aristoteles 2006.
12 Aristoteles 1837, V, 1022a-b.
13 (2.a) "As the building knowledge is a type of manufacturing knowledge (techne) and by its nature is a certain with consideration affiliated diposition of manufacturing [. . .] are knowledge of manufacturing and with true reasoning associated disposition of manufacturing be the same. [. . .] (b) Because the knowledge of manufacturing does not relate to what is necessarily or what is produced even to what occurs by nature because it has its origin in itself. But as making and action are different, has to belong to the knowledge of manufacturing making, not the action." Aristoteles 2006, 1139 a 5-10.

14 Heidegger 2005.
15 "The tool-being of the Equipment, the reliability, holds all things according to their kind and comprehensiveness collected in itself. [...] The individual tool is worn out and exhausted." Heidegger 1960, 28-29.
16 "But what about the third case - nature? [...] Heidegger repeatedly reminds us that such objects are abstractions that reduce the things of the world to a set of present-at-hand traits that fail to capture the cryptic, withdrawn reality of things. If we weigh and measure a thing, describe its physical properties, or note its objective position in space-time, these qualities hold good for the thing only insofar as it is relates to us or to something else. In short, the thing as portrayed by natural sciences is the thing made dependent on our knowledge, and not in its untamed, subterranean reality." Harman 2011, 52.
17 Heidegger 1960, 41.
18 Latour and Porter 2004, 21.
19 Latour 2006.
20 "The sacrilege is that the opposition between tool and broken tool can actually be restated as the competition between a thing and its parts. When a house is assembled from pillars, beams, baseboards, chimneys, and carpets, it siphons from these objects only the limited number of features that it needs. The house never fully grasps or even deploys the total reality of its stairwells and electrical cords, which withdraw from the house into the shadows of their private reality. In other words, a thing relates to its parts in the same way that it relates to other things, and indeed in the same way that we ourselves relate to things: namely by distorting them, caricaturing them, bringing them into play only partially." Harman 2005, 172.
21 Hays 1992, 187-194.
22 Padovan 1986, revised in: Padovan 2002, 146-173.
23 Riegl 1901, 64.
24 210.
25 Deleuze and Guattari 1992, 682-693.
26 43-59.
27 "The determination of the size of a unit within the residential area will depend mainly on the total inhabitants, the density of population and the type of building." Hilberseimer 12/ 1940, page 9.
28 Hilberseimer 1925b.
29 Hilberseimer 1925b.
30 Hilberseimer 12/ 1940.
31 Hilberseimer 1925e.
32 Hilberseimer in an interview about the temporal aspect of a city: "Surely a city is an organism that needs as any other specific conditions, in order to exist. If the livelihoods taken from it, the city is destroyed like any other organism." Interviewer, n.d. 1.
33 Hilberseimer 1925e.

34 Hilberseimer 1923d.
35 Hilberseimer 1925b.
36 Hilberseimer 1924.
37 "But the quality of an apartment is less dependent on their height position as the fulfillment of other conditions such as sunlight, ventilation, appropriate distances and the organization of the floor plan" Hilberseimer 1929d, 5.
38 Sir Gwilyn Gibbon suggests a plan to avoid the complications which ensue when individual owners must be dealt with separately. He proposes the compulsory pooling of ownership, each owner to be reimbursed according the value of his property. Freed from the obstacles of property boundaries and rights, the reconstruction of some city districts, and the creation of new traffic routes, could thus be more easily effected. Hilberseimer 1944, 164.
39 Aristoteles. and Schwarz 1989.
40 1252a-1253a.
41 "So far we know, the Polis was the result of the process of synoicism: the condensation of a clan into a city" Hilberseimer 1955, 42; similar in: Hilberseimer 1963a, 6.
42 Aristotle, however, recognized other considerations influencing the size of a city. It should be small enough, he thought, so that every citizen could hear the speaker on the Agora; large enough lo provide as many hoplites as any neighboring city with which it might come into conflict. It had to be prepared against aggression. Hilberseimer 1955, 42.
43 Aristotle's measure of the physical size of his ideal territory was the need of its people. It should be of such size, he said, "as may enable the inhabitants to live at once temperately and liberally in the enjoyment of leisure. It should be a territory which is all-producing, for to have all things and to want nothing is sufficiency" 43.
44 Hilberseimer 1949c, XIV.
45 Hilberseimer 1955, 193.
46 42-43.
47 The schools do not seem to be supported by an institution but are run by the congregation of the neighboring settlement units. Although there is a schematic layout of a school, which is a kind of placeholder in the drawings of the Settlement Unit. But this type of building designed Hilberseimer or his students never specifically.
48 196.
49 Weber and Nippel 1999, 110.
50 Hilberseimer 1949b.
51 Limitation of the analysis: The studies of the Flat-Building and the Settlement-Unit extend a time frame from the first Bauhaus seminars 1928 until the last studies at IIT in 1967. Most of the drawings thus do not come from Hilberseimer himself but are student works under his supervision as teacher. For this reason, I will restrict my analysis to drawings, which were selected by Hilberseimer himself before. As part of publications, also part of academic work, such as master's thesis; as kept works and today part of archives. The index numbers in the

analytic drawings refer to the original drawings: (0.1): Fig. 17, p. 3; (0.2): Fig. 18, p. 3 in: Hilberseimer 1929b; (1.1): p. 266 in: Hilberseimer 1931a; (2.1-2.4.): Fig. 6, p. 776 in Hilberseimer 1931b; (2.5-2.8): Fig. 13; (2.9, 2.10): Fig. 12, p. 778 in Hilberseimer 1931b; (3.1-3.3): Fig. 6, p. 474 in: Hilberseimer 1932, (3.4, 3.5): Fig. 7, p. 474, (3.6, 3.7): Fig. 9, p. 475 in: Hilberseimer 1932; (3.8, 3.9): Fig. 10, p. 475; (3.10): Fig, 12, p. 477; (3.11): Fig. 16, p. 478; in: Hilberseimer 1932; (4.1-4.3): p. 11 in: Hilberseimer 12/ 1940; (5.1): Fig. 67, p. 92; (5.2-5.4): Fig. 68, p. 94 in: Hilberseimer 1944; (6.1-6.4): Fig. 68, p. 136 in: Hilberseimer 1949c; (7.1-7.6): Fig. 186, p. 208 in: Hilberseimer 1955; (8.1-8.6): 1947 Projekt Evergreen II, Chicago, Hausgrundrisse Fig. 113; (8.7-8.8): L-förmige Häuser Fig. 114, p. 130 in: Hilberseimer 1963b; (9.1-9.9): 1950 Chicago neu geplant, Wohnungsgrundrisse, Fig. 72, p.90 in: Hilberseimer 1963b; (12.1-12.15): n.d. House Plan Study; (13.1-13.16): n.d. one-family-houses, Series 10.1 Box 3 Folder 9 in: Ryerson and Burnham Archives Finding Aids, The Art Institute of Chicago.

52   Hilberseimer 1949b.

53   Hilberseimer here takes on a concept of Peter Kropotkin, Kropotkin 1913; compare Alfred Caldwell's Master-Thesis, supervised by Hilberseimer: Caldwell 1948; in more detail Hilberseimer writes: "The location of the vegetable gardens in the open area instead of beside the homes has certain advantages other than economy. Such an arrangement would create a productive park system. The recreational area would thus be increased and the cost of its maintenance considerably decreased." Hilberseimer 1944, 125.

54   Hilberseimer 2.1936.

55   For his very existence, man must change nature's way and adjust it to his needs.Hilberseimer 1949c, 125.

56   The city, in fact, becomes part of the landscape. The one-storey house in the settlement unit disappears among trees and behind shrubs and a natural camouflage results. The city will be within the landscape and the landscape within the city. Hilberseimer 1944, 126.

57   Spaeth 1988, 56.

58   In the manuscript Hilberseimer 1963a, 21 illustrates Hilberseimer his architectural intention with the element nature: "Low density in itself can be architecturally very undistinctive [...] If low density is combined with the mixed type of settlement, [...] architectural values may become possible and the feeling of spaciousness and openness may be achieved. This becomes possible because the single family houses optically disappear behind the trees and bushes of their gardens and the community surrounding parks. What remains to be seen are the few freestanding multi storied apartment buildings, which gain through their disposition in space a new architectural importance and make also the realization of a new space concept, based on openness, possible."

59   Ecology, the branch of biology which deals with the relation of organisms to their environments, has taught us that the landscape, with all its vital force, man the animal included, is an integrated whole, based on a natural cooperation, on a comprehensive symbiosis Hilberseimer 1949c, 121.

60   Hilberseimer 1963b, 101.

61   Zenbei Furya, Mito and its Region Replanned; IIT Master Thesis, Advisor Ludwig Hilberseimer, 1961, Chicago.

62   *The New Regional Pattern: Industries and Gardens, Workshops and Farms*, shows parallels to Kropotkin 1913. As a role model of the regional pattern lists Hilberseimer also Geddes and Branford 1917.

63   Hilberseimer 1949c, 88-89.

64   110.

Conclusion: The Art of City-Planning

1   Hilberseimer 1944, 190-191.

2   Hilberseimer 1925b, page 290.

3   Rescher and Oppenheim 1955, page 93.

4   Compare parallels of Aristotle and Hilberseimer in: Jimeno 1973.

5   Aristoteles 2006, 1139 a 5-10.

6   The room it's generating elements, floor, walls, ceiling, openings in the walls, material and color, the furniture and its layout, the link with the neighboring rooms result in a large complex of creative constructive possibilities. Hilberseimer 1923a, page 138.

7   Hilberseimer 1949b, 1.

8   Hilberseimer used all three words synonymous.

9   Hilberseimer 1963a, 2.

10   If the form of a thing is its condition, this form is always simultaneously its negative, since the form of a thing is not a thing. Form is what determines each thing and is simultaneously its surrounding, its reverse side, and its negative. Garcia 2014, 77.

11   Hilberseimer 1944, 171.

12   Hilberseimer 1963a, 1.

13   Hilberseimer 1944, 172-173.

14   Albert O. Hirschman. 1977. *The passions and the interests: Political arguments for capitalism before its triumph*. First Princeton classics edition. Princeton University Press.

15   92.

16   Christian Meier. 1985. *Politik und anmut*. Berlin: Siedler, 77-78.

List of Figures

The works shown are located in the respective institution. The copyright lies – unless stated otherwise – with the photographers or their legal successors. Not in all cases it was possible to make the holders of image rights identified. Individuals and institutions who claim rights to depicted works, we ask you to contact the editors in conjunction.

2.1	Ludwig Hilberseimer, Portraits, A: Series 10/1 Box 1 Folder 1.2; B: Series 10/1 Box 1 Folder 1.6; C: Series 10/2b Box 2 Folder 14.15, Ludwig Karl Hilberseimer Papers, Ryerson and Burnham Archives, The Art Institute of Chicago	23
2.2	left, middle: Christopher Alexander: Diagram Lattice (a), Semi-Lattice (b), p. 5 in: Alexander 1966; right: Ludwig Hilberseimer, A new Settlement-Unit and the orientation of houses, version C, fig. 82, p. 106 in: Hilberseimer 1944	26
2.3	Ludwig Hilberseimerleft: A new settlement unit, Fig. 80, S. 106 in: Hilberseimer 1944; right: Settlement Unit, detail, Fig. 88, S. 136 in: Hilberseimer 1949c	27
2.4	Ludwig Hilberseimer, A: Trabantenstadt, in: Fig. 4, p.11 in: Hilberseimer 1925d; B: Combination of Elements of a City for 4,000.000 People, p. 13 in: Hilberseimer 12/ 1940	33
2.5	Stanislaw Lesnievski, the line as mereological whole, 1916; redrawn by author	45
2.6	Greg Lynn, Spline-Diagram, in: Lynn 1999	48
2.7	Daniel Köhler, Greg Lynn's line as mereological composition, 2014	49
2.8	Daniel Köhler, Gothine04, 2014	53
2.9	Daniel Köhler, Gothine04 detail, 2014	54
2.10	Daniel Köhler, mereological line, 2014	55

240 The Mereological City: a reading of the works of Ludwig Hilberseimer

2.11 Petras Vestartas, student work, seminar: "The Figure and its Figuration", supervisor: Daniel Köhler, Rasa Navasaityte, Vilnius Academy of Arts, 2014 57
2.12 Hilberseimer, Sketches from the classroom, 1908-11, Bauhaus-Archiv Berlin, Mappe 2-6, Inv. Nr. 5550 - 5553 59

3.1 Alois Riegl, middle: Fig. 7: Lotus flower in profile 1893, right: Fig. 8: Lotus flower in profile, p. 48; links: Fig. 18: Lotus flower with mugging sepals by Goodyear, p. 61 in: Riegl 1893 64
3.2 Alois Riegl, Fig. 101, 102, 103, p. 201, handle ornaments from Greek amphorae in: Riegl 1893 65
3.3 Daniel Köhler, Rasa Navasaityte, Choreograments, 2010 67
3.4 Ludwig Hilberseimer, The Geometrical and the Organic City, Fig. 90: Castellazzo di Fontanellato, Fig. 91: Glastonbury, p. 131 in: Hilberseimer 1955 69
3.5 Alois Riegl, Late Roman sarcophagus, Fig. 13, p. 74 in: Riegl 1901 . 72
3.6 Ludwig Hilberseimer, draft of a factory building, left: p. 140 in: Hilberseimer 1923a, middle: Fig. 28: High-rise floor plan, p. 26: Hilberseimer 1925d; redrawn by author 77
3.7 Ludwig Hilberseimer, living house 1, top: original drawing: fig. 31: Wohnhaus, p. 28 in: Hilberseimer 1925d 78
3.8 Ludwig Hilberseimer, Development of the high-rise typology, top: p. 39, 40 in: Hilberseimer 1927b; bottom: highrise studies in: Hilberseimer 1923b 82
3.9 Ludwig Hilberseimer, Chicago Tribune Tower, 1922, drawing by author 83
3.10 Daniel Köhler, Collage: The City as a democracy of architectural elements, original photographs from Hilberseimer 1927b 85
3.11 Ludwig Hilberseimer, Vertical-City, perspective North-South Street, left: Fig. 5, p. 14. Hilberseimer 1925d, right: first published: Fig. 23, p. 18 in: Hilberseimer 1927b; original: Series 10/2a, Box.FF 1.4, Ludwig Karl Hilberseimer Papers, Ryerson and Burnham Archives, The Art Institute of Chicago 86
3.12 Ludwig Hilberseimer, Vertical-City, perspective East-West Street; Left: Fig. 5, p. 12 in: Hilberseimer 1925d, right: first published: Fig. 24, p. 19 in: Hilberseimer 1927b, original: Series 10/2a, Box.FF 1.5, Ludwig Karl Hilberseimer Papers, Ryerson and Burnham Archives, The Art Institute of Chicago 86

3.13 Ludwig Hilberseimer, Schema of a Vertical-City, city plan, 1927, first published: Fig. 22, p 17 in: Hilberseimer 1927b; original: Series 10/2a, OP 15, Ludwig Karl Hilberseimer Papers, Ryerson and Burnham Archives, The Art Institute of Chicago 88

3.14 Ludwig Hilberseimer, schema of a Vertical-City, city plan, 1927, Series 10/2a, OP 15, Ludwig Karl Hilberseimer Papers, Ryerson and Burnham Archives, The Art Institute of Chicago, overlaid diagram . 89

3.15 Ludwig Hilberseimer, schema of a Vertical-City, city plan, 1927; drawing No 1: city for 4 million inhabitants, redrawn by author . . . 92

3.16 Ludwig Hilberseimer, schema of a Vertical-City, city plan, 1927; drawing No 2: plan schema, redrawn by author 93

3.17 Ludwig Hilberseimer, schema of a Vertical-City, city plan, 1927; drawing No 4-8, redrawn by author 94

3.18 Ludwig Hilberseimer, Vertical-City , perspective East-West-Street, 1927: Series 10/2a, Box.FF 1.5, Ludwig Karl Hilberseimer Papers, Ryerson and Burnham Archives, The Art Institute of Chicago 96

3.19 Ludwig Hilberseimer, Vertical-City, perspective North-South-Street, 1927: Series 10/2a, Box.FF 1.4, Ludwig Karl Hilberseimer Papers, Ryerson and Burnham Archives, The Art Institute of Chicago 98

3.20 Ludwig Hilberseimer, Vertical-City, perspective North-South-Street, 1927: Series 10/2a, Box.FF 1.4, Ludwig Karl Hilberseimer Papers, Ryerson and Burnham Archives, The Art Institute of Chicago 99

3.21 Ludwig Hilberseimer, Vertical-City, perspective North-South-Street, 1927, analytical representations by author, original: Series 10/2a, Box.FF 1.4, Ludwig Karl Hilberseimer Papers, Ryerson and Burnham Archives, The Art Institute of Chicago; bottom: rebuilt perspective North-South-Street, drawing by author 100

3.22 Daniel Köhler, Vertical-City rebuilt, top: perspective North-South-Street, 2014; possible division of the facades; bottom: perspective of an exemplary city-block, color coding of the different units 101

3.23 Daniel Köhler, Vertical-City rebuilt, axonometric of one city element, color coding of the different units, 2014 102

3.24 Daniel Köhler, mereological analysis of the Vertical-City, 2015 . . . 106

3.25 Ludwig Hilberseimer, schema of a Vertical-City, 1927, top: drawing No. 11; midle: drawing No 9; bottom: drawing No 10; redrawn by author, original: Series 10/2a, OP 15, Ludwig Karl Hilberseimer Papers, Ryerson and Burnham Archives, The Art Institute of Chicago 107

3.26 Daniel Köhler, mereological composition (A) according to the schema of the Vertical-City, plans, 2015 108
3.27 Daniel Köhler, mereological composition (A) according to the schema of the Vertical-City, perspectives, 2015 109
3.28 Daniel Köhler, mereological composition (B) according to the schema of the Vertical-City, plans, 2015 110
3.29 Daniel Köhler, mereological composition (B) according to the schema of the Vertical-City, perspectives, 2015 111
3.30 Daniel Köhler, mereological composition (C) according to the schema of the Vertical-City, plans, 2015 112
3.31 Daniel Köhler, mereological composition (C) according to the schema of the Vertical-City, perspectives, 2015 113
3.32 Daniel Köhler, selection of three possible mereological compositions inherent in the schema of the Vertical-City, 2015 114
3.33 Daniel Köhler, model foto of three mereological compositions inherent in the schema of the Vertical-City, 2015 115
3.34 Karl Friedrich Schinkel: Schloss Charlottenhof, Potsdam, 1822-23, top: engraving of the East-Side/terrace garden, middle: WestSide (Middle); bottom sections in: Schinkel 1829 117
3.35 Ludwig Hilberseimer, residential city, Interior perspective views of apartment, Fig. 9, p. 16 in: Hilberseimer 1925d 119
4.1 Ludwig Hilberseimer, Welfare City, Stuttgart, 1927, Series 10/1 Box 1 Folder 6, Ludwig Karl Hilberseimer Papers, Ryerson and Burnham Archives, The Art Institute of Chicago 124
4.2 Ludwig Hilberseimer, Proposal to City-Building, 1930, drawing by author 127
4.3 Hugo Häring, L-House Schema, 1934. p. 205 in: Kremer 1984 . . . 131
4.4 Ludwig Hilberseimer, Fig. 14-16, p. 3, in: Hilberseimer 1929b; Copyright Wilhelm Ernst & Sohn Verlag für Architektur und technische Wissenschaften GmbH & Co. KG. Reproduced with permission. . . 132
4.5 Ludwig Hilberseimer, Mixed-Building ratio form to surface; original drawings in: Hilberseimer 1931b; based on: A-C: fig. 2, D: Fig. 3; E: Fig. 10; F: Fig. 8; G, N: Fig. 2a in: Hilberseimer 1932; H: student design by Pius Pahl; I,L,M: student design by Wilhelm Jacob Hess; J,K: student design by Heinz Neuy; O: student design by Waldemar Hüsing in: p. 64-71, Bauhaus Archiv 1986; drawing by author 136

List of Figures   243

4.6 Student work at the IIT, course: City Planning 201, studies, 1948, top: author unknown, bottom: Eric Anderson, Series 10.1, Box 3, Folder 9, Ludwig Karl Hilberseimer Papers, Ryerson and Burnham Archives, The Art Institute of Chicago 137

4.7 Student works at the Bauhaus, supervisor Mies van der Rohe; top: Heinz Neuy, one family house study, 1931, Inv. Nr. 7176/1, Inv. Nr. 7179/1, Bauhaus-Archiv Berlin; bottom: Ernst Hegel: 3 single family houses, 1933, Inv. Nr. 7165/1, Bauhaus-Archiv Berlin 142

4.8 Anthony Clyde Lewis, sun penetration study, drawing as part of the Master-Thesis "Survey And Replanning Of Montreal" at the Illinois Institute of Technology, supervisor Ludwig Hilberseimer, 1943, Graham Resource Center, Chicago 146

4.9 Ludwig Hilberseimer, historical structure of the architectural elements, Photographic material in: Series 10.2, Box 14, Ludwig Karl Hilberseimer Papers, Ryerson and Burnham Archives, The Art Institute of Chicago; drawing by author..................... 147

4.10 Ludwig Hilberseimer: The City in the Landscape, 1940 in: Hilberseimer 12/ 1940 149

4.11 Ludwig Hilberseimer: study settlement and transport, in: Hilberseimer 12/ 1940 151

4.12 Ludwig Hilberseimer: Basic City Unit, 1940, in: Hilberseimer 12/ 1940 152

4.13 Ludwig Hilberseimer: Mixed-Building 1, free standing L-Shape houses and porch houses, Fig. 1, 3, 5, 6, 7, in: Hilberseimer 1931b; Copyright Wilhelm Ernst & Sohn Verlag für Architektur und technische Wissenschaften GmbH & Co. KG. Reproduced with permission. . . 156

4.14 Ludwig Hilberseimer: Mixed-Building 2, row houses, appartment houses and porch houses, Fig. 7, 10, 11, 14, 15, 16 in: Hilberseimer 1931b; Copyright Wilhelm Ernst & Sohn Verlag für Architektur und technische Wissenschaften GmbH & Co. KG. Reproduced with permission. 157

4.15 Ludwig Hilberseimer: Mixed-Building 3, free standing L-Shape houses and porch houses, Fig. 7, 8, 9, 12, 13 in: Hilberseimer 1931b; Copyright Wilhelm Ernst & Sohn Verlag für Architektur und technische Wissenschaften GmbH & Co. KG. Reproduced with permission. . . 158

4.16 Pius Pahl, top: Inv. Nr.: 4485/2, Bauhaus-Archiv Berlin; bottom: Inv. Nr.: 4484, Bauhaus-Archiv Berlin, Foto: Markus Hawlik 159

244 The Mereological City: a reading of the works of Ludwig Hilberseimer

4.17 Daniel Köhler, L-Shape house as settlement, the effect of room composition on settlement figuration, 2015 160
4.18 Daniel Köhler, L-Shape house as settlement, the effect of room composition on settlement figuration, 2015 161
4.19 Daniel Köhler, L-Shape house as settlement, study housetype C, 2015 162
4.20 Daniel Köhler, L-Shape house as settlement, study housetyp F, H, 2015 163

5.1 Alois Riegl, perforated bronzes, table XV in: Riegl 1901 169
5.2 Daniel Köhler, schema: influence of road segments on the assignability of plots, 2014 175
5.3 Ludwig Hilberseimer, Plan of Chicago, Southside District, Chicago, IL, 1951; original Fig. 216-219, p. 240, 241 in: Hilberseimer 1955; redrawn by author 177
5.4 Daniel Köhler, Plan of Chicago rebuilt, according to the schema of removing street segments, 2015 180
5.5 Ludwig Hilberseimer, exhibition Open House, c. 1950, Series 10.1 Box 6 Folder 3, Ludwig Karl Hilberseimer Papers, Ryerson and Burnham Archives, The Art Institute of Chicago; photographer unknown . 183
5.6 Daniel Köhler, mereological analysis room-insolation; original drawings: Ludwig Hilberseimer, study Room-Insolation, 1935, Series 4/3 Box 4 Folder 27, Ludwig Karl Hilberseimer Papers, Ryerson and Burnham Archives, The Art Institute of Chicago 190
5.7 Daniel Köhler, mereological analysis of rooms designed by Ludwig Hilberseimer, 2015 191
5.8 Daniel Köhler, mereological analysis of rooms designed by Ludwig Hilberseimer, 2015 192
5.9 Daniel Köhler, mereological analysis of rooms designed by Ludwig Hilberseimer, 2015 193
5.10 Daniel Köhler, mereological analysis of room to house to settlement designed by Ludwig Hilberseimer, 2015 194
5.11 Daniel Köhler, mereological analysis house as parthood relation of rooms designed by Ludwig Hilberseimer, 2015 195
5.12 Daniel Köhler, mereological analysis house to settlement designed by Ludwig Hilberseimer, 2015 196
5.13 Daniel Köhler, mereological analysis of the house figure depending on settlement density, top: Ludwig Hilberseimer, Effects of different densities, Fig. 68, S. 94 in: Hilberseimer 1944 197

5.14 Daniel Köhler, mereological analysis sun-insolation, original drawings: Ludwig Hilberseimer, sun insolation study, top: Fig. 3, p.3; bottom: Fig. 7, p. 5 in: Hilberseimer 2.1936 198

5.15 Daniel Köhler, mereological analysis sun-insolation, original drawings: Ludwig Hilberseimer, sun insolation study, top: Fig. 3, p.3; bottom: Fig. 7, p. 5 in: Hilberseimer 2.1936 199

5.16 Daniel Köhler, variation in the peripheral area of the settlement; original drawings: Ludwig Hilberseimer, top: settlement unit detail, Fig. 171, p. 195, in: Hilberseimer 1955; bottom: settlement unit detail, Fig. 88, p. 136, in: Hilberseimer 1949c; drawing by author 200

5.17 Daniel Köhler, mereological analysis orientation house – settlement; original drawing: Ludwig Hilberseimer, A new Settlement-Unit and the orientation of houses, Fig. 82, p. 109 in: Hilberseimer 1944 ... 201

5.18 John Ast, San Juan Replanned, 1964, Master Thesis at the Illinois Institute of Technology, supervisor Ludwig Hilberseimer, Graham Resource Center, Chicago 202

5.19 Ludwig Hilberseimer, A, B, C: Fig. 96, p. 127; D: Fig. 69, p. 95 in: Hilberseimer 1944 203

5.20 Ludwig Hilberseimer, Influence of prevailing winds, wind diagram 1,2; Fig. 86, 87, p. 113 in: Hilberseimer 1944 204

5.21 Zenbei Furya, Replanning Mito, 1961, top: Fig. 9: Houses built along the street; bottom: Fig. 10: Mito and its Region Replanned; Master Thesis at the Illinois Institute of Technology, supervisor Ludwig Hilberseimer, Graham Resource Center, Chicago 205

5.22 Cesar Solis, Santa River Valley Peru, 1957, top: Fig. 12, Types of Villages, bottom: Fig. 13, proposed plan, Master Thesis at the Illinois Institute of Technology, supervisor Ludwig Hilberseimer, Graham Resource Center, Chicago 206

6.1 John Frega, Island of Jamaica, IIT Master Thesis, 1957; Series 10.1 Box 3 Folder 16 in: Ryerson and Burnham Archives Finding Aids, The Art Institute of Chicago 210

Bibliography

Alberti, Leon Baptista, and Max Theuer. 1452. *Zehn bücher über die baukunst.* 1. ed. Wien. 1912. Darmstadt: Wiss. Buchges.
Alberti, Leon Battista. 1456. *De l'architettura.* Vinegia.
Alberti, Leon Battista. 1541. *De re aedificatoria.* Mainz: Jacobus Cammer.
Alberti, Leon Battista, and Edward Owen. 1755. *Ten books on archtiecture.* London.
Alexander, Christopher. 1966. A city is not a tree. *Design, London: Council of Industrial Design* 206.
Anderson, Richard. No date. An end to speculation. In *Metropolisarchitecture and selected essays*, edited by Richard Anderson, volume 2, pages 17–81. 2.
Aristoteles, and Immanuel Bekker. 1837. *Metaphysics.*
Aristoteles 2006. *Nikomachische Ethik.* Orig.-Ausg. Reinbek bei Hamburg: Rowohlt-Taschenbuch-Verlag
Aristoteles. and Franz Ferdinand Schwarz. 1989. *Politik: Schriften zur Staatstheorie.* Stuttgart: Reclam.
Aristoteles, Horst Seidl,Wilhelm von Christ, and Hermann Bonitz. 1978. *Aristoteles' metaphysik: Griechisch – deutsch.* 1. Aufl. Volume 307. Hamburg: Meiner
Augustinus, Aurelius and Johann Perl. 386 / 1940. *Die ordnung.* Paderborn: Verlag Ferdinand Schöningh.
Aureli, Pier Vittorio. 2012. In Hilberseimer's footsteps. In *Metropolisarchitecture and selected essays*, edited by Richard Anderson, volume 2, pages 334–363. 2.
Aureli, Pier Vittorio. 2008. *The project of autonomy: Politics and architecture within and against capitalism.* New York: Temple Hoyne Buell Center for the Study of American Architecture / Princeton Architectural Press.
Aureli, Pier Vittorio. 2011. *The possibility of an absolute architecture.* Cambridge and Mass: MIT press.
Aureli, Pier Vittorio. 2012. Architecture for barbarians: Ludwig hilberseimer and the rise of the generic city. *AA Files* 63:3–18.

Bauhaus Archiv, editor. 1986. *Mies van der Rohe, Ludwig: der vorbildliche Architekt: Mies van der Rohes Architekturunterricht 1930-1958 am Bauhaus und in Chicago*. 1st edition. Berlin: Das Archiv / Nicolaische Verlagsbuchh.

Baumeister, Reinhard. 1876. *Stadterweiterungen in technischer baupolizeilicher und wirtschaftlicher Beziehung*. Berlin: Ernst & Korn.

Bergdoll, Barry. 1994. *Karl Friedrich Schinkel: Preussens berühmtester Baumeister*. München: Klinkhardt & Biermann.

Blaser, Werner. 1977. Mies von der Rohe, Lehre und Schule. Volume 3. Basel and Stuttgart: Birkhaeuser.

Blum, Betty J. 1990. Oral history of Reginald Malcolmson. Chicago.

Blum, Betty J. 2000. *Oral history of James Ingo Freed: Chicago architects oral history project*. The Art Institute of Chicago.

Bohrer, Karl Heinz. 2007. Die stile des dionysos. In *Grosser Stil: Form und Formlosigkeit in der Moderne*, edited by Karl Heinz Bohrer, pages 216–235. München: Hanser.

Branzi, Andrea. 2006. *W & W: weak and widespread*. Milan and London: Skira / Thames & Hudson.

Bryant, Levi R. 2011. *The democracy of objects*. Ann Arbor: University of Michigan Library.

Caldwell, Alfred. 1948. *City in the landscape: A preface for planning*. Master Thesis. Chicago.

Carpo, Mario. 2011. *The alphabet and the algorithm*. Cambridge, Mass: mit press.

Casati, Roberto, and Achille C. Varzi. 1999. *Parts and places: The structures of spatial representation*. Cambridge, Mass: mit press.

Cepl, Jasper. 2007. *Oswald Mathias Ungers: Eine intellektuelle Biographie*. Volume Bd. 33. Köln: König.

Danforth, George E. 1988. Hilberseimer remembered. In *Ludwig Hilbereimer: in the shadow of mies*, edited by The Art Institute of Chicago. Chicago: Rizzoli.

Deleuze, Gilles, and Félix Guattari. 1992. *Tausend plateaus: Kapitalismus und Schizophrenie*. Berlin: Merve

Descola, Philippe. 2011. Jenseits von natur und kultur. Volume 2076. Berlin: Suhrkamp

Dorn, Nico. 2006. *Das apollinische und das dionysische: Nietzsches gegensatzpaar im antiken mythos*. Visited on September 9, 2013. $http://www.texttexturen.de/arbeiten/apollondionysos$.

Droste, Magdalena. 1989. Unterrichtsstruktur und werkstattarbeit am bauhaus unter hannes meyer. In *Hannes Meyer: 1889-1954 ; Architekt, Urbanist, Lehrer*, edited by Magdalena Droste. Berlin: Ernst.

Ehrenfels, Christian. 1890. Über Gestaltqualitäten. In *Vierteljahrsschrift für wissenschaftliche Philosophie* 14: 249–292.

Eisenman, Peter. 2010. *Architecture or design: wither the discipline*. Cornell University, New York.

Endell, August. 1908, 1984. *Die Schönheit der grossen Stadt*. Volume Nr. 4. Berlin: Archibook.

Focillon, Henri. 1989. *The life of forms in art*. New York: Zone Books.

Frobenius, Leo, and Douglas C. Fox. 1999. *African genesis: Folk tales and myths of africa*. Mineola and N.Y: Dover Publications.

Garcia, Tristan. 2014. *Form and object: A treatise on things*. Edinburgh: Edinburgh University Press.

Geddes, Patrick, and Victor Branford. 1917. *The coming polity*. London: Williams and Norgate.

Graham Foundation, editor. 21.03.1987. *Hilbs concordia: L. Hilberseimer, the man and the work*. Graham Foundation.

Hake, Sabine. 2008. *Topographies of class: Modern architecture and mass society in weimar berlin*. Ann Arbor: University of Michigan Press.

Häring, Hugo. 1926. Zwei Städte. Die Form (8): 172–175.

Harman, Graham. 2005. *Guerrilla metaphysics: Phenomenology and the carpentry of things*. Chicago: Open Court.

Harman, Graham. 2011. *The quadruple object*. Winchester: Zero Books.

Harman, Graham. 2012. *The third table*. Hatje Cantz

Hays, Michael. 1992. *Modernism and the posthumanist subject: The architecture of Hannes Meyer and Ludwig Hilberseimer*. cambridge and massachusetts: mit press.

Heidegger, Martin and Hans-Georg Gadamer. 1960. Der Ursprung des Kunstwerkes. Reclam

Heidegger, Martin. 1961. *Nietzsche: Der Wille zur Macht als Kunst: Freiburger Vorlesung WS 1936/37*. Volume 43. Gesamtausgabe. Frankfurt am Main: Vitorio Klostermann GmbH.

Heidegger, Martin. 1991. *Kant und das Problem der Metaphysik*. Volume 3. Gesamtausgabe. Frankfurt am Main: Vitorio Klostermann GmbH.

Heidegger, Martin. 2005. *Bremer und Freiburger Vorträge*. Volume 79 Gesamtausgabe. 2. Frankfurt am Main: Vitorio Klostermann GmbH.

Hilberseimer, Ludwig. 1908-1911. Werksaufzeichnungen: Mitschriften aus dem architekturunterricht, hochschule karlsruhe, 1908-1911. Mappe 2-6, Inventarnummer 5550 - 5553, Bauhaus Archiv and Berlin.

Hilberseimer, Ludwig. 1914. Die Architektur der Groszstadt. Manuscript. Ryerson & Burnham Archive. Series 8/3, Box 1, Folder 1. The Art Institute of Chicago.

Hilberseimer, Ludwig. 26.01.1919. Umwertung in der Kunst. *Der Einzige* (2): 16–17.

Hilberseimer, Ludwig. 2.02.1919. Form und individuum. Der Einzige (3): 30–31.

Hilberseimer, Ludwig. 1919. Paul scheerbart und die architekten. In *Das Kunstblatt* (3): 271–274.

Hilberseimer, Ludwig. 28.06.1920. Afrikanische Kunst. *Socialistische Monatshefte*: 520–523.

Hilberseimer, Ludwig. 1920. Amerikanische architektur. *Kunst und Künstler* (20): 537–545.

Hilberseimer, Ludwig. 1921. Exotische Kunst. Manuscript. In Ryerson & Burnham Archive. Series 8/3, Box 1, Folder 7, The Art Institute of Chicago.

Hilberseimer, Ludwig. 1922a. Das Hochhaus. *Das Kunstblatt* (6): 525–531.

Hilberseimer, Ludwig. 1922b. Mexikanische baukunst. *Das Kunstblatt* 6 (4): 163–171.

Hilberseimer, Ludwig. 1922c. Schöpfung und Entwicklung. Ryerson & Burnham Archive, Series 8/3, Box 1, Folder 10, The Art Institute of Chicago.

Hilberseimer, Ludwig. 1922d. Schöpfung und entwicklung. *Socialistische Monatshefte* 28 (16): 993–997.

Hilberseimer, Ludwig. 1923a. Der Wille zur Wrchitektur. *Das Kunstblatt* (7): 133–140.

Hilberseimer, Ludwig. 1923b. Hochhaus. G (2): 3.

Hilberseimer, Ludwig. 1923c. J.j.p. Oud's Wohnungsbauten. *Das Kunstblatt* (7): 289–292.

Hilberseimer, Ludwig. 1923d. Vom städtebaulichen Problem der Grossstadt. *Socialistische Monatshefte* 29 (6): 352–357.

Hilberseimer, Ludwig. 1924. Raumgestaltung. Socialistische Monatshefte (1): 65–66.

Hilberseimer, Ludwig. 1925a. Attrappen architektur. *Qualität* (4/5): 102–103. 1925b. Bauwirtschaft und Wohnungsbau. *Sozialistische Monatshefte* 31 (5): 285-291.

Hilberseimer, Ludwig. 1925c. Dänische Architektur: Ausstellung des Architekturverlags Ernst Wasmuth. *Die Form* 1: 352.

Hilberseimer, Ludwig. 1925d. Groszstadtbauten. Hannover: Apossverlag

Hilberseimer, Ludwig. 1925e. Stadt- und Wohnungsbau. *Soziale Bauwirtschaft* 5 (14).

Hilberseimer, Ludwig. 03 1926. Amerikanische Architektur: Ausstellung in der Akademie der bildenden Künste. *G* (4): 86–90.

Hilberseimer, Ludwig. 1926. Über die typisierung des Mietshauses. *Die Form* 1 (15): 338–340.

Hilberseimer, Ludwig. 1927a. Die Wohnung als Gebrauchsgegenstand. *Bau und Wohnung*: 68–75.

Hilberseimer, Ludwig. 1927b. *Groszstadt Architektur.* Stuttgart: Julius Hoffmann.

Hilberseimer, Ludwig. 1928. Berlin und seine Bauprobleme. *Sozialistische Monatshefte* 34 (12): 1074–1078.

Hilberseimer, Ludwig. 1929a. Die neue Geschäftsstrasse. *Das neue Frankfurt* (4).

Hilberseimer, Ludwig. 1929b. Groszstädtische Kleinstwohnungen. *Zentralblatt der Bauverwaltung; Sonderdruck des Preussischen Finanzministeriums.* Ernst & Sohn. 49 (32).

Hilberseimer, Ludwig. 1929c. Kleinstwohnungen. Bauhaus (2).

Hilberseimer, Ludwig. 1929d. Stadt- und Wohnungsbau. Manuscript. Mappe 7, Bauhaus Archiv and Berlin.

Hilberseimer, Ludwig. 1929e. Vorschlag zur City-Bebauung. *Das Kunstblatt* 13 (40): 93–95.

Hilberseimer, Ludwig. 1930. Vorschlag zur City-Bebauung. *Die Form* 5 (23/24): 608–611.

Hilberseimer, Ludwig. 1931a. Die wohnung unserer Zeit. *Die Form* 6 (7): 249–270.

Hilberseimer, Ludwig. 1931b. Flachbau und Stadtraum. *Zentralblatt der Bauverwaltung.* Ernst & Sohn. 51 (53/54): 773–778.

Hilberseimer, Ludwig. 1931c. *Hallenbauten: Stadt- und Festhallen, Turn- und Sporthallen, Ausstellungshallen, Ausstellungsanlagen.* Handbuch der Architektur. 4 volumes. Leipzig: J. M. Gebhardt's Verlag.

Hilberseimer, Ludwig. 1932. Flachbau und Flachbautypen. *Moderne Bauformen* (31): 471–478.

Hilberseimer, Ludwig. 1933. Vorläufiges Literaturverzeichnis: Die Frage Der Besonnung im Wohnungsbau. Ryerson & Burnham Archive. Art Institue of Chicago.

Hilberseimer, Ludwig. 1935. Raumdurchsonnung. *Moderne Bauformen* 34: 29–36.

Hilberseimer, Ludwig. 2.1936. Raumdurchsonnung und siedlungsdichtigkeit. In *Moderne Bauformen* (Sonderdruck).

Hilberseimer, Ludwig. 12/ 1940. Elements of city planning. In *Armour Engineer and Alumnus*:4–14.

Hilberseimer, Ludwig. 1940. The literature of City Planning. *Architectural Forum* (73): 100–101.

Hilberseimer, Ludwig. 1944. *The new City: Principles of Planning*. Chicago: Paul Theobald.
Hilberseimer, Ludwig. 1947. Elemente der Stadtplanung. *Der Bauhelfer* 2 (19): 3–8.
Hilberseimer, Ludwig. 1949a. Architecture: Structure and Form. Manuscript. Ryerson & Burnham Archive, Series 8 / 2, Box 1, Folder 1-7, Chicago.
Hilberseimer, Ludwig. 1949b. Physical planning, a textbook: Room, house, site, and town. Mansucript. Ryerson & Burnham Archive, Series 8/2, Box 2, Folder 22, Chicago.
Hilberseimer, Ludwig. 1949c. *The new regional pattern: Industries and gardens; workshops and farms*. Chicago: Paul Theobald.
Hilberseimer, Ludwig. 1955. *The nature of cities*. Chicago: Paul Theobald.
Hilberseimer, Ludwig. 1956. *Mies van der Rohe*. Chicago: Paul Theobald.
Hilberseimer, Ludwig. 1963a. City architecture: The trend towards openess. Ryerson & Burnham Archive, Series 8/2, Box2, Folder 17-21, Chicago.
Hilberseimer, Ludwig. 1963b. *Entfaltung einer Planungsidee*. Bauwelt Fundamente. Frankfurt/M and Wien: Ullstein Verlag Berlin.
Hilberseimer, Ludwig. 1964. *Contemporary architecture: Its roots and trends*. Chicago: Paul Theobald and Company.
Hilberseimer, Ludwig. 1965. Can city traffic be reduced?. Ryerson & Burnham Archive, Series 8/3, Box3, Folder 6. Chicago.
Hilberseimer, Ludwig. 1988. The art of architecture. In *Ludwig Hilbereimer: in the shadow of Mies*, edited by The Art Institute of Chicago, pages 94–99. Chicago: Rizzoli.
Hilberseimer, Ludwig. n.d. Principles of city planning. Ryerson & Burnham Archive, Series 8/3, Box 4, Folder 20, Chicago.
Hilberseimer, Ludwig and Interviewer. n.d. Interview regarding the city as an organism. Ryerson & Burnham Archive, Series 8/3, Box 4, Folder 29. Chicago.
Hildebrand, Adolf. 1918. *Das Problem der Form in der bildenden Kunst*. 3. Strassbourg: J.H. ED. Heitz.
Holl, Steven. 1980. *The alphabetical City*. Volume 5. New York: Pamphlet Architecture.
Hoyningen-Huene, Paul. 1998. *Formale Logik: Eine philosophische Einführung*. Volume 9692. Stuttgart: Reclam.
Husserl, Edmund. 1901. *Logische Untersuchungen: Zweiter Teil Untersuchungen zur Phänomenologie und Theorie der Erkenntnis*. Halle an der Saale: Max Niemeyer.
Jameson, Fredric. 1986. Postmodernism, or, the cultural logic of late capitalism. Duke University Press.

Jennings, Michael William, and Detlef Mertins. 2011. *G: Material for elemental form-creation*. London: Tate.

Jimeno, Oswaldo. 1973. *Hilberseimer y Aristoteles*. Lima: Cuadernos de Arquitectura y Urbanismo.

Kadinsky, Wassily. 1926. *Punkt und Linie zu Fläche*. Weimar: Bauhaus Books.

Kant, Immanuel. 1919. *Kritik der reinen Vernunft*. 11th edition. Leipzig: Verlag von Felix Meiner.

Kaufmann, Emil. 1933. *Von Ledoux bis Le Corbusier: Ursprung und Entwicklung der autonomen Architektur*. Stuttgart: Gerd Hatje.

Kieren, Martin. 1998. Ein imaginäres Museum. In *Internationale neue Baukunst*, edited by Ludwig Hilberseimer and Martin Kieren, pages 57–68. Berlin: Gebr. Mann

Kilian, Markus. 2002. *Großstadtarchitektur und New City: Eine planungsmethodische Untersuchung der Stadtplanungsmodelle Ludwig Hilberseimers*. Köln.

Kohlmeyer, Agnes. 1986. Appolo and dionysus. In *Ludwig hilberseimer 1885/1967 (rassegna 27)*, edited by Marco Michelis, Agnes Kohlmeyer de Vittorio Gregotti, Ludwig Hilberseimer, Pierluigi Cerri, Giampiero Bosoni, and Giovanni Vragnaz. Bologna: Cipea / C.I.P.I.A.

Koolhaas, Rem. 1998a. Imagine Nothingness. In *S,M,L,XL*, edited by Rem Koolhaas, pages 199–203. New-York: Sigler.

Koolhaas, Rem. editor. 1998b. *S,m,l,xl*. New-York: Sigler.

Kremer, Sabine. 1984. *Hugo Häring (1882-1958): Wohnungsbau, Theorie und Praxis*. Stuttgart: K. Krämer.

Kropotkin, Peter. 1913. *Fields, Factories and Workshops*. New York and London: G. P. Putnam's and Sons.

Latour, Bruno. 2006. *Die hoffnung der Pandora: Untersuchungen zur Wirklichkeit der Wissenschaft*. 1st edition. Frankfurt am Main: Suhrkamp

Latour, Bruno. 2010. An attempt at a *"compositionist manifesto"*. In collaboration with Ludwig-Maximilians-Universität München. Münchener Universitätsgesellschaft, München.

Latour, Bruno. 2014. *Existenzweisen: Eine anthropologie der Modernen*. 1. Aufl., neue Ausg. In collaboration with Gustav Roßler. Berlin: Suhrkamp.

Latour, Bruno, and Catherine Porter. 2004. *Politics of Nature*. Cambridge (Mass.): Harvard University Press.

Law, John. 1992. Notes on the theory of the actor network: Ordering, strategy and heterogeneity. *Systems Practice* 5:379–393.

Le Corbusier. 1925, 1987. *The city of tomorrow and its planning*. New York: Dover.

Lévi-Strauss, Claude. 1973. *Das wilde Denken*. Volume 14. Frankfurt am Main: Suhrkamp Taschenbuch Verlag.

Lipps, Theodor. 1906. Zur ästhetischen mechanik. in *Zeitschrift für Ästhetik* (1).

Lynn, Greg. 1998. Multiplicitous and inorganic bodies. In *Folds, bodies & blobs: Collected essays*, edited by Greg Lynn. Bruxelles: La Lettre volée.

Lynn, Greg. 1999. *Animate form*. New York: Princeton Architectural Press.

Mackay, Robin, and Armen Avanessian, editors. 2014. #accelerate#. Falmouth, United Kingdom and Berlin: Urbanomic Media Ltd. / in association with Merve.

Mallgrave, Harry Francis, and Gottfried Semper. 2001. *Gottfried Semper: Ein Architekt des 19. Jahrhunderts*. Zürich: gta-Verlag

Mengin, Christine. 1986a. Lists of works and projects 1885/1938. In *Ludwig hilberseimer 1885/1967 (rassegna 27)*. Bologna: Cipea / C.I.P.I.A.

Mengin, Christine. 1986b. The architecture of the groszstadt. In *Ludwig hilberseimer 1885/1967 (rassegna 27)*. Bologna: Cipea / C.I.P.I.A.

Mertins, Detlef, and Phyllis Lambert. 2014. *Mies*. New York: Phaidon.

Michelis, Marco de. 1986. Portrait of an architect as a young artist. In *Ludwig hilberseimer 1885/1967 (rassegna 27)*. Bologna: Cipea / C.I.P.I.A.

Müller-Sievers, Helmut. 1997. *Self-generation: Biology, philosophy, and literature around 1800*. Stanford, Calif.: Stanford University Press.

Nietzsche, Friedrich Wilhelm. 1922. Nachgelassene werke: Der Wille zur Macht. Nietzsche's Werke. Leipzig: Alfred Kröner Verlag.

Nietzsche, Friedrich, and GünterWohlfart. 1872, 2010. *Die Geburt der Tragödie oder: Griechenthum und Pessimismus*. Stuttgart: Reclam.

Ostendorf, Friedrich. 1918. *Sechs Bücher vom Bauen, enthaltend eine Theorie des architektonischen Entwerfens*. 3rd edition. Berlin: W. Ernst und Sohn.

Otto, Frei, and Bodo Rasch. 2001. *Gestalt finden: Auf dem Weg zu einer Baukunst des Minimalen*. 3. Aufl. Stuttgart: Ed. Menges.

Padovan, Richard. 1986. Machines a mediter. In *Mies van der Rohe, Ludwig: der vorbildliche Architekt*, edited by Bauhaus Archiv, pages 32–41. Berlin: Das Archiv / Nicolaische Verlagsbuchh.

Padovan, Richard. 2002. *Towards Universality: Le corbusier, Mies, and de Stijl*. London and New York: Routledge.

Panofsky, Erwin. 1920. Der Begriff des Kunstwollens. *Zeitschrift für Ästhetik und Allgemeine Kunstwissenschaft* XIV:321–339.

Pommer, Richard. 1988. More a necropolis than a Metropolis. In *Ludwig Hilbereimer: in the Shadow of Mies*, edited by The Art Institute of Chicago. Chicago: Rizzoli.

Pope, Albert. 1996. *Ladders*. Volume 34. Houston and New York: Princeton Architectural Press / Rice School of Architecture.

Posener, Julius. 2013a. *Vorlesungen zur Geschichte der neuen Architektur*. Aachen: ARCH+ Verlag.

Rescher, Nicholas, and Paul Oppenheim. 1955. Logical analysis of gestalt concepts. *The British Journal for the Philosophy of Science* 6 (22): 89–106.

Ridder, Lothar. 2002. *Mereologie: Ein Beitrag zur Ontologie und Erkenntnistheorie*. Volume Bd. 83. Frankfurt am Main: V. Klostermann.

Riegl, Alois. 1889. *Altorientalische Teppiche*. Mittenwald: Mäander.

Riegl, Alois. 1893. *Stilfragen: Geschichte der Ornamentik*. Berlin: Verlag von Georg Siemens.

Riegl, Alois. 1901. *Spätrömische Kunstindustrie*. Wien: Verlag der kaiserlichen und königlichen Hof- und Staatsdruckerei.

Riegl, Alois. 1928. Naturwerk und Kunstwerk. In *Gesammelte Aufsätze*, edited by Karl M. Swoboda and Alois Riegl, pages 51–64. Augsburg: Dr. Benno Filser Verlag.

Riegl, Alois. 1966. *Historische Grammatik der bildenden Künste: Buchmanuskript der Jahre 1897/98*. Graz-Köln: Hermann Böhlaus Nachf.

Rossi, Aldo. 1988. *The Architecture of the City*. Cambridge, Mass: Graham Foundation for Advanced Studies in the Fine Arts and the Institute for Architecture and Urban Studies by MIT.

Rowe, Colin, and Fred Koetter. 1978. *Collage City*. Basel and Boston: Birkhaüser.

Ryerson and Burnham Archives Finding Aids, The Art Institute of Chicago. Accessionnumber: 070383; Hilberseimer, Ludwig Karl, Papers.

Saliga, Pauline. 1993. Oral history of George Edson Danforth, faia. The Art Institute of Chicago.

Schäfer, Rainer. 2011. Die Wandlungen des Dionysischen bei Nietzsche. *Internationales Jahrbuch für die Nietzsche-Forschung* 40:178–202.

Schaur, Eda, and Frei Otto. 1992. *Ungeplante Siedlungen*. Volume Nr. 39. Stuttgart: Institut für leichte Flächentragwerke.

Scheffler, Karl. 1913. *Die Architektur der Groszstadt*. Berlin: Bruno Gassierer Verlag.

Schmarsow, August. 1893. *Das wesen der architektonischen Schöpfung*. Universität Leipzig.

Schumacher, Patrik. 2012a. Parametric order: Architectural order via an agent based parametric semiology. www.patrikschumacher.com.

Schumacher, Patrik. 2012b. The autopoiesis of architecture 2. 1st edition. Hoboken and N.J: Wiley.

Schwarzer, Mitchell. 1995. *German architectural theory and the search for modern identity*. Cambridge, England and New York: Cambridge University Press.

Sedlmayr, Hans. 1928. Einleitung: Die Quintessenz der Lehren Riegls. In *Gesammelte Aufsätze*, edited by Karl M. Swoboda and Alois Riegl. Augsburg: Dr. Benno Filser Verlag.

Shaviro, Steven. 2014. *The universe of things: On speculative realism*. Volume v.30. Minneapolis: University of Minnesota Press.

Simondon, Gilbert. 2012. *Die Existenzweise technischer Objekte*. Volume Bd. 11. Zürich: Diaphanes.

Simons, Peter M. 2000. *Parts: A study in ontology*. Pbk. ed. Oxford, New York: Clarendon Press / Oxford University Press.

Sitte, Camillo. 2002. *Der Städtebau nach seinen künstlerischen Grundsätzen*; Reprint der 4. Aufl. Wien, Graeser, Leipzig, Teubner von 1909. Basel, Boston, and Berlin: Birkhäuser.

Smith, Barry. 1982. Annotated bibliography of writings on part-whole relations since brentano. In *Parts and moments: Studies in logic and formal ontology*, edited by Barry Smith, pages 481–552. München and Wien: Philosophia Verlag.

Spaeth, David. 1981. *Ludwig Karl Hilberseimer, an annotated bibliography and chronology*. New York and London: Garland Publishing, Inc.

Spaeth, David. 1988. Ludwig hilbeiseimer's settlement unit, origins and applications. In *Ludwig hilbereimer: in the shadow of mies*, edited by The Art Institute of Chicago. Chicago: Rizzoli.

Spuybroek, Lars. 2011. *The sympathy of things: Ruskin and the ecology of design*. Rotterdam: V2 Publishing / NAi Publishing.

Spuybroek, Lars, and Hildegard Rudolph. 2004. *Nox: Machining architecture; Bauten und Projekte*. München: Dt. Verl.-Anst.

Stanislaw Lesniewski. 1929. Grundzüge eines neuen Systems der Grundlagen der Mathematik. *Fundamenta Mathematicae* (XIV): 1–82.

Sungho Choi, Michael Fara. 2006. Dispositions. Visited on October 20, 2013. $http://plato.stanford.edu/entries/dispositions$.

Tafuri, Manfredo. 1985, c1976. *Architecture and utopia: Design and capitalist development*. Cambridge and Mass: mit press.

Tatarkiewicz, Władysław. 1980. A history of six ideas: An essay in aesthetics. The Hague, Boston, and Hingham, MA: Nijhoff / Distribution for the U.S. and Canada, Kluwer Boston.

The Art Institute of Chicago, editor. 1988. *Ludwig hilbereimer: in the shadow of Mies*. Chicago: Rizzoli.

Ungers, Oswald Mathias, Rem Koolhaas, Peter Riemann, and Florian Hertweck. 2013. *The city in the city: Berlin: a green archipelago*. Baden: Lars Müller.

Ungers, Oswald Mathias. 1978. *The urban garden: Student projects for the Südliche Friedrichstadt Berlin*. Berlin Summer Academy for Architecture, Berlin, Studio Press for Architecture.

Unwin, Raymond. 1929. Ribbon development and sporadic building. In *First report of the greater london regional planning comitee*, edited by Knapp, Drewett and Sons Ldt, pages 27–33. London.

Varzi, Achille. 2014. Mereology. Stanford Enceclopedia of Philosophie. Visited on May 12, 2014. $http://plato.stanford.edu/archives/spr2014/entries/mereology$.

Venturi, Robert, Denise Scott Brown, and Steven Izenour. 1977. *Learning from Las Vegas*. Rev. ed. Cambridge, Mass.: mit press.

Vittorio Gregotti, Marco Michelis Agnes Kohlmeyer de, Ludwig Hilberseimer, Pierluigi Cerri, Giampiero Bosoni, and Giovanni Vragnaz, editors. 1986. *Ludwig Hilberseimer 1885/1967 (rassegna 27)*. Bologna: Cipea / C.I.P.I.A.

Wagner, Martin. 1932. 1932. *Das wachsende Haus: Ein Beitrag zur Lösung der städtischen Wohnungsfrage*. Berlin: Bong & Co.

Wagner, Otto. 1911. *Die Groszstadt: Eine Studie über diese*. Wien: Schroll-Verlag.

Weber, Max, and Wilfried Nippel. 1999. *Wirtschaft und Gesellschaft*: nachlass. Volume 22,5. Tübingen: Mohr Siebeck.

Whitehead, Alfred North. 1987. *Prozess und Realität*. 1. Aufl. Volume 690. Frankfurt am Main: Suhrkamp.

William J. R. Curtis. 1996. *Modern architecture since 1900*. 3rd. London: Phaidon.

Winkler, Klaus-Jürgen. 2003. *Baulehre und entwerfen am bauhaus: 1919-1933*. Weimar: Bauhaus-Universität Weimar.

Wölfflin, Heinrich. 1915. *Kunstgeschichtliche Kunstbegriffe: Das Problem der Stilentwicklung in der neueren Kunst*. München: Hugo Bruckmann Verlag.

Wolsdorff, Christian. 1986. Das bauhaus unter Mies van der Rohe – ein Mies-Bauhaus? In *Mies van der Rohe, ludwig: der vorbildliche Architekt*, 1st edition, edited by Bauhaus Archiv, pages 43–45. Berlin: Das Archiv / Nicolaische Verlagsbuchh.

Worringer, Wilhelm. 2004a. Abstraktion und Einfühlung. In *Schriften*, edited by Wilhelm Worringer. München: Wilhelm Fink.

Worringer, Wilhelm. 2004b. Formprobleme der gotik. In *Schriften*, edited by Wilhelm Worringer. München: Wilhelm Fink.

GPSR Authorized Representative: Easy Access System Europe, Mustamäe tee 50, 10621 Tallinn, Estonia, gpsr.requests@easproject.com